CW00675379

THE GODDESS NUT
And the Wisdom of the Sky

PUBLISHED BY AVALONIA

BM AVALONIA
LONDON
WC1N 3XX
ENGLAND, UK
WWW.AVALONIABOOKS.COM

THE GODDESS NUT AND THE WISDOM OF THE SKY

ISBN: 978-1-910191-25-5
(PAPERBACK)

FIRST EDITION, JUNE 2021

TYPESET AND DESIGN BY SATORI.

COVER DESIGN BY SATORI.

ILLUSTRATIONS BY BRIAN ANDREWS © 2020

BRITISH LIBRARY CATALOGUING IN PUBLICATION DATA. A CATALOGUE RECORD FOR THIS
BOOK IS AVAILABLE FROM THE BRITISH LIBRARY.

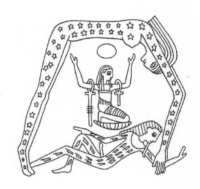

The Goddess Nut

And the Wisdom of the Sky

Lesley Jackson

PUBLISHED BY AVALONIA

WWW.AVALONIABOOKS.COM

DEDICATION

This book is dedicated to Nut
the Goddess of the Northern Sky, the Lady of the Stars
and also to Ann and John.

BIOGRAPHY

Lesley Jackson has a lifelong interest in archaeology, ancient history and sacred myth and a fascination with the mysterious geographical be they lost worlds, otherworlds or the sacred places of this world. She is a devotee of the Egyptian deities and since being blessed with early retirement has devoted much of her time to researching and writing about them.

Lesley is the author of *Thoth: The History of the Ancient Egyptian God of Wisdom*, *Hathor: A Reintroduction to an Ancient Egyptian Goddess*, *Isis: The Eternal Goddess of Egypt and Rome*, *Sekhmet and Bastet: The Feline Powers of Egypt* and *The Cobra Goddess & The Chaos Serpent*, all published by Avalonia. She has also written a number of articles about Egyptian religion, some of which have been published in Pagan Dawn and Nile Magazine.

Despite the strong call of Egypt she is a Northerner at heart, preferring cooler climes and wooded landscapes. She lives in the East Riding of Yorkshire, close to the lost world of Doggerland.

ACKNOWLEDGEMENTS

No study of Egyptian religion would be possible without access to their writings. I am indebted to all of those who have studied these ancient languages and have provided translations for the rest of us to use.

I would like to thank the British Library and the Egyptian Exploration Society for the use of their libraries.

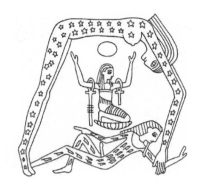

Table of Contents

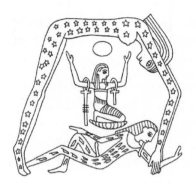

CHAPTER 1

Introduction

*"As for the sky, the earth, and the horizon, that which is
in them is the way of the goddess."* [1]

The Goddess Nut graces many beautiful ceilings in Egyptian
tombs and temples, but one inspiring image of Nut I encountered
in the early days of my Egyptian journey came from elsewhere. It
was a picture by the artist Wendy Andrew who portrayed Nut as a
dancing Goddess with galaxies spiralling from her fingers. Being of
such galactic dimensions Nut and her planets and stars can seem
remote and removed from daily life, unless you have an interest in
astrology. Often, it is only the moon who sails across her dual skies
who comes close into our lives. The first impression is that the
Ancient Egyptians appeared to have felt this way, especially as the
solar and Osirian cults gained and maintained their dominance. A
closer investigation reveals the stellar and lunar influences which
still sparkle beneath the too-bright solar cults and flow through the
many myths. The patterns of the cosmos show order and meaning

---

[1] The Ancient Egyptian Book of Two Ways, Lesko, 1977:39 spell 1146

in the heavens, revealing the hands of the Creators and the unknowable business of the deities. For the Egyptians the sky showed a model of consistency and order which could be reflected on earth because the patterns seen in the sky were imbued with the power of the deities. Studying the cosmos revealed a hint of the secrets of the deities and brought people closer to them.

I start at the beginning of the universe and then look at Nut in detail as well as the planets and stars that sail across her body. While acknowledging that our sun is a star I have largely omitted the diurnal sky of the Sun Gods and Solar Goddesses, having covered much of them in my previous books. I then return to the Moon, my guide, who connects the day and night and leads us to wisdom. I live too close to a city to see the stars reflect Nut's glory. Only the moon and Thoth are close and personal, and so the Way of Nut became a distant background. But the deities have a way of directing the writing, and astral snakes and Thoth have guided me thus far.

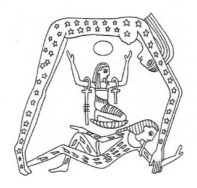

CHAPTER 2

Building the Cosmos

"Great One who came into being as the sky, you have achieved power, you have achieved strength, and have filled every place with your beauty; the entire land is yours…you have enclosed the earth and all things are within your embrace."[2]

BEFORE THE BEGINNING

Before time and space had even been thought about there was only the primordial ocean, which the Egyptians called the *nun*, described as being of *"uniform darkness"* the *"limits of which are unknown"*.[3] It was a chaotic non-place of non-being but within it, for some unfathomable reason, small eddies occurred which formed into currents of potential. The cenotaph of Sety I (19th dynasty) describes the *nun* as *"the fount of the gods, the place from which*

---

[2] The Ancient Egyptian Pyramid Texts, Faulkner, 2007: 142 utt 432
[3] Genesis in Egypt: The Philosophy of Ancient Egyptian Creation Accounts, Allen, 1988:4

birds come".[4] From this place of nothing something happened and a tiny fragile bubble of being burst into existence. Now this bubble, which contains the created universe, floats in the hostile waters of the *nun* which forever threaten its existence. For the Egyptians the created world was not infinite but was bounded by the *nun*. Although we tend to think of space as being more or less a vacuum, Galfard says the fabric of the universe, being a mixture of space and time, is *"not a band, nor is it flat. It is everywhere. A planet or a star, in outer space, is therefore better represented by a ball...immersed in an ocean filling the whole universe. No surface above, no ground below. Just water everywhere."*[5]

THE CELESTIAL CREATOR COW

The Egyptians had a number of creation theories, but only those relevant to Nut are covered here. To explain why they envisaged a Creator Cow we need to go back to the Pre-dynastic and Neolithic and the earliest origins of Egyptian culture. Before they became an agricultural society, the peoples who were to become the Egyptians were cattle herders and as such cattle played a central role in their culture and beliefs. The cow seems to have been one of the earliest manifestations of their Mother Goddess. The link between the cow and the Goddess is clear as both are nurturing and protective of their young. There are female figurines from the Pre-dynastic period sculpted with arms raised to mimic the horns of a cow. The link between cows and the cosmos seems less clear to us but it was obvious to the Egyptians and the concept was well established during the Pre-dynastic. Climate change in the 6th and 5th millennia BCE brought drier conditions and forced the cattle herders to settle along the Nile and start farming. It may have been a new way of life but cattle retained their importance both in the economy and in religious beliefs. By the time of the Early Dynastic the Divine Cow was a symbol of creation with strong stellar connections as well as having nurturing, fertility and rebirth aspects.

---

[4] Genesis in Egypt: The Philosophy of Ancient Egyptian Creation Accounts, Allen, 1988:1
[5] The Universe in Your Hand, Galfard, 2015:108

Rock art at Wadi Barramiya (dating to about 4000 BCE) depicts a cow, or perhaps a statue of a cow, being dragged in a boat. Reflecting this ancient pedigree there is a very similar depiction of the Hathor Cow in the 18ᵗʰ dynasty tomb of Hatshepsut.[6] In the late Pre-Dynastic there are depictions of the Cow Goddess on slate palettes. The Narmer palette commemorates the unification of Egypt and so is a very important artefact. Above the battle scenes are two forward-facing human heads with cow ears and curling horns. Another, the Gerzean palette, emphasises the cosmic link. It shows a stylised cow's head facing forwards. A star marks the tuft of hair between her horns, and there is a star next to each ear and at the tip of her horns. We know virtually nothing of the beliefs of the Pre-dynastic other than the importance of cows and their association with the cosmos and stars. The Sky Goddess who took the form of a Cow was one of the earliest known deities of the Pre-dynastic Period. Regardless of her various names, the Cow represented the loving and nurturing aspects of the protecting, overarching sky – both nocturnal and diurnal. The cow depictions on the slate palettes are thought to represent Bat who was a Celestial Cow Goddess of the late Pre-dynastic and early Dynastic Periods. Bat was important until the early Dynastic Period, after which she was absorbed by Hathor. Her name is the feminine version of the word *ba* meaning soul or spirit and in the *Pyramid Texts* she is referred to as having two faces.

The main Creator Cow Goddess is Mehet-Weret who was a Theban Goddess. Her name means Great Swimmer. She existed as a fertile current in the pre-creation *nun*. After creation she was associated with the night sky and was identified as the Milky Way, the celestial river of stars which the Egyptians called the Winding Waterway. Mehet-Weret also gave birth to the Sun God for the first time, giving light to the darkness. She is associated with both Nut and Hathor. After the Middle Kingdom she was considered a form of the Hathor Cow of Thebes. Mehet-Weret is also associated with the Creator Goddess Neith. Hathor absorbed many of the early Cow Goddesses and became the main, and best known, Cow Goddess. The deceased are frequently welcomed into the

---

[6] Genesis of the Pharaohs, Wilkinson, 2003:151

underworld by Hathor as the Cow Goddess. Nut, as the Cosmic Cow, straddles the earth and her limbs mark the cardinal points and support the sky. Her belly forms the star-studded night sky and she is depicted lifting the Sun God into the heavens between her horns. Her eye is usually depicted as the *wedjat* eye (a human eye with the facial markings of a falcon).

THE STRUCTURE OF CREATION

Having created the sun and the cosmos, the Cosmic Cow appears to have left the consolidation work to various Gods. Or, more likely, her role was usurped by them. According to the Heliopolitan tradition the Sun God (Ra or Atum) self-generated Shu and Tefnut. Shu is the God of air, and it is thought that his name means emptiness or *"he who rises up"*.[7] His sister-wife Tefnut represents moisture, as well as being a Solar Eye Goddess. It has been suggested that Tefnut personified the lower layers of the atmosphere with its mist and rain while Shu formed the upper levels. Shu and Tefnut did not stay with their father in the created world but drifted away into the *nun*. Here they were watched over by the Eye of the Sun God. She brought them back to be reunited with their father and then transformed into the *Uraeus* Goddess, the fire-spitting cobra who adorns the brow of deities and royals. Jackson (2018) discusses the myth in detail. This myth, in part, explains the creation of space and time, which was essential for the development of life and movement. Together Shu and Tefnut are associated with the horizon, space and time and the sun and moon. Their children are the Earth God Geb and the Sky Goddess Nut.

It is said that Geb and Nut fell in love and embraced each other so closely that there was no space between them. They could be viewed as trying to revert back to the original pre-creation unity. Creation could only progress if it moved towards diversity. On orders from Ra, their father Shu separated them and in doing so created a gap between the earth and sky, allowing the entry of air to breathe and space for life to exist. *"I have separated you from Geb in*

---

[7] The Complete Gods and Goddesses of Ancient Egypt, Wilkinson, 2003:129

your name of Sky; and yet I have united all earth everywhere to you."[8] Shu
stands with his arms raised and bent at the elbow. His arms form
the shape of the hieroglyph symbol for *ka*, which is the life force
or vital essence. This emphasises his role in making creation
suitable for life. "*The arms of Shu which support the sky.*"[9] When Shu
lifted up the sky he enabled the sun to be born and its light to shine
for the first time. In one *Coffin Texts* spell the deceased align
themselves with Shu saying "*I am Life that is under Nut*".[10] Shu is
sometimes given the role of Creator who "*fixed the sky on its four
pillars...when he separated the land from the waters*".[11] Shu is assisted by
the eight Heh Gods of Eternity. They are depicted as squatting men
with upraised arms. Their posture forms the hieroglyph sign for
eternity.

THE STRUCTURE OF THE COSMOS

Regardless of the varying creation theories, the Egyptians had a
clear and precise understanding of the actual structure of the
created universe. Surrounding everything that had been created was
the *nun* and in the middle of creation was the earth, of which Egypt
was the centre and its perfect image. This was the realm of the
Earth God Geb. The air was the realm of Shu and where his realm
ended was the realm of Nut. There is also reference to the space
"*beyond the limits of the circumference of the sky*".[12] This is described as
being in total darkness, as the sun never shines there, and its
boundaries are limitless. The waters of the *nun*, everything beyond
Nut's protective embrace, lay beyond the power of the Sun God,
"*he does not appear there*".[13] Hatshepsut admitted "*I rule as far as the
realm of the primaeval darkness*".[14] In modern terminology this is
beyond the limits of the observable universe, which consists of

---

[8] Hymns, Prayers and Songs, Foster, 1995:20
[9] The Ancient Egyptian Pyramid Texts, Faulkner, 2007:66 utt 255
[10] The Secrets of Tomb 10A, Freed, 2009:124
[11] The Genesis of the Stars in Ancient Egypt, According to the Naos of the Decades, Bomhard, 2016:127
[12] Ancient Egyptian Science Volume II: Calendars, Clocks and Astronomy, Clagett, 1995:371
[13] Genesis in Egypt: The Philosophy of Ancient Egyptian Creation Accounts, Allen, 1988:5
[14] The Sun God's Journey Through the Netherworld, Schweizer, 2010:34

everything that can be seen either from earth or from our space telescopes. Beyond this sphere is a region so distant that light from there has not yet travelled far enough to reach us.

Below the earth lay the netherworld, the realm of Osiris and the deceased, often referred to as the *duat*. The location of the *duat* wasn't clearly defined, it was a place that was neither sky nor land. Parts of it lay underground as this was where the deceased were placed so that they could begin their journey. As the Sun God and some of the stars were considered to spend time in the *duat* it was also thought of as within the body of Nut. The Egyptians were trying to describe and locate a place which we would now say was in a different dimension. On the cenotaph of Sety I it explains that *"as for every place void of sky and void of land, that is the entire Duat"*.[15]

Although the entire sky can be seen, most of its light comes from the stars in the Milky Way or from the sun and moon following the ecliptic. This is a narrow band across the sky which the sun, moon and planets meander along. Areas of the night sky away from this were sometimes thought to be where the absolute darkness of the *nun* touches against our world. It was labelled *"what constricts the intestines"* a very good description of the effects of feeling very vulnerable in total darkness.[16] *"No one is strong at night; no one can fight alone."* Night was to be feared for it hid many potential hazards; dangerous creatures, malevolent humans and spirits and the more mundane but equally serious hazards which accompany trying to move around in the dark. *"Earth is in darkness as if in death...one eye does not see another...every lion comes from its den. All the serpents bite."*[17] Little wonder then that dawn was greeted with joy and the full moon welcomed.

The Egyptians saw no contradiction in viewing the sky in multiple ways. When trying to describe something beyond understanding a number of different approaches can give a better overall impression. The vault of the sky was also viewed as a ceiling and so was considered flat. It could be a transparent barrier

[15] Genesis in Egypt: The Philosophy of Ancient Egyptian Creation Accounts, Allen, 1988:2
[16] Genesis in Egypt: The Philosophy of Ancient Egyptian Creation Accounts, Allen, 1988:5
[17] 100 Hieroglyph: Think Like an Egyptian, Kemp, 2005:108

between creation and the waters of the *nun*, which explained the blue of the sky. Either way it needed supports which rested upon the earth, usually at the cardinal points. These could be the limbs of either Nut or the Cosmic Cow. One relief at Dendera shows four Goddesses supporting the hieroglyph for sky. They are named according to the cardinal directions, such as "*she who carries the East*".[18] The hieroglyph for sky is a plinth with two short supports. Its basic outline is the same as that made by Nut as she arches over the earth. The supports were referred to as the Two Pillars of Heaven which were Mount Bakhau in the east and Mount Manu in the west. It was here that Nut touched the earth. Joining the realms of the sky, earth and *duat* was the horizon. It was viewed as a place of passage between two states, such as day and night or yesterday and tomorrow. As such it was a liminal place where the critical events of death and rebirth took place and it was depicted in a variety of ways, usually as mountains, trees or lions.

The word for firmament is *bia*. This is related to the words *biau*, marvel or wonder, and *biat*, iron.[19] Before the 3rd Intermediate Period the only iron which the Egyptians had access to came from meteorites which were found lying on the surface of the desert. The substance of the sky could be thought of as being some form of iron canopy, bits of which fell to earth. "*The metal that is in the midst of the sky.*" Iron, meteors and lightning strikes were closely connected, as they were in other neighbouring cultures such as Mesopotamia. One *Pyramid Texts* spell refers to the "*cords of bj3 to go up to the sky*".[20] A number of the spells refer to the king ascending in the midst of a storm or becoming a flash of lightning.

The concept of the cosmos as a building is reflected in the architecture of temples which were considered to be an earthly representation of creation. "*Columns in the form of papyrus plants and date-palms support the heaven of its roof, just as the four goddesses support the heaven of the world. There is an Offering Court with surrounding columns in front of it, as light as the sky-goddess Nut when she has given birth to the daylight.*"[21] Perimeter walls, often inscribed with the hieroglyph for

---

[18] The Theology of Hathor of Dendera, Richter, 2016:140
[19] Ancient Egyptian Cosmogenesis and Cosmology, Lesko, 1991:117
[20] The Cultural Indexicality of the N41 sign for b3j, Almanso-Villatoro, 2019:73-81
[21] The Temple of Edfu, Kurth, 2004:48

water, formed the boundary which protected the temple from the chaos of the outside world just as Nut protected creation from the chaos of the *nun*. The structure of the cosmos is also seen in some of the ways in which rituals are enacted and the deceased ascend to heaven. Ladders, staircases, doors and gates are important symbols. Ladders and staircases are symbolic as they depict a way of transitioning between states such as life and death and between the worlds.

The sky hieroglyph was used on the top of walls, doors and gateways. Passing through the portal corresponded to walking under the arched, protecting body of Nut. To further emphasise the link, the hieroglyph was often covered with stars. Sacred portals, in the form of arches or gateways, are common concepts in many cultures. They mark the boundary between the sacred and the profane, forming both a visible boundary and an entrance. A spell for opening the doors of a shrine states that "*the two door-leaves of the sky are open*".[22] In the Chapel of Nefertem is a request that "*thy mother, Nut, may open for thee the two doors of the sky*".[23] Inscriptions in some 5th dynasty burial chambers refer to the Gate of Nut as the symbolic doorway to heaven.[24] There is reference to the horizon as the gates or doors of earth. "*The door of Geb has been made to draw aside.*"[25] All these will lie at the rim of the sky, the horizon. No living person can approach them because the horizon will always move away from the observer, unless you are approaching a sheer rock face. This may be one reason why mountains were considered liminal places with entrances to the underworld.

The Nile dominated the lives of the majority of the Egyptians; Egypt wouldn't exist without the Nile. It is no surprise that they envisaged a celestial river above them and various rivers below them in the *duat*. Their deities used boats for transport, the most important being the Solar and Lunar Barques. The edges of the Milky Way could be viewed as the banks of the Celestial River which divides the sky in two. The position of the Milky Way moves across the sky over the year. To the north are the constellations and

[22] Temple Ritual at Abydos, David, 2016:137
[23] Temple Ritual at Abydos, David, 2016:219
[24] Reading Egyptian Art, Wilkinson, 2011:147
[25] The Cosmology of the Pyramid Texts, Allen, 1989:22

the circumpolar or imperishable stars and to the south are the unwearying stars and the decan stars (these are used for timekeeping and are discussed in chapter 7). The imperishable stars are those that never die, that is they never set below the horizon. The unwearying stars disappear and reappear showing a cycle of death and rebirth.

The sky contains both beings and places. Within it are the planets, stars, sun, moon, the deities and the *bas* of the deceased. The word *ba* is often translated as soul though it may be more accurate to describe it as the manifestation of the spirit or personality of the deceased. In effect it is the essence of the person without any physical attributes or constraints. Deities usually have multiple *bas*. The deities might manifest on earth but their domain is in the sky. "*When the sky was split from the earth and the gods went to the sky.*"[26] The celestial inhabitants will be covered in later chapters. Two important afterlife places are the Field of Offerings, in the northern sky, and the Field of Reeds in the southern sky. The *Pyramid Texts* describe a "*great island in the midst of the Field of Offerings on which the swallow-gods alight; the swallows are the Imperishable Stars*".[27] As on earth there are pathways across the sky. The Milky Way forms the "*beaten path of the stars*".[28] In one *Pyramid Texts* spell the deceased king is led on "*the goodly roads which are in the sky in the Field of Rushes*".[29]

GENDER DIFFERENCES

Even among the civilisations of their time the Egyptians frequently perceived things differently to the rest of the world. Everyone else had Sky Gods while the Egyptians had the Goddess Nut, Hathor as a Sky Goddess and the Cosmic Cow. The Falcon God Horus the Elder is a Sky God but he is contained within the realm of Hathor in her aspect of the diurnal sky. Likewise, other cultures had an Earth Goddess but the Egyptians had the Earth God Geb as well as the Lion Gods of Earth, Ruty and Aker,

---

[26] The Cosmology of the Pyramid Texts, Allen, 1989:3
[27] The Ancient Egyptian Pyramid Texts, Faulkner, 2007:193 utt 519
[28] The Cosmology of the Pyramid Texts, Allen, 1989:7
[29] The Ancient Egyptian Pyramid Texts, Faulkner, 2007:148 utt 442

although they tend to be associated more with the horizon. The Egyptian word for sky was a feminine noun and that for earth a masculine one, but there has to be more to it than grammar. One suggestion is that the Earth Goddess was removed by the patriarchal powers, but the fact that she exists in other very patriarchal, male-dominated cultures at the same period makes this unlikely. The role of the cow is too important to ignore and perhaps the image of a suckling calf beneath her mother evolved into the Great Cow Goddess above us all. In Egypt the earth was seen in the context of solidity rather than as a womb. The horizon connects the earth to the sky and has a more fluid gender, as might be expected of a liminal place. The word for horizon is a feminine noun but its determinative connected it to the masculine which was a pair of mountains representing earth.[30] (A determinative is a sign which clarifies the meaning of a word but which isn't part of the pronunciation.)

MAINTAINING THE COSMOS

Once created everything needs to be protected, maintained and regulated lest it slip back into unformed chaos. The cosmos is no exception. Allen describes Egyptian cosmology as a *"construct of opposites in balance: nonexistence and potentiality balanced against existence and reality"*.[31] Everything is interconnected and events have an impact throughout the structure of the cosmos. There is also a balance between the static and the dynamic which is reflected in the two terms that the Egyptians used for eternity. *Neheh* is cyclical time; the ever-renewing cycles of nature which give the seasons and the processes of birth-life-death-rebirth. *Djet* is continuous time; the apparently eternal presence of the earth and the circumpolar stars.

The Goddess Maat personifies the order of the cosmos and the laws of physics and nature. She keeps both the divine world in order and the stars and atoms spinning. Without her, all of creation would quickly return to the chaotic waters of the *nun*. *"Order is effective. Its*

---

[30] Nut: The Goddess of Life in Text and Iconography, Billing, 2002:201
[31] Genesis in Egypt: The Philosophy of Ancient Egyptian Creation Accounts, Allen, 1988:57

appropriateness lasts. It has not been disturbed since the time of the one who made it."[32] The endless task of regulation and protection is carried out by many of the deities and, in theory at least, has to be mirrored on earth from the actions of the king down to those of ordinary individuals. Nut has a major role in keeping the destructive forces of chaos away as it is her body which forms the protective shield around the cosmos. This shield was viewed as permeable and invisible which is why the blue waters of the *nun* can be seen through it and why the life-giving water, as well as the destructive Chaos Serpent Apophis, can enter. Nut is the boundary or interface between the *nun* and creation and the force which holds back the eternally threatening waters of the *nun*. In some ways she can be likened to the earth's magnetic field which protects the earth from the damaging effects of cosmic radiation and encloses our atmosphere, protecting it from being stripped away by the solar wind. Shu, as the atmosphere, can only exist beneath her.

WHY IS THE NIGHT SKY IMPORTANT?

The night sky has been important for most of human history. Only now, when many of us live in light-polluted areas, has it become a minor background. The Enlightenment of the 18th century might have split science and religion and removed the divine from our skies, but the ensuing technological developments and science have given us a phenomenal amount of information and wonderful photography. Our universe is far bigger for us than it was for ancient cultures and in some ways can be viewed as cold, remote and indifferent – which it actually is in physical terms. However, the patterns and wonder might be science but they should also be appreciated for what Heath calls their *"poetic cosmology"*.[33] The ancient astronomers were studying the night sky in a scientific way. Understanding the workings of the cosmos allowed a glimpse into the divine world. Ancient societies used the night sky in a number of different ways, some of which are used today for the same purpose; for timekeeping and ascertaining the

---

[32] Genesis in Egypt: The Philosophy of Ancient Egyptian Creation Accounts, Allen, 1988:57
[33] Sun, Moon & Earth, Heath, 2006:1

future, for navigation and for storytelling (both serious such as divine mythology and for entertainment). It gives us patterns and cycles which need explaining and also assists in connecting to the divine – something tangible and awe-inspiring.

CHAPTER 3

Introducing the Goddess Nut

"Hail, O Nut, far-striding Goddess who strews the
greenstone, malachite and turquoise of the stars."[34]

THE NAME OF THE GODDESS

Nut's name is written as *Nwt* using the hieroglyph symbols of a circular water pot and a loaf above the sky symbol which is the determinative. The pot gives the syllable *nw* and was an appropriate symbol given her key aspects which are discussed below. Her name may have been derived from the word *nw*, water, hence the water pot symbol. Allen suggests that her name means She of the Waters.[35] We may not consider the sky and cosmos to be watery but to the Egyptians the water alluded to is the water of the *nun*. As well as giving the syllable *t* the bread loaf alludes to the life-giving power of food both in life and as offerings in the afterlife. The

---

[34] Hymns, Prayers and Songs, Foster, 1995:21
[35] Genesis in Egypt: The Philosophy of Ancient Egyptian Creation Accounts, Allen, 1988:5

Greeks completely misunderstood the power and presence of Nut as they equated her with Rhea who was the daughter of the Sky God Cronos and the Earth Goddess Gaia.

EPITHETS

Nut has the generic epithets of many Goddesses such as Mother, Great One, Lady of Heliopolis and Mistress of the Two Lands. She is the Mother of the Gods, a reference to her giving birth to both Ra and to her five children with Geb. Many other epithets refer to her as a Sky Goddess. Her name is virtually interchangeable with that of sky. "*O Great Sky, give your hand to the King; O Great Nut, give your hand to the King.*"[36] She is Lady of the Sky[37] and Goddess of the Northern Sky.[38] The northern sky contained the circumpolar stars and the Egyptian constellations. The north in general was a positive concept, associated with cool and refreshing breezes rather than the stifling heat of the south. In the *Litany of Re* there is reference to Nut as the Lady of the Mountains.[39] These are the mountains of the horizon. One *Pyramid Texts* epithet is Great Horizon and she is also Lady of the Horizon.[40] Nut is closely connected with tombs, coffins and sarcophagi so can be referred to simply as in "*her name of sarcophagus*" or "*name of tomb*".[41] In this role she is Protector and the Great Encloser. Sometimes she is called Encloser of the Frightened, which is probably the best description of a deceased but aware person. One epithet of hers is Shentayet – the Mysterious One. This alludes both to her role in rebirth and the mysteries of the cosmos. Other epithets are Nut the Granary[42] and the Effective One.[43]

---

[36] The Ancient Egyptian Pyramid Texts, Faulkner, 2007:292 utt 681
[37] Spread Your Wings Over Me, Sousa, 2014:102
[38] Egyptian Astronomical Texts I: The Early Decans, Neugebauer & Parker, 1960:44
[39] The Litany of Re, Piankoff, 1964:134
[40] Spread Your Wings Over Me, Sousa, 2014:102
[41] The Routledge Dictionary of Egyptian Gods and Goddesses, Hart, 2005:112
[42] The Ancient Egyptian Pyramid Texts, Faulkner, 2007:143 utt 435
[43] The Great Goddesses of Egypt, Lesko, 1999:42

DEPICTIONS OF NUT

Nut is normally depicted as a woman. Sometimes she has a water pot or sky hieroglyph on her head to identify her. At other times she just wears a tie around her head. She can be depicted standing, kneeling or arching over the ground to form the protecting sky. On coffins she is often shown kneeling and with wings. Kneeling is associated with mourning. Wings symbolise protection based on the way that a bird will use their wings to shelter or protect their young. On a Late Period coffin there is a depiction of Nut found nowhere else. Here she arches over a circle which represents the world. This is believed to have been a Greek or western Asiatic influence.[44]

Nudity is rare in Egyptian depictions of deities. Usually only child Gods are shown nude as a sign of their youth. Nut is the main exception and she is portrayed nude when she is shown arching over the earth. Hathor is occasionally shown nude as the Goddess of the West. (The West is a euphemism for the afterlife.) This was to emphasise her sky aspect by aligning her more closely with Nut. When Nut is depicted as a standing or kneeling woman she is clothed. Her dress is frequently blue sometimes with long sleeves, as on the lid of a 21st dynasty coffin from Tanis.[45] Her dress is decorated with stars (representing the deceased) because she was *"the one with a thousand souls"* as well as being Mother of the Stars.[46] On the base of the sarcophagus of Sety I (19th dynasty) she is depicted wearing a tight-fitting dress which has a pattern of feathers.

Nut and Hathor share a number of depictions, and the close associations of these two Goddesses is discussed in the following chapter. Like Hathor, Nut can take the form of a cow. One *Pyramid Texts* spell refers to Nut as *"she the long-horned, the pendulous of breast"*.[47] Nut is not depicted with a cow's head, Hathor is rarely depicted in this form either. Forward-facing deities are rare in Egyptian art probably because it is hard to create an elegant form in two dimensions. The protective dwarf God Bes is shown in this way, as

---

[44] Hieroglyphs & the Afterlife, Foreman & Quirke, 1996:137
[45] Reading Egyptian Art, Wilkinson, 2011:130
[46] Ancient Egyptian Religion, Cerny, 1957:82
[47] The Ancient Egyptian Pyramid Texts, Faulkner, 2007:211 utt 548

is Hathor with whom he had a close relationship. Nut is shown facing forward on a few Netherworld Texts and on coffins. Nut and Hathor have a close association with the sycamore tree in the afterlife and can be depicted as a tree or in a composite woman-tree form.

One unusual depiction of Nut, indeed of any Goddess, is found on a coffin from the 3rd Intermediate Period. She is pregnant with a rounded stomach. In Egyptian art women are depicted with a flat stomach even when it is clear from other information that they are pregnant or in the process of giving birth.

This linked them with the concept of emergence both of creation out of the *nun* and the dawn sun rising as the scarab Khepri from the body of Nut. In the New Kingdom the Celestial Cow (as Hathor or Mehet-Weret) is frequently depicted emerging from the Western Mountains. The fact that some flint nodules have the stylised appearance of a pregnant woman seems to have associated them with Nut. Flint was considered to be of celestial origin, further strengthening this connection.[48]

HER SACRED ANIMALS

Nut's principal animal form is the cow but it doesn't appear to have been particularly sacred to her. In the temple of Sety I at Abydos Nut is likened to a sow eating her piglets when she swallows the stars. From the 3rd Intermediate Period Nut was depicted on glazed amulets as a sow, sometimes with up to seven piglets around her. Is this related to the seven stars of the Plough, or another asterism, or is it because seven is a magic number? Isis has amulets in a similar form; by this time she was assimilating many Goddesses and adopting their forms. The Goddess the amulet refers to can only be discerned if there is an inscription. One amulet is in the shape of a sow with a head at each end. Andrews suggests it may show a dual Nut-Isis aspect.[49] Such amulets were worn as fertility amulets.

---

[48] Emergent Flints, Graves-Brown, 2006:53-54
[49] Amulets of Ancient Egypt, Andrews, 1994:35

Nut as woman – based on an image found in a burial chamber of Djehuti

Two *Pyramid Texts* spells refer to Nut *"who appeared as a bee"*. In this she has *"power over the gods, their doubles, their heritages, their provisions and all their possessions"*. [50] Bees were economically important providing honey and wax, the latter used to make ointments. They had religious significance as they were said to have sprung from the tears of Ra. Neith was a Creator Goddess and was linked to Nut in her aspect of the Cosmic Cow. She was associated with the bee and her temple at Sais was called the *per-bit*, the house of the bee.

ASPECTS

Nut's aspects will be covered in more detail in the following chapters. In one way Nut's main role is that of firmament, the personification of the vault of heaven. *"I am Nut the Great, the Mighty...the earth is under me to its limit."*[51] However, no deity can be just a personification of a concept or a thing. Nut's main aspect is at a cosmic level where she is a very active force intricately involved in the maintenance of the cosmos and natural cycles. Sometimes she is equated to the entire sky, at others she is seen in the Milky Way.

Nut has a strong water element which isn't the first quality we would think of for a Sky deity, especially in a country with a very dry climate. I use the term sky as the Egyptians understood it, weather taking place in the atmosphere which is the realm of Shu. The womb is both dark and watery and for an individual is like the primeval waters of the *nun* which preceded light and life. The source of life is in the watery darkness. One *Pyramid Texts* spell refers to *"the waters of life which are in the sky"*.[52] Water is also associated with purification, a very symbolic and important ritual for the Egyptians. Nut's symbol of the water pot links her aspect of water with her very important one of enclosure. In the spelling of her name the Egyptians described her core attributes; a Sky Goddess associated with a contained space filled with life and water. In one Greco-Roman spell she is addressed as Nut, Mother of Water.[53] The

---

[50] The Ancient Egyptian Pyramid Texts, Faulkner, 2007:142 utt 431
[51] The Great Goddesses of Egypt, Lesko, 1999:42
[52] The Ancient Egyptian Pyramid Texts, Faulkner, 2007:295 utt 685
[53] The Leyden Papyrus, Griffith & Thompson, 1974:53

Egyptians believed that all water on earth originally came from the waters of the *nun*. Most scientists now believe that water was brought to earth by comets and asteroids.

Nut is the all-encompassing Great Mother but a very different one to those of most other cultures. Normally the Great Mother is seen as the natural regenerative force of the individual womb and the womb of earth. Nut however is the Great Round who encloses the universe. Hers is the womb of the generative *nun*. She is a creative space in which life is constantly regenerated. By providing the attributes of contained space and water Nut can be viewed as life itself. Nut is the source of everything. The cosmos is her body and she births and nourishes all living things taking them back into her body at death. Unlike virtually all the other Mother Goddesses Nut isn't remotely chthonic, despite being associated with the tomb and coffin.

Nut is the eternal mother of the Sun God as she gives birth to Ra each morning. *"Nut, who gave birth to the gods, lady of heaven, mistress of the Two Lands, lady of eternity, who creates everlastingness."*[54] Because Nut is the mother of Osiris she is the mother of all the deceased, who identify with Osiris so they too can be resurrected. She is often shown on coffin lids as a vulture which has a strong association with motherhood and protection. The word for mother is written with the vulture hieroglyph. A papyrus from the Roman Period includes a prayer to Nut. *"O Mother, I desire to conceive a daughter...she being conceived within me in a free time, there being nothing odious forever."*[55] This is the only reference we have to Nut in terms of a Fertility Goddess on an individual basis but she is an obvious choice as she is *"Nut the Greatly Fruitful"* and as the Sow represents fecundity.[56] *"Nut who is in the Necropolis"* becomes a very personal Goddess at the moment of death and in the afterlife.[57] In funerary contexts Nut is associated with trees, both in the provision of water and food and also with enclosure, by their branches or in a more literal sense as the wood which makes the coffin.

---

[54] The Tomb of Maya and Meryt I, Martin, 2012:44
[55] An Appeal to Nut in a Papyrus of the Roman Era, Griffiths:182-183
[56] The Dialogue of Geb and Nut in Relation to the Royal Sarcophagus in the Pyramid of King Pepy I, Billing, 2016:6
[57] Nut: The Goddess of Life in Text and Iconography, Billing, 2002:284

HER PARENTS – SHU AND TEFNUT

Little is mentioned about Tefnut in relation to Nut. A hymn to Nut emphasises her innate greatness when it describes how the *"splendour is yours and the power was yours from the body of your mother, Tefnut…make this king a spirit within you"*.[58] Some versions and translations use the word *akh* instead of spirit or power. This term describes a transfigured being and has associations with light and luminosity as well as alluding to powerful abilities. Being an *akh* was a description of deities associated with the power of creation and regeneration. Atum, Ra, Osiris, Isis and Horus were also described as *akh*. As Nut was *akh* within the womb of her mother she is able to give the same to the king who is within the sarcophagus which is her womb. The *akh* is also the form that the vindicated deceased take and is an imperishable and celestial form.

In a text on the shrine of Tutankhamun (18th dynasty) Nut describes herself as the *Uraeus* Serpent, which is an unusual role for her to take as it is Tefnut who is a *Uraeus* Serpent. In assuming this role Nut appears to have absorbed the power and aspect of her mother. The *uraeus* is closely associated with the Eye of the Sun and Nut must contain solar elements because the sun and stars exist within her. Shu's main role is to support Nut in the heavens and to ensure that she remains separate from Geb to enable life to flourish. Unlike Ra he is not upset by their wanting to lie together but knows that their separation is essential.

HER CONSORT GEB

As discussed previously, Nut and Geb had to be forced apart because they were lovers. Geb is often depicted as a man lying on his side leaning on his elbow, sometimes with an erect phallus to show their forced separation and to emphasise his fertility aspects. His symbolic animal is the goose and the goose hieroglyph is used in his name. Osiris is often referred to via his parents as *"son of Geb, born of Nut"*.[59] In the New Kingdom *Book of Nut* Geb is reported as having an argument with Nut, he accuses her of eating her children

---

[58] Hymns, Prayers and Songs, Foster, 1995:19
[59] The Tomb of Maya and Meryt I, Martin, 2012:21

when she appears to swallow the stars each night. This is discussed in chapter 7.

RA – THE TROUBLED SUN GOD

Ra does not come across well in a number of myths. He has become a jealous and angry God, unwilling to take responsibility and unable to deal effectively with problems. He is both Nut's son, reflecting the original concept, and her grandfather once the solar religion gained supremacy. Nut as the Sun God's mother is covered in chapter 5. The *Book of the Heavenly Cow* appears on one of Tutankhamun's shrines. It was first attested to in the New Kingdom but is thought to have existed in the Middle Kingdom. On the shrine it depicts Nut as a Cow supported by Shu and the Heh Gods. The sun, moon and stars sail across her stomach. This text describes how humans rebelled against Ra and were punished by the Lioness Goddess Sekhmet. She is one of the Daughters of Ra and the Solar Eye. This is covered in detail in Jackson (2018). At the end of this episode Ra decides that he doesn't want to remain on earth with humans as they cause too much trouble. *"As I live for myself, my heart is too weary to remain with them, that I should slay them to the very last one."*[60] Nut transforms herself into a cow and takes Ra on her back. Soon Ra discovers that humans are continuing in their war-like ways and orders Nut to lift him further up into the heavens far away from the rebellious humans. *"And so she came to be there in both the heavens...she became the sky. Then the majesty of god was visible within her."* Ra then created the Milky Way and the Field of Rushes. When the Cow of Nut started shaking under the weight of all this Ra asked Shu to *"place yourself under my granddaughter Nut"*.[61] He is assisted in this by the Heh Gods, who live in the twilight at the rim of the sky. The Cow form of Nut as the mother of the Sun God is referenced in a morning hymn to the sun. *"Hail to thee, Great One, who came forth from the Heavenly Cow."*[62]

---

[60] The Literature of Ancient Egypt, Simpson, 2003:292
[61] The Literature of Ancient Egypt, Simpson, 2003:293
[62] Ancient Egyptian Religion, Frankfort, 1948:17

THE CHILDREN OF NUT

The children of Nut and Geb in birth order are Osiris, Horus the Elder, Seth, Isis and Nephthys. Horus the Elder isn't part of the Osirian mythology. It is thought that he was included because of the need for five extra days in the calendar. His presence may have been to show that the Falcon Sky God existed within Nut and came from her. Seth, in keeping with his violent and chaotic nature, wasn't born in the normal manner. *"Typhon, neither in season nor in place, but breaking through with a blow, leapt forth from her side."*[63] (The Greeks associated Seth with Typhon, their deadliest monster who was the son of the Earth Goddess Gaia and Tartarus, a God of the underworld.) Nut is the only Goddess who has a multiple birth, another reason perhaps for her association with the fecund sow.

The story we have is told by Plutarch, which will differ from the earlier and original Egyptian versions. Ra is angry when Nut becomes pregnant and he forbids her to give birth *"in month and year"*, that is at any time of the year. As the creator of time this is apparently within Ra's control. Thoth comes to her assistance with the help of the moon. Plutarch explains that by *"playing draughts against Selene, and winning the seventieth of each of the lights, he conduced from all five days and induced them into the three hundred and sixty"*.[64] Because these days hadn't been created by Ra, Nut was able to give birth to her children without contravening the curse laid on her. 1/70th of 360 days gives 5.1, which is enough light to make five additional days. The need for these five extra days, referred to as the epagomenal days, to add to the 360 day year is discussed in chapter 12. The *Pyramid Texts* refer to these as the *"birth of the gods"*. Each of the five deities were associated with a specific day. Because these five days were created out of time they were considered dangerous and liminal, forming a bridge from the old to the new year. Normal time had been suspended, so that the five extra days could be inserted, and there was the fear that it couldn't be restarted. The end of the year was at the hottest time when food and water levels were low and pests and diseases were rampant. Referred to as *"the*

---

[63] Plutarch: Concerning the Mysteries of Isis and Osiris, Mead, 2002:195
[64] Plutarch: Concerning the Mysteries of Isis and Osiris, Mead, 2002:194

five days above the year" they became associated with Sekhmet and her demons who brought plague and disaster at the end of the year.[65]

Nut doesn't have much of a maternal role because she is the Great Mother, not the individual, personal mother as exemplified by Isis. She does play a part in the resurrection of Osiris as she does for all the deceased. Osiris is frequently referred to as the Son of Nut or Firstborn of Nut as this emphasises his important ancestry. He is also *"beloved of his mother Nut".*[66] Her other children Isis, Nephthys and Seth are referred to in a similar way. Nut isn't blamed for her wayward son Seth. *"Nut, the great one...who dispels chaos from her son."*[67] In the *Book of the Dead* Seth addresses Apophis reminding him that he is the *"greatest magician, the son of Nut".*[68] His father, Geb, does have power over snakes but chthonic power is no use against Apophis, which may be why Seth stresses his inheritance from his mother. Being in such close proximity to the *nun* she is better placed to understand chaos and to deal with it. Nut lets her children go their own ways, as she does with all of us, until she enfolds them back within her at death. Unlike her mother Nut, Isis is very involved with the lives of her husband and son. This is one reason why Nut didn't have a cult following whilst Isis did.

NUT'S CHANGING ROLE AND STATUS

Why was Ra so upset when Nut became pregnant? He wasn't when Shu and Tefnut had children but they were essential components in the structure of creation providing time and space. Nut was going to do what no man or God could – conceive a child through sexual intercourse and create independent life. In doing so she threatened his role as creator. Jealousy also plays a part. Ra is reborn each morning from the body of Nut and these additional five offspring can be viewed as his younger siblings. He was frightened that they or their offspring would challenge his position of absolute authority. Osiris, Seth, Isis and Nephthys belong to the Osirian mythological cycle and cult and as such were a threat to the

---

[65] Some Remarks on the Epagomenal Days in Ancient Egypt, Spalinger, 1995:33-47
[66] Ancient Egyptian Literature Volume II, Lichtheim, 2006:82
[67] The Tomb of Maya and Meryt I, Martin, 2012:45
[68] The Sun God's Journey Through the Netherworld, Schweizer, 2010:141

dominance of the Heliopolitan solar tradition. It is Osiris who is central to the rebirth and resurrection mythic cycles and he and Isis became very popular amongst the ordinary people as well as in the official cults. As such they were incorporated into the solar cult and pantheon because of their growing popularity, as a way of avoiding any loss of status and power by the solar cult.

Originally, the Great Mother Goddess gave birth to us all. Throughout all cultures she lost this role with the rise of the patriarchy when one God usurped her role and generated life by other means. It is in Nut's relationship with Ra that the decline and demotion of the Great Mother Goddess is illustrated. The creator God and his priests are filled with jealousy and anger when the Goddess gives birth naturally. The decline of feminine power and status is seen in the fact that creator Gods give birth to all life without the need of the Goddess. Nut, once Mother of all, becomes the granddaughter of the creator Sun God.

OUR GALACTIC GODDESS

Nut is a light-bringer who *"chases away the shadows and makes the light shine everywhere"*.[69] She gives birth to the light-giving stars, including our own sun, and also transforms the deceased, taking them out of the darkness of death into the light of eternal life within her body. She has no dedicated temples, no cult and apparently no followers, yet she is one of the most helpful of the afterlife Goddesses. So why wasn't Nut worshipped in everyday life? There appear to be three main reasons for this. Nut as the night sky might be awe-inspiring but as such she can appear very remote from the concerns of daily life. The known universe is far larger for us than it was for the Egyptians and for many, the larger it gets the more remote and incomprehensible it appears. Secondly, although Nut is important in the myths there is little in them that can be reinterpreted on a human level unlike in those about deities such as Isis and Osiris. Finally, Nut is very much a Funerary Goddess. Would this have dissuaded people from worshipping her? You will meet the afterlife deities soon enough, why call to them and risk

---

[69] The Myth of the Goddess: Evolution of an Image, Barring & Cashford, 1993:259-260

shortening your life? They knew that Nut never demanded worship as a prerequisite for helping the deceased, unlike the jealous sole god of some religions. Perhaps the Egyptians felt no compulsion to set up temples to her as they saw and acknowledged her regularly in the night sky.

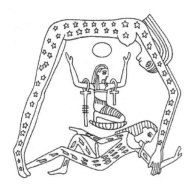

CHAPTER 4

The Great Encloser

*"I am Nut, tall and great in the horizon...you shall sit
under me and cool yourself under my branches."*[70]

NUT AS THE ENCLOSER

In her enclosure aspect Nut defines the boundaries of a space,
whether of the universe, the earth or the coffin. Life may need
space to exist in, but it also needs boundaries to contain it so that
it can work as a single entity, be it an individual cell or an entire
ecosystem. Space and water are the media through which life exists.
Nut defines the space in the afterlife, or night, where Ra and Osiris
can meet and unite. In the *Pyramid Texts* and *Coffin Texts* there are
many references to Nut as the Great Encloser. In the *Pyramid Texts*
Encloser or Protector is Nut's most common epithet. The Egyptian
word, *hnmt*, uses a basket as its determinative.[71] Nut embraces,

---

[70] The Painted Tomb-Chapel of Nebamun, Parkinson, 2008:135
[71] Nut: The Goddess of Life in Text and Iconography, Billing, 2002:179

spreads herself over and covers the deceased. *"The embrace of your mother Nut will enfold you."*[72] Her actions both protect the deceased and provide a womb-like space for them to regenerate in. One of Nut's most important manifestations is as an enclosed space where death is transformed back into life.

THE SYCAMORE FIG

It is surprising that a Sky Goddess should also be a Tree Goddess but Nut's attributes of enclosed space and water tie in well with tree symbolism. She is identified with the Sycamore Fig (*Ficus sycomorus*) which is a different species to the European sycamore. Called *nehet*, its hieroglyph was used to represent trees in general. This is a stylised form of the shape of the leaf which is a smooth oval. In paintings this symbol can be used as the actual tree, scaled up and coloured green often bearing fruit. Mature trees can reach up to 12m with a trunk girth of over 6m which produces a canopy of up to 36m in diameter. The word *nehet*, when written with a house determinative, gives it the meaning of refuge. Standing beneath the enclosing canopy of a densely foliaged tree, the bright sky can be seen between small gaps in the leaves. These points of light against the dark green appear like stars against the black of the night sky. The sycamore's fruit is smaller than that of true figs and Classical writers report them yielding over three crops a year. Fruit-bearing trees have an obvious connection to the Goddess. When the tree is cut its sap, a milky colour, runs out providing a visual link to a nursing mother.

TREE GODDESSES AND THEIR DEPICTIONS

A number of Goddesses can take the form of a Tree Goddess including Nut, Hathor and later Isis. The Goddess Nehet is the embodiment of the tree itself. They can all be the Lady of the Sycamore, but this title is more often used for Hathor. The Goddesses appear identical, only when there is a caption can they be identified. Tree Goddesses became a popular motif in the 18th

---

[72] The Ancient Egyptian Pyramid Texts, Faulkner, 200:50 utt 222

dynasty when they appear on tomb paintings and coffins. The Tree Goddesses are shown in a number of different forms. In the tomb of Nebamun Nut is depicted with her torso emerging from the foliage and she offers fruit and drink to the deceased and his wife. In later periods it is often just a pair of arms which emerge from the tree holding food and drink for the deceased. Sometimes the Tree Goddess is depicted next to a tree or with the tree hieroglyph on her head. If the Tree Goddess is Nut she sometimes stands on a platform depicted as a pool of water. In the papyrus Louvre Nut tells the deceased *"I am together with you that I may unite you with your ba; I shall not be far away from you, ever"*.[73]

THE TREE GODDESS IN THE AFTERLIFE

Nut welcomes the deceased into a garden of paradise with a pool full of fish and ducks surrounded by large trees. While certainly considered a paradise, particularly to people in dry countries, it seems a strange contradiction for a Goddess who welcomes the deceased as a star. Trees, gardens and ponds were full of symbolism. The pool, like the *nun* and Nut, was a source of regeneration as well as life. Trees around an oasis or on the banks of the Nile suggested the life-generating waters of the *nun*. Trees only grow if they are near a water source but conversely the presence of trees points to the presence of water which could be viewed as the gift of the tree. Technically this is true as trees are an important part of the water cycle. They store and release water vapour controlling rainfall and the presence of trees in arid lands stops desertification.

The enclosed garden can be seen as a space for the deceased provided by Nut. Like a single star, it is a distinct entity within the much larger context of the cosmic space of Nut. In the same way as a traveller coming across an oasis in the desert, the deceased finds water, food and sanctuary in the barren afterlife. *"Nut the great one, working wonders in her name of sycamore…your ba sits in my shade and drinks water to its heart's content."*[74]

---

[73] Nut: The Goddess of Life in Text and Iconography, Billing, 2002:307
[74] The Sycamore in Ancient Egypt, Azzazy & Ezzat, 2016:212

Nut as Tree Goddess. From tomb of Nakht.

It is the Tree Goddess who enables the deceased to breathe air and she provides them with food and water in the afterlife. "*O you Sycamore of Nut, give me the water and air in you.*"[75] The cool air under the shade of a tree is pleasanter to breathe than the hot desert air. The Egyptians knew instinctively that trees provide us with cleaner, cooler air and so were associated with the ability to breathe. Sycamores were often planted near the tombs to symbolise their gifts in the afterlife. A mature sycamore fig creates a natural sacred space which is shady and cool beneath its massive lateral branches. Given the temperatures in Egypt it is no surprise that sitting in the shade was considered a necessity in the afterlife. Tomb paintings often depict the deceased sitting under a tree.

Sacred places can sometimes have an air of menace or exclusivity, but the sycamore fig and its kindly Goddess makes it an approachable natural sacred space. The Egyptians didn't have the heavy forests that some other cultures had to bring any negative concepts to trees and shade. Burial in a wooden coffin was symbolic of a return to the womb of the Mother Tree Goddess. A cedar tree was said to have grown around the coffin of Osiris when it was washed up on the shore at Byblos. "*Hail to you, you tree which encloses the god.*"[76] The trunk of a tree can easily be viewed as a coffin and sycamore wood was often used for coffins. Nut assures everyone that she will "*cover the corpses of those who have no tomb. I shall be with you and unite you with your ba, I shall not depart from you, forever*".[77] This would have been a very comforting thought for the poorer majority of Egyptians or those whose corpses were damaged or never found. "*Thy mother Nut has spread over thee that she may protect thee from evil.*" This is equally appropriate of both the sycamore of Nut and the coffin lid of Nut. "*I have embraced the sycamore and I have joined the sycamore.*"[78]

One address to Nut in a 19th dynasty tomb refers to her as the "*Great and Transformed in this her name of Sycamore*".[79] One vignette for the spell shows a man adoring a tree and the sun disc rising over

---

[75] Ancient Egyptian Literature Volume II, Lichtheim, 2006:122
[76] The Ancient Egyptian Pyramid Texts, Faulkner, 2007:229 utt 574
[77] Death and Salvation in Ancient Egypt, Assman, 2005:359
[78] The Goddesses of the Egyptian Tree Cult, Buhl, 1947:80-97
[79] Nut: The Goddess of Life in Text and Iconography, Billing, 2002:250

its top. Nut is the celestial body where the deceased are placed and are given eternal or recurring life. A much more personal and relatable image is that of the deceased receiving these gifts whilst sitting under her tree.

THE WORLD AND HORIZON TREES

One of the markers and guardians of the eastern horizon were two sycamore trees of turquoise. The sun rose between these two trees, equating them with the Sun God's birth from Nut. The soul of Osiris, as a *ba*-bird, was said to rest on the tree where the sun was reborn. The *Pyramid Texts* speak of a *"tall sycamore in the east of the sky, quivering of leaves, on which the gods sit"*.[80] One depiction of Nut is as a large tree with human-headed *ba*-birds flying around and perching in her branches. The *ba*-birds sitting on the body of the Tree Goddess were like the *bas* of the stars within the body of Nut. In some ways Nut can be seen as the all-encompassing World Tree but she is not a Tree Goddess in terms of being a presiding deity of trees, forests or nature. She has a Tree Goddess aspect because the sycamore tree forms an excellent metaphor for her funerary role as well as encompassing her two primary aspects of space and water.

NUT AS THE COFFIN AND SARCOPHAGUS.

As Nut is the mother of Osiris she is also the mother of all the deceased. The enclosing coffin symbolised the body of Nut which enclosed and protected the deceased and also her womb in which they were reborn. Nut was shown both inside and outside of the coffin or sarcophagus, on the base or on its lid. In Old Kingdom texts the sarcophagus chest was sometimes referred to as *mwt* – mother. [81] Nut is frequently requested to spread herself over the deceased. *"O Nut, spread yourself out over your son...conceal him...protect him."*[82] Like the temple, the coffin was a reflection of creation and during the Middle Kingdom cosmological elements were important design motifs. The lid was associated with the sky and Nut. The

[80] The Ancient Egyptian Pyramid Texts, Faulkner, 2007:159 utt 470
[81] Spread Your Wings Over Me, Sousa, 2014:103
[82] Hymns, Prayers and Songs, Foster, 1995:19

inner part of the lid was decorated with star clocks and constellations linking them to the stars which sailed across her body. The lid could also be decorated with repeating star hieroglyphs. It was the cosmic reference which was the most important rather than the astronomical accuracy of the representations. The coffin now had cosmic space which could enclose the deceased. The corners of the coffin could be aligned with the four pillars which held up the sky.

Nut as the embracing Mother is a very common decorative motif on coffins. Decoration on the outer coffin of Djedhor (Ptolemaic Period) shows Nut as a kneeling Goddess with outstretched wings.[83] This posture is not confined to Nut. Isis, Nephthys, Hathor and Maat are also shown on coffins in this pose.

During the Ramesside Period many coffins display Nut as a kneeling winged Goddess in the central panel. Above this is a composite block often in the form of a pectoral or amulet. Wearing a dress similar to other Goddesses of the period Nut usually has a long red belt and a head tie. During the 21st dynasty these compositions get increasingly complex and crowded. After the 3rd Intermediate Period the scene of Shu separating Nut and Geb becomes popular on coffins.[84] By separating Nut and Geb Shu enabled the creation of life and so this vignette is seen as a symbol of the eternal renewal of life. A coffin fragment from the 21st dynasty depicts sunrise. The God Nun (who personified the *nun*) lifts the Solar Barque into the arms of Nut who reaches through the top of the frieze to take the newborn sun.[85]

The base of the sarcophagus of Sety I (19th dynasty) is dominated by a depiction of Nut as a standing woman. She doesn't wear a crown, her hair is tied with a ribbon, and the hieroglyphic signs for her name are placed above her head. The text around her includes speeches by the king, Geb and Nut. Spells 72 and 89 of the *Book of the Dead* are also included. Spell 89 is an important one as it unites the *ba* with the corpse. The bulk of the text and decoration of the sarcophagus is from the *Book of Gates*. The uniting

---

[83] Death & the Afterlife in Ancient Egypt, Taylor, 201:88
[84] Hieroglyphs & the Afterlife, Foreman & Quirke, 1996:147
[85] Death & the Afterlife in Ancient Egypt, Taylor, 201:29

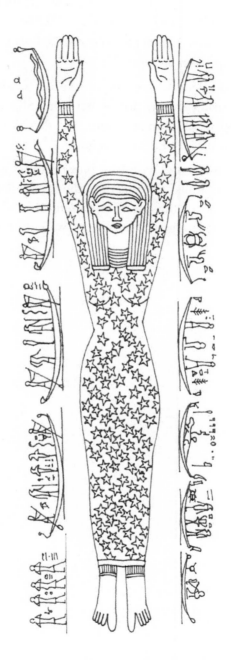

Nut on the coffin of Merenptah.

of the *ba* with the body as a prerequisite for rebirth is an important theme in this text.[86] *"You have been given to your mother Nut in her name of Sarcophagus, she has embraced you in her name of Coffin, and you have been brought to her in her name of Tomb."*[87]

The Roman Period wooden coffin of Soter from Thebes depicts Nut wearing a water pot on her head. She is flanked by the signs of the zodiac and personifications of the 24 hours of the day. She faces forwards with her arms upraised.[88]

The coffin, tomb and womb of Nut becomes a mythical space of manifestation, similar in concept to the manifestation of creation out of the disorder of the *nun* but on an individual basis. Here the disorder and non-being of death gives way to the rebirth of the deceased.

---

[86] Sir John Soane's Greatest Treasure, Taylor, 2017:76
[87] The Ancient Egyptian Pyramid Texts, Faulkner, 2007:119 utt 364
[88] The British Museum Dictionary of Ancient Egypt, Shaw & Nicholson, 2008:46

NUT IN THE BURIAL CHAMBER

In the 6th dynasty pyramids of Pepy I, Pepy II, Merenra and queen Neit a selection of short spells (426-434) are inscribed on the western wall of the sarcophagus hall closest to the sarcophagus. All but one pertain to Nut. The first two spells ask Nut, as the Great Protectress, to protect and conceal the king from Seth (who mutilated the body of Osiris). The next four praise Nut as the daughter *"mighty in her mother"*.[89] Nut is asked to *"set this king as an imperishable Star who is within you"*.[90] These spells may have been recited as the sarcophagus lid was closed.[91] The sarcophagus then became the king's cosmic mother and his new kingdom while his spirit did the same within the celestial body of Nut.

Djehuty was the overseer of the treasury and the overseer of works during the reign of Hatshepsut. The walls and ceiling of his burial chamber are decorated with passages from the *Book of the Dead*. In the centre of the ceiling, directly over the coffin, is a depiction of Nut wearing a blue dress. Her arms are raised in a protective pose, arms extended and bent at the elbows. This echoes the one used by Shu when he separates Nut and Geb and follows the shape of the *ka* hieroglyph. *"Oh mother Nut, spread yourself over me, may you place me among the imperishable stars which are in you, as I shall not die. Raise me up... remove weariness from me. Protect me."*[92]

---

[89] The Ancient Egyptian Pyramid Texts, Faulkner, 2007:142 utt 431
[90] The Ancient Egyptian Pyramid Texts, Faulkner, 2007: 142 utt 432
[91] The Dialogue of Geb and Nut in Relation to the Royal Sarcophagus in the Pyramid of King Pepy I, Billing, 2016:9
[92] The Book of the Dead in Djehuty's burial chamber, Galan, 2013:21-24

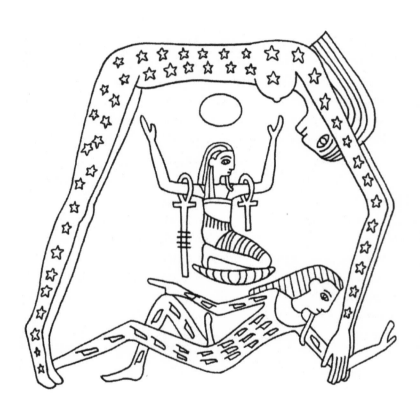

Separation of Nut and Geb

FUNERARY ACCESSORIES

It was common practice from the 25th dynasty to the Ptolemaic Period to dress the mummy in a net of large blue-green faience beads, which form a lozenge pattern. The colour and lustre of the beads were symbolic of the heavens. The net symbolised protection by Nut. A net is made by knotting, another potent form of magical protection. Osiris was depicted wearing such a net in a tomb at Kom el-Shuqafa. The sun, moon and stars are shown in some of the spaces of the net while some examples from Memphis have the face of Nut woven in, echoing depictions of her on coffins.[93] Amulets were incorporated into the bandages, placed on the mummy and also attached to the net.

Stars have an association with rebirth but for some reason they only appear on amulets at three specific times, as far as excavations can tell. The traditional symbols of resurrection were more popular; perhaps the star gave too broad an image. A 12th dynasty burial of Princess Khnumet at Dashur contained two gold star amulets and a private burial of the same period contained a glazed star. Glazed star amulets have been found in Amarna burials and also in Ptolemaic ones at Dendera.[94]

NUT, HATHOR AND THE GREAT MOTHER GODDESS

Hathor is a Sky Goddess but a very different one to Nut. Both are linked to the Cosmic Cow. Hathor is the Lady of the Sky and this is seen in the meaning of her Egyptian name, *Hwt-Hrw*. This translates as the *"Domain of Horus"* or the *"Womb of Horus"* namely the sky that the Falcon God, Horus the Elder, flies through and as such she is his mother. Unlike Nut she is very much connected with the diurnal sky and the Sun God. She is his daughter, the Solar Eye Goddess, and can also be his mother. Her epithet Lady of Turquoise suggests the blue of the sky. Hathor has a very wide range of aspects and can also be a Stellar Goddess as the Lady of

---

[93] Death & the Afterlife in Ancient Egypt, Taylor, 201:207
[94] Amulets of Ancient Egypt, Andrews, 1994:90

the Stars. Nut herself can be the diurnal sky. In the *Book of the Day* the Solar Barque travels across her body during the day.

Like Nut, Hathor is a Tree Goddess. Without an accompanying inscription it is usually impossible to identify which Goddess is represented. This implies that the specific Goddess is either obvious through the context (to those who can interpret the symbols) or else it doesn't matter what her name is as all Tree Goddesses have identical roles. One coffin from the Persian Period is decorated with a pair of sycamores at each end, one labelled Hathor and the other Nut. These two Tree Goddesses mirror the Two Trees of the Horizon so the deceased can be reborn between them like the rising sun. They can also symbolise the diurnal and nocturnal sky. On many coffins Nut is depicted as a winged Goddess embracing the deceased. The transformation of the deceased within the body of Nut paralleled the daily rebirth of Ra as he journeyed through her body at night. After the New Kingdom Hathor was sometimes depicted in the same manner.

Nut and Hathor share ritual objects known as cosmetic spoons. These elaborately carved wooden spoons occur from the Old Kingdom with some of the finest examples coming from the 18th Dynasty. Once dismissed because of their seemingly trivial nature, more sympathetic studies revealed their importance as ritual objects. The spoons are very fragile and the majority appear to be unused. They have all been found in tombs, predominantly in the northern part of Egypt. One was found with ointment in the bowl, which would have been perfumed. It is believed that their form and decoration form a rebus (a play on words using symbols and double meanings) which in turn points to important religious concepts. The most conspicuous symbol is the *ankh*, the symbol for life, which forms the stem of the spoon with the looped head forming the bowl. Although the *ankh* is associated with all deities Hathor is probably the most frequently depicted Goddess carrying the *ankh*. When the themes and symbols are studied it becomes clear that they relate largely to Hathor and then to Nut but to no other deity in their own right.

The handles of the spoons are often in the form of a nude girl swimming which equates to Nut swimming in the celestial ocean. Her arms enclose the bowl emphasising her protecting and enclosing aspect. She normally holds a waterfowl usually in the form of a goose. This is the symbol of her consort Geb and also of the constellation of Cygnus (the Swan), as there were no swans in Egypt. One spoon with a long-necked goose echoes the position of this constellation which appears between the two branches of the Milky Way.[95] On Tutankhamun's shrine is the request to Nut to "*spread thyself over thy son*". Osiris is her son and the word for son puns with that for duck. Another style of the spoons is Nut holding a gazelle and that word puns with that of heir and Osiris is the heir of Geb.[96] These spoons only occur in funerary contexts so must have been symbols of rebirth as an aide for the deceased. Many deities are associated with the afterlife and rebirth, such as Isis and Osiris, but only Nut and Hathor are Sky Goddesses. These spoons must therefore have been important in committing the deceased into the care of the Sky Goddesses and possibly in indicating the nature of the heaven the deceased hoped for; rebirth either as a star in Nut's body or in the Solar Barque with Hathor.

Cosmetic spoon showing Nut & Geb as a goose.

---

[95] Egypt's Dazzling Sun: Amenhotep III and his World, Kozloff & Bryan, 1992:337
[96] Egypt's Dazzling Sun: Amenhotep III and his World, Kozloff & Bryan, 1992:333

Egyptian religion is fluid and all deities can assume the aspect of another as a way of highlighting a specific aspect or as their cult gains power. In eulogies it is a way of emphasising their greatness and power. *"Nut will position her arms so as to receive you in her aspect as Hathor, mistress of the West."*[97] Hathor shares a number of roles with Nut but she doesn't appear to have assimilated Nut who has retained a distinct and independent personality. Nut doesn't have any other aspects whilst Hathor has a wide range, as would be expected of an ancient and widely worshipped Goddess. In addition, there is no relationship between these two Goddesses in any the surviving mythologies. Why is this? Coincidences are rare in Egyptian religion, so it is safe to assume that there is an explanation somewhere.

The Great Mother Goddess is the source of everything. The world, indeed the entire cosmos, is her body. Through her the universe is a living, sacred whole. She presides over the mystery of birth, making the un-manifest manifest. Giving birth to all things she nourishes them and upon their death receives them back into herself. The importance of the Cow Goddess in the Pre-dynastic suggests that the Egyptians perceived the cow as the manifestation of the Great Mother Goddess. With the Great Mother as the Cosmic Cow the emphasis was not on sexuality or even fertility but rather on her loving, protective and nurturing aspects. In the Mother Goddess is the reconnection to the security of the mother's breast and her protective embrace. This protective embrace, an act of containment and wholeness, was an important concept for the Egyptians. This is seen at all levels from Nut the Sky Goddess who embraces the earth, Nut as the coffin and tomb, through Hathor and Nut as the Tree Goddess down to the image of a cow nursing her calf with her head turned around to protect and connect with her calf.

As small tribal communities developed into nation-states there was a shift from the Goddess cults associated with vegetation and the cycles of life and death to a religious doctrine focused on kingship. The Great Goddess began to splinter into a variety of deities. Can we see an echo of the Pre-dynastic Mother Goddess of

---

[97] Traversing Eternity, Smith, 2009:326

the Egyptians in Hathor and Nut? They both manifest in the form of Goddesses of three of the Egyptian's most important and interconnected concepts; sky, tree and cow. The Cow Goddess Bat was referred to as *"Bat with her two faces"* in the *Pyramid Texts*. On the Pre-dynastic Narmer palette each side has two faces, with cow ears and horns, at the top. Does this hint at a Double Goddess, the first step in the splitting of the Great Mother Goddess? The Double Goddess can demonstrate the dual aspects of the Great Mother with each Goddess representing her opposing aspects, such as life and death. I don't think that this is the case here because the underlying aspects of Hathor and Nut are not in opposition; they are both protectors and providers.

Hathor can be viewed as a Great Mother Goddess in her own right given her extensive aspects. As well as those already mentioned she was also associated with music, dance, wine and fragrance. She was a Goddess of sex, love, fertility and childbirth and oversaw trade and foreign lands. Strongly associated with gold, as well as other precious metals and gemstones, she was also the protector of prospectors and miners. Hathor was a well-loved Goddess at all levels of society and had an extensive cult. She was benevolent and wanted people to enjoy themselves and looked after them both during life and in the afterlife.

In Nut we do see some contrasting aspects to those of Hathor, and combining both Goddesses gives us a more complete view of the Great Mother. As the Eye of the Sun Hathor is fire whilst Nut has a strong water element. The elements of earth and air are missing from Hathor and Nut but it is significant that the Gods providing these elements are both related to Nut. Her father is Shu, the God of Air, and her consort is Geb, the Earth God. Hathor is predominately associated with the sun and the diurnal sky whilst Nut is the nocturnal sky and has a strong stellar component. Nut is an enclosing Goddess at all levels whilst Hathor is not, she is the solar energy which drives all natural cycles. Nut is the darkness of the womb, essential for the generation of life, and Hathor is the spark of energy which ignites the life-force and the sun's rays which are essential for the continuation of life. Hathor is an active and a very involved, physical Goddess. Nut takes a more passive role being more remote and celestial and she did not have a cult, despite her important role in the afterlife. The lack of a relationship between the two Goddesses in the surviving mythologies is more difficult to explain. I don't think that it points to Nut being an aspect of Hathor. It is more likely to be because Nut was not a particularly pro-active Goddess but as we only have a selection of the religious literature we cannot say for definite that they never interacted.

It is easy to view either Goddess as the Great Mother. Nut can be seen as a Great Cosmic Mother encompassing the entire universe to the limits of light rather than just our Earth. Life is generated within her and it returns into her at death to be reborn. No matter how incomprehensibly large the universe becomes Nut remains our Mother, she is just infinitely more than we can ever grasp. Hathor is such a wide-ranging and Great Goddess that she can be the Great Mother Goddess but in a different manner to that of Nut. Hathor connects to individuals on a much more personal day-to-day level. The Egyptians happily accepted the various contradictions of their religion and in a polytheist society the deities had many overlapping roles. It is my belief that Hathor and Nut, through their shared aspects, with slightly different nuances, point back to a single origin in the Cosmic Cow as the Great Mother.

HOLDING NOT RESTRAINING

Nut as the protecting barrier between the earth and the *nun* and Nut as the tree does not form an impassable barrier. She is not a prison guard. Sitting under the spreading branches of a tree you are enclosed but not constrained and can get up and walk out of their shelter. Nut as the barrier between us and the *nun* is equally permeable – hence the presence of the Chaos Serpent and the water which seeps through. Only in the coffin do we see the apparently unyielding container. Even this is only a temporary containment – the justifiable deceased will be reborn from this seemingly ultimate place of confinement. *"I place you within me, I bear you a second time, that you may go out and in among the Imperishable Stars and be elevated, alive and rejuvenated like the Sun God, daily...I surround you in my name of coffin, I give you the sweet breath of the north wind...your existence lasts forever."*[98]

---

[98] Death and Salvation in Ancient Egypt, Assman, 2005:170

CHAPTER 5

Reborn in Nut

"May you go forth to your mother Nut that she may take your hand and lead you to the sky." [99]

NUT AND THE AFTERLIFE

The concept of Nut as the Mother of the sun, giving birth to him each morning and taking him back into her at dusk to be regenerated, was present from the Old Kingdom. She was the mother of Osiris and, because the deceased identified with Osiris, she became the mother and protector of all. Although the focus in this chapter is on Nut there are many deities guiding the deceased, protecting them and working towards their resurrection; such as Isis, Nephthys, Anubis and Thoth.

---

[99] Nut: The Goddess of Life in Text and Iconography, Billing, 2002:144

THE ANNUAL BIRTH OF THE SUN

The daily birth of Ra is a common theme in Egyptian religion but Wells (1992) suggests that it was an annual event which formed the origin of this myth. He studied the star patterns as they would have been in the early Old Kingdom as seen from the latitude of Cairo and suggests that Nut was originally perceived as a personification of the Milky Way who gave birth to the Sun God at the winter solstice. What we call the Milky Way is a view of stars along the outermost arm of our galaxy. Under perfect viewing conditions, which I admit I have never experienced, the band can be interpreted as a woman wearing a gauzy dress. In the northern hemisphere it splits into two branches at the constellation of Cygnus which form her legs. At the other end, near Gemini, the Milky Way thickens and forms a pattern hinting at the arms and head of the Goddess.

> *"It is from the southeastern side behind Punt that this God exists."*[100]

For the Egyptians, Punt lay as far south on the eastern horizon as the sun went in winter. Punt was an almost mythical land, the land of the deities, which scholars have been unable to identify. It was probably in southern Sudan or Eritrea. At the spring equinox, about an hour after sunset, the head of Nut would have lain due west near Gemini on the horizon. The setting sun appeared to enter the body of Nut through her mouth and nine months later, at the winter solstice, the sun was born. Star charts for 3500 BCE show that the sun would rise at the winter solstice following the rise of Cygnus, therefore the sun could be seen being born from Nut. Cygnus and this part of the Milky Way are only visible close to sunrise for a few days prior to the winter solstice. In a text on a New Kingdom coffin Nut says *"I have conceived you in Lower Egypt, I have given you birth in Upper Egypt"*.[101] Could this allude to the winter solstice birth of the sun when it is at its furthest point south compared to its more northerly position at the equinox? The papyrus Carlsberg says of Nut *"her western position is on the northwestern*

---

[100] The Mythology of Nut and the Birth of Ra, Wells, 1992:305-321
[101] Nut: The Goddess of Life in Text and Iconography, Billing, 2002:147

side, her eastern on the southeastern side" which was the orientation of the Milky Way during the winter.[102] Regardless of the position of the constellations, sunrise at the winter solstice marks the turning point in the solar cycle. From then on, in the northern hemisphere, the days lengthen and the sun starts to move northwards and Pagan religions of all persuasions celebrate the birth of the sun.

The annual birth of the sun was paralleled each day when the sun rose and set. It was this very noticeable daily cycle of the death and rebirth of the sun which became the predominant myth. The concept of Nut giving birth to the sun each morning was present in the funerary texts but only in the *Pyramid Texts* is it clearly stated:

> *"His mother, the sky, bears him alive every day like Re, and he appears with him in the East, he goes to rest with him in the West, and his mother Nut is not free from him any day."*[103]

THE BOOKS OF THE SKY

The New Kingdom saw the development of the Books of the Sky which consist of the *Book of the Day*, the *Book of the Night* and the *Book of Nut*. These all place emphasis on the Sun God's journey through the body of Nut during both the day and night. These were complementary to the Books of the Netherworld which described the Sun God's journey through the underworld. His nocturnal journey in the body of Nut is very similar to his journey as described in the Netherworld Books. The *Book of the Day* and *Book of the Night* are displayed together on the ceiling of the tomb of Ramesses VI (20th dynasty). Positioning them this way enabled Nut to be shown back to back, making it a very distinctive image and also doubling the potency and magic of her presence. Her arching body forms the boundary of the composition and text and images below her describe the sun's journey. As well as the sun other celestial bodies such as the decans are depicted. There is an emphasis on the cosmological details of the sky. The *Book of the Day* also appears on

---

102 Egypt's Dazzling Sun: Amenhotep III and his World, Kozloff & Bryan, 1992:337
103 The Ancient Egyptian Pyramid Texts, Faulkner, 2007:268 utt 650

its own in a number of 22nd dynasty tombs at Tanis, such as those of Osorkon II and Sheshonq III.

The Book of the Day

As the name suggests, this book describes the diurnal journey of the sun from its birth at dawn, along the celestial river which is upon the body of the Goddess, until she swallows the sun disc in the evening, when the Sun God begins his cycle of regeneration. A total eclipse of the sun shows that the stars in the diurnal sky are always present even though they are usually obliterated by the light of the sun. This proved that the sun did indeed travel on the body of Nut during the day. The Sun God is depicted with a falcon's head unlike in the other funerary books where he is in his nocturnal ram-headed form. The word for ram puns with that for *ba* and emphasises that it is the *ba* of the Sun God which traverses the underworld. In the first hour the birth of the Sun God is depicted in a number of forms. The sun disc is shown next to Nut's vulva and is supported and protected by a winged scarab. This is Khepri, the form of the Sun God at dawn. Below the scarab Isis and Nephthys kneel next to a depiction of Nut as a pregnant woman. She is shown kneeling and facing forward and holds a sun disc inside of which is the Sun-child. Forward-facing figures are rare in Egyptian art and Nut is shown with her hair tucked behind her ears in a style reminiscent of a Hathor Head. (On a Hathor Head the Goddess is shown facing forwards with cow's ears. Her head is normally depicted in this way when it is part of an object such as the capital of a pillar.) Beneath this trio Shu stands with upraised arms. Ra is described as coming out of the "*thighs of Nut*" when he appears on the horizon.[104] Another scene beneath the barque of Shu summarises the passage from night to day. Nephthys in the night barque hands over the solar disc to Isis in the day barque. The second hour of day is called the Hour of Jubilation and Adoration of Ra.

Apophis attacks in the sixth hour and the crew of the Solar Barque, usually Isis and Seth, repulse his attack. The next hour consists of navigating the sandbank in the sky. Apophis was seen

---

[104] The Tomb of Rameses VI, Piankoff, 1954: 389

as a water snake who drank the celestial waters. His coils were the sandbanks that could ground the Solar Barque. In the eighth hour they are safely past the danger and it was a time of jubilation. These hours mirror the midnight hours of the *duat* when the Barque is nearest to the dangers of the *nun*. In contrast the dangers of the day occur when the sun is at its highest and hottest and shade is at a minimum. The Field of Reeds is encountered at the ninth hour and we are told that it grows barley 5 cubits (2.25 m) high, a similar description to that given in the *Book of the Dead*. At the tenth hour the sun begins its descent into the Barge of Evening. The composition ends at the twelfth hour when the Solar Disc, accompanied by four protective jackals, heads into the mouth of Nut. No mention is made of Nut swallowing the solar disc, just that Re *"rests in life in the west"*.[105]

The Book of the Night

The earliest surviving version of the *Book of the Night* is that of Sety I (19th dynasty) on the ceiling of the Osireion at Abydos, but it is only partially completed. In the tomb of Ramesses VI there are two versions. Like its complementary book it also appears in some of the royal tombs of Tanis. The twelve hours of night are divided by columns of text which act as the gates between the hours. The nocturnal journey of the Solar Barque is depicted as it is towed through the hours of night by a large group of stellar deities known as the Unwearying Ones. These are the decan stars and the justified deceased. The first hour of night is not included because it was considered a liminal time and was positioned between the arms of Nut. The sun disc is no longer visible but it is not yet dark because its light still illuminates the land, albeit dimly. Like the corresponding Netherworld books, the hours are filled with scenes of the punishment of enemies, fights with adversaries and the regeneration of both Osiris and the Sun God. It is surprising that Apophis does not make an appearance, perhaps this is because the journey is taking place within Nut's body.

With the exception of the Unwearying Stars there is little to suggest a cosmic setting, which is disappointing for such a

---

[105] The Tomb of Rameses VI, Piankoff, 1954:403

promising title. The constellation of Ursa Major (the Great Bear) is mentioned in the sixth hour, underlying its importance. In the second, eighth and ninth hours there is reference to *"those who belong to the opposite sky"*.[106] It is not clear who this is referring to, it may be the deities of the equivalent hour of the day. Even the birth of the Sun God is low-key compared with that of the *Book of the Day*. Isis and Nephthys are shown lifting up the Solar Disc.

The Book of Nut

The *Book of Nut* is found on the ceiling of the cenotaph of Sety I and the tomb of Rameses VI. It gives a topography of the sky and shows the daily cycle of the sun. Nut is described as the Goddess of the Northern Sky and also *"the water from which Re rises."*[107] Her arching body provides the margins of the composition. Shu stands beneath her, his arms supporting her body. Pictorial motifs appear next to her body. A winged sun disc is shown next to her mouth, other sun discs are placed throughout and a winged scarab is next to her knees. Behind her legs is a vulture perching on a lotus representing Nekhbet the tutelary Goddess of Upper Egypt. The main body of the text is placed either side of Shu. A large amount of space is given over to a detailed description of the decan stars, which are covered in chapter 7.

"It is by her mouth…that the god Ra enters within the Duat. Look at the picture…the disk which is in her mouth…with him these stars set and with him they rise."[108] The text often refers the reader back to the picture. They were designed to be understood as a coherent whole and both words and images are essential for understanding. The Sun God enters Nut at the first hour of night, but it is not until the second hour that he enters the *duat*. During that first hour, at sunset, the text says he becomes glorious and beautiful. Tying up with the concept of the *duat* being within the body of Nut, texts near the thigh of the Goddess explain how the Sun God goes forth from the *duat* at the ninth hour. It also refers to the *mesqet*-region where he is reared and revived. It is not clear where or what this is. Clagett

---

[106] The Tomb of Rameses VI, Piankoff, 1954:411
[107] Egyptian Astronomical Texts I: The Early Decans, Neugebauer & Parker, 1960:44
[108] Ancient Egyptian Science Volume II: Calendars, Clocks and Astronomy, Clagett, 1995:382

suggests it is the eastern part of the *duat* close to the horizon. The text says this area provides him with strength which alludes to the liminal mysterious energies which interact to regenerate the Sun God. There is reference to the God's glowing, which is the light before sunrise, and the fact that he *"sees Geb"* as he rises above the mountains. On Nut's thigh it reads *"he opens the thighs of his mother Nut; he rises towards the sky"*. Lower down her leg *"he moves towards earth, rising and being born"*. The hour of Ra's emergence is called *"She who causes the beauty of Re to appear"* and it is this which enables life on earth.[109]

Text related to the winged scarab say that the Sun God assumes the form of Khepri as he is born and rises. *"He enters as this scarabaeus. He comes into existence as he came into existence the first time on earth, in primaeval time...he goes into the sky...the form of Kheprer."* It explains that the *"redness comes after birth. It is in the colour which comes in the sun disc at dawn...his rays being upon the earth in the colour named"*. It then directs the reader to *"look at the picture"*.[110] Text next to Nekhbet says that she flies before the sun. This suggests that she has a guardian role, making sure his path is secure. Vultures do not tend to fly until the sun has warmed the earth as they like to use thermals to gain height. One text refers to the nests of the *ba*-birds which are near the western horizon, the western gateway to the *duat*. This area is called the Marshes of Heaven. The *ba* manifests as a separate entity at the point of death, before that it was an integral part of the person. The hieroglyph sign for *ba* is a human-headed bird. The human head denotes an individual and their personality and the bird's body depicts freedom of movement. *"Their faces as people and their nature as birds, one of them speaking to the other with the speech of crying. After they come to eat plants and to get nourished in the Black Land, alighting under the brightness of sky, then they change into their nature of birds."*[111] Birds in the marshes go silent and disappear to roost at night reappearing noisily at dawn. Were the *ba*-birds thought to fly back to the heavens and assume the form of a star? A high-flying flock does appear to vanish into the sky.

---

[109] The Sky-Goddess Nut and the Night Journey of the Sun, Piankoff, 1934:57-61
[110] Egyptian Astronomical Texts I: The Early Decans, Neugebauer & Parker, 1960:46
[111] Genesis in Egypt: The Philosophy of Ancient Egyptian Creation Accounts, Allen, 1988:1

The Shadow Clock Text

This is found in the Osireion of Sety I. Text below Nut's feet lists the twelve hours of night and the twelve stations of Nut's body through which the Sun God passes during his nocturnal journey. Starting from the first hour these are hand, lip, tooth, throat and breast. The sixth and seventh hours are unreadable. Roberts suggests it might be lungs and liver. The eighth hour is gall bladder then intestine and vulva. The eleventh hour is unreadable and the twelfth is thigh.[112] Preserving the body was a critical component in the process of rebirth. Aligning the body of the deceased with that of Nut and the rejuvenation of the Sun God would give extra protection. Is this related to the concept of energy centres of the body, like the chakras? A map of the energy of the body mirroring the cosmic energy needed for rebirth. Were the various components renewed at different hours of the night? Or was it more mundane and an approximate division of the human body into twelve parts, perhaps echoing the gates which the Solar Barque and the deceased have to pass through in the *Book of the Night*. These gates are described as dangerous and protective Goddesses, such as She Who Causes Pain and She Who Fights for her Lord. Roberts suggests that the development of the *Book of the Night* and the *Shadow Clock Text* were a reaction to the theology of the heretic Akhenaten (18th dynasty) who, by denying all but the Aten (the sun disc), had severed the divine world from its equilibrium of male-female and light-dark polarities. The emphasis on the underground journey of the Solar Barque in the Netherworld Texts and the Books of Sky was a response to this unnatural action.

THE BIRTH OF THE SUN IN THE NETHERWORLD TEXTS

In illustrations for the Netherworld Texts, and many others, the scene is divided into a number of horizontal sections which are arranged one above the other and are separated by lines. The convention is to describe these sections as registers.

---

[112] My Heart, My Mother, Roberts, 2000:105

Although not focusing on Nut, the Netherworld Texts do mention the birth of the sun from Nut. The *Book of the Amduat* depicts the journey of the Sun God through the underworld with little reference to Nut, but in the last hour it reiterates that the Sun God "*appears from the thighs of Nut*" and later adds that he "*sets at the body of Nut*".[113] In the *Book of Gates*, although set in the underworld, there is frequent reference to the sky and Nut as heaven in the tenth hour. "*They proceed with him to the sky...they cause him to appear in heaven.*"[114] There is also reference to the Sun God's *ba* resting in Nut. "*Opened for you are the doors which are in Earth, for you Ba-soul that she rests in heaven.*" The Sun God is described as sailing "*between the thighs of your mother*".[115] In the eleventh hour three Star Gods tow the solar barque. They carry a star in their hands rather than wearing them. "*They praise with their stars...when they have entered heaven (Nut).*"[116] At the twelfth gate, the horizon, it says that Ra "*has gone forth from the Shetit, that he may rest in the womb of Nut*".[117] This appears to be the merging of two traditions, possibly for added potency. Having gone through the process of rejuvenation in the *duat* the Sun God then enters the womb of Nut to be reborn.

The *Book of Caverns* also references the birth of Ra from Nut in the final vignette. The Solar Barque is hauled by twelve deities to the eastern horizon. Various deities praise Ra-Horakhty (Horus of the Horizon) "*when he enters into the belly of Nut*" and there is mention of birth-bricks.[118] The three registers then form an arrangement of triangles focusing on the end of the central register where the sun disc emerges with the newborn solar child. A band of water is shown across these triangles. Is this a stylised depiction of the birth canal and vulva?

In the *Book of Earth* and the *Book of Caverns* there is a repeating motif of a large standing Goddess referred to as the Secret or Mysterious One who is believed to be Nut. "*She with the mysterious form.*"[119] In her upraised arms she holds various items such as a

---

[113] The Egyptian Amduat, Abt & Hornung, 2007:358
[114] The Egyptian Book of Gates, Abt & Hornung, 2014:351-352
[115] The Egyptian Book of Gates, Abt & Hornung, 2014:363
[116] The Egyptian Book of Gates, Abt & Hornung, 2014:384-385
[117] The Egyptian Book of Gates, Abt & Hornung, 2014:449
[118] The Ancient Egyptian Netherworld Books, Darnell, 2018:455
[119] The Ancient Egyptian Books of the Afterlife, Hornung, 1999:88

solar disc and a ram-headed *ba*-bird which is a manifestation of the Sun God in the underworld. There are usually standing snakes and crocodiles beside her. The *Book of Earth* describes her as *"this goddess in this fashion…the head of the Mysterious One is in the Upper Netherworld, her feet in the Lower Netherworld"*. The Sun God travels *"over her two hands"*.[120] An almost identical text is given in the *Book of Caverns*. *"Her head in the upper Netherworld, her feet in the lower Netherworld of the gods. On the arms of the Mysterious One does this great god travel through the cavern."*[121] Litanies to Re are interspersed throughout the *Book of Caverns*. Ra says *"behold, I am travelling through the Mysterious One"*.[122] As in the *Book of the Night* the Sun God travels through the body of Nut, which is also the location of the *duat*. The caverns of the underworld can be viewed as the womb of Nut which is inside her rather than below her. It also reflects the stellar life cycle where Nut swallows the stars and they regenerate within her. Billing says that one of Nut's epithets could be interpreted as *"the Secrecy of the Sky"* which incorporates a pun on a word used to define spaces.[123] In her everyday role Nut defines the limits of the sky but in terms of rebirth the space defined by Nut is beyond our perception and understanding. Despite the fact that the Earth manifests as Gods in Egypt we can see in parts of the *Book of Caverns* and *Book of Earth* the presence of the Goddess whose body is the regenerative earth-based *duat*.

REBIRTH OF THE DECEASED

As she gave birth to Osiris and rebirths the Sun God daily, so Nut will give rebirth to all the justified deceased. She *"spends the night transfiguring you"*.[124] In the *Coffin Texts* there is reference to the deceased following the solar cycle and to the deceased being reborn each day.[125] *"Re rises in the east, and he finds N there. Re goes towards the west, he finds N there living and enduring."*[126] Less of Nut birthing the

---

[120] The Ancient Egyptian Netherworld Books, Darnell, 2018:466
[121] The Ancient Egyptian Netherworld Books, Darnell, 2018:401
[122] The Ancient Egyptian Netherworld Books, Darnell, 2018:404
[123] The Secret One. An Analysis of a Core Motif in the Books of the Netherworld, Billing, 2006:51-71
[124] Nut: The Goddess of Life in Text and Iconography, Billing, 2002:106
[125] The Ancient Egyptian Coffin Texts, Vol I, Faulkner, 2007:225 Spell 306
[126] The Sky-Goddess Nut and the Night Journey of the Sun, Piankoff, 1934:57-61

sun is seen in the *Book of the Dead*. Nut is called the mother of the Sun God but there is no reference to her swallowing and birthing him. *"Thy mother Nut embraces thee, thou settest in beauty."*[127]

Osiris is referred to as the *"lord of splendour in the womb of Nut"*.[128] The rebirth of Osiris is complicated and varying, especially when it is incorporated into the Solar religion. In the *Book of the Dead* Ra and Osiris are intertwined and complementary. In one spell Osiris is compared to Ra. *"You cross the sky daily, you convey him to his mother Nut, when he goes to rest daily in the West."*[129] In other texts Osiris remains underground. Texts from Dendera address Osiris saying *"your mother Nut is pregnant with you…she rejuvenates your body…she renews you at your time of year"*.[130] In doing so Nut *"imbues the Mistress of the House, Senebtisi justified, with life stability and power so that she not die ever"*.[131] One spell asks Nut to enclose the deceased *"with the life which is in you"*.[132] The womb of Nut is very similar to the cauldron of rebirth found in some other traditions. Nut provides the uterine space in which all the deceased are reborn. The deceased are not delivered from the body of Nut, which is the coffin. Their physical body remains in the earthly realm. It is their *ba* which is reborn and joins in the eternal cycles of the sun, moon and stars. *"Spirit to the sky, corpse into the earth."*[133] However, another tradition emphasises the resurrection of the physical body. *"Nut has come so that she may join your bones together, knit up your sinews, make your members firm, take away your corruption and take hold of your hand, so that you may live."*[134] The deceased seem to follow both patterns; the Egyptians were always given plenty of leeway in their beliefs and options. *"May you traverse the hall of Nut and cross the hall of Geb."*[135]

The funerary texts illustrate the demise of Nut's importance. Nut is one of the most important deities in the *Pyramid Texts* where she appears almost 100 times and plays a central role in the rebirth

---

[127] The Sky-Goddess Nut and the Night Journey of the Sun, Piankoff, 1934:57-61
[128] The Tomb of Maya and Meryt I, Martin, 2012:18
[129] How to Read the Egyptian Book of the Dead, Kemp, 2007:31
[130] Hathor's Alchemy, Roberts, 2019:111
[131] The Great Goddesses of Egypt, Lesko, 1999:29
[132] Nut: The Goddess of Life in Text and Iconography, Billing, 2002:90
[133] Ancient Egyptian Religion, Frankfort, 1948:100
[134] The Great Goddesses of Egypt, Lesko, 1999:39
[135] The Tomb of Maya and Meryt I, Martin, 2012:22

of the king. She is still prominent in the *Coffin Texts* acting as mother of the deceased. On the coffin of Dahshur Nut states that she loves her daughter, the deceased, as much as she loves her husband Geb and her son Osiris. *"N is my daughter, N is my beloved with whom I am pleased."*[136] Other spells refer to seeing Nut, when the deceased are reborn as stars they see Nut as the starry night sky. *"I pass through Heaven, I walk upon Nut."*[137] Nut the Great will resurrect and raise the deceased. *"O my mother Nut, come to me that you may remove my bandages...O Nut, raise me up! I am this son of yours. May you remove my weariness."*[138] Although references to the ladder of Nut are common in the *Pyramid Texts* only one spell in the *Coffin Texts* references it. Her rank and roles decline steadily in the New Kingdom. She is referenced a lot less in the *Book of the Dead*. The emphasis is more on the deceased joining the crew of the Solar Barque and being reborn like Ra. There is no mention of the deceased being reborn within Nut. She is more prominent in her role as the Sycamore Goddess who receives and nourishes the deceased. Was this due in part to the rise in prominence and popularity of Isis and Hathor? On some coffins and sarcophagus Nut is replaced by Neith and after the New Kingdom it was common to have Hathor, Lady of the West. However Nut still retains the role of the Great Mother in heaven and a protector of the deceased in their coffins. On one Late Period coffin Nut greets the deceased *"welcome in peace to your coffin, the place of my heart"*.[139]

LOCATING THE AFTERWORLD

In the *Pyramid Texts* the *duat* is not fixed in the underground. Even though it is not a desirable place to stay it was considered a celestial region. In the *Pyramid Texts* the word *duat* is usually given the determinative of a star within a circle and in concept is more of a cosmic region. One text refers to Sothis and Orion being *"encircled by the duat"*. Another reference to the *duat* being within Nut comes

---

[136] Permeable Containers: Body and Cosmos in Middle Kingdom Coffins, Nyord, 2014:39
[137] Ancient Egyptian Religion, Frankfort, 1948:112
[138] Permeable Containers: Body and Cosmos in Middle Kingdom Coffins, Nyord, 2014:36
[139] Death and Salvation in Ancient Egypt, Assman, 2005:171

from the cenotaph of Sety I. "*When the incarnation of this god enters her mouth, inside the Duat.*"[140] After the Old Kingdom the *duat* tends to be viewed as an underground region. Placing the afterlife, or at least part of it, underground is quite logical. The corpse returns to the earth and new life springs from the earth. Caverns have long been associated with the womb of the Earth Goddess who births all life. The Egyptians didn't think in quite the same way. For a start the corpse was mummified to preserve it for eternity, they had no desire for the body to return to the earth. As in many areas of their religion the location of the *duat* did vary. The Netherworld Texts include books which are set in an underground world, such as the *Book of Caverns*, and they refer to the deceased and Sun God traversing this dark region. At dawn the revived Sun God is lifted up into the sky. But rebirth underground is the way of Earth. It has its counterpart in celestial rebirth which is the way of Nut. Here the deceased live on within the body of Nut which is the body of the cosmos. On one of the shrines of Tutankhamun the deceased king asks of Nut "*that I may exist inside you*".[141]

ASCENDING TO HEAVEN

A staircase, or ladder, is symbolic of a transition from one state to another. The deceased descend into the netherworld when the coffin is placed underground, often taken down steps. Correspondingly the ascent to heaven, from death to rebirth, is via steps or a ladder. Wooden ladders have been found in Old and Middle Kingdom tombs and these symbolise the ladder called *maqet* which was used by Osiris to ascend into the celestial realms.[142] "*A ladder to the sky will be knotted together for you, and Nut will stretch her arms out to you.*"[143] Pools in gardens and temples often had steps leading down into them, as did depictions of them in tombs. This associated them with the celestial waters and the ascension into the afterlife. For this reason a ladder can be one of Nut's symbols. "*Pepi*

[140] The Cosmology of the Pyramid Texts, Allen, 1989:21-22
[141] The Great Goddesses of Egypt, Lesko, 1999:40
[142] Staircases in Ancient Egyptian Pools, Ezzat, 2016:68
[143] Death and Salvation in Ancient Egypt, Assman, 2005:272

is therewith to his mother Nut; Pepi rises up on her, in this her name of ladder."[144]

Ascension to heaven requires effort on the part of the deceased, they have to climb the ladder or reach out as the deities reach down. Like enclosure in the coffin, ascension with Nut is an act of enclosure. The *Pyramid Texts* talk of her extending her arms to the deceased. "*She takes him to herself at the sky, she does not drop him to earth.*"[145] The concept of Nut reaching down from the sky to lift up the sun at dawn is illustrated in the final vignette of the *Book of Gates*. As the Solar Barque is lifted up from the *duat* Nut is depicted upside-down reaching into the *duat* to take the solar disc which is pushed up to her by Khepri. "*This is Nut. She receives Re.*"[146] Doors at the horizon separated the underworld from the sky. Spells in the *Coffin Texts* and the *Book of the Dead* refer to the doors or gates of the sky being opened for the deceased. Sometimes this is carried out by Nut, at other times it is by Thoth.

Heaven, or the afterlife, can be considered as being within the body of Nut. The Egyptians held many views of the afterlife and it appears that the justified deceased did have some say in the matter. You could join the Solar or Lunar Barques working as the crew. "*You will see the moon in its rising. You will see Re in his rising...your ba will be taken to the sky.*"[147] At other times it was considered a place very much like Egypt, without the unpleasant elements, however the deceased would be expected to work. Those who chose the way of Nut hoped for rebirth as one of the stars within her – an afterlife among the stars that was without obligations. "*Nut the Great will raise you in your beauty, she will enclose you in her arms.*"[148]

THE MILKY WAY AND THE PATHS OF NUT

The Winding Waterway and descriptions of the sky are common in the *Pyramid* and *Coffin Texts*. It is treated as though it was an actual celestial river. There are references to its banks and

---

[144] Staircases in Ancient Egyptian Pools, Ezzat, 2016:69
[145] The Ancient Egyptian Pyramid Texts, Faulkner, 2007: 211 utt 548
[146] The Egyptian Book of Gates, Abt & Hornung, 2014:453
[147] The Liturgy of Opening the Mouth for Breathing, Smith, 1993:31-32
[148] The Great Goddesses of Egypt, Lesko, 1999:39

there are many spells to cross over it. It is a river to be crossed on the way to the northern sky and Field of Reeds, rather than a destination. One spell is to become Sobek (the Crocodile God) as Lord of the Winding Waterway. In the *Book of the Dead* there are many references to the Winding Waterway and the Paths of Nut, the latter being the paths travelled by the stars, sun and moon. In a spell for becoming a divine falcon in the *Coffin Texts* the deceased state that they know the Paths of Nut. The falcon is associated with Horus, or Ra-Horakhty, and his roads are the path of the ecliptic. The ferry boat was used to cross the Winding Waterway and there are requests that the deceased not be rejected by the Milky Way. *"I will go forth to the sky, I will sail in it to Nut."*[149]

Purification of the deceased was an important part of the funerary rites. One spell in the *Book of the Dead* implies that it is the Milky Way which purifies the deceased as they continue their journey after bathing in the Milky Way. Other spells hint that the deceased need to be pure before they can enter the Milky Way. Various deities are involved with purification especially Anubis, through his mummification rites, and Sothis (the Goddess associated with the star Sirius) through her role of bringing the inundation. The *Coffin Texts* also refer to Nut, possibly as the Milky Way, cleansing the deceased. In the *Pyramid Texts* the Celestial Serpent Kebehwet, who is the daughter of Anubis, takes on this role.

OUR COSMIC MOTHER

Despite the constant propaganda about the Sun God being the sole creator and grandfather of Nut, he sails along the body of Nut during the day and travels within her at night. She is the realm where the sun is born and dies, not the realm that the sun rules over. The Sun God, and the deceased who travel with him, are in constant contact with the Great Goddess and hence the divine feminine. Whatever the various details of the journey, the deceased can follow the Sun God and achieve eternal rebirth through the Great Cosmic Mother. Adding a further feminine element, the *Pyramid Texts* refer

---

[149] An Ancient Egyptian Book of the Dead, O'Rourke, 2016:86 spell 136A

to the dawn light as the daughter of Nut. *"The sky is pregnant with wine, Nut has given birth to her daughter the dawn-light."*[150] Although she gives birth to the Sun God the actual light-giving Eye of the Sun is a Goddess so the dawn light can be considered a daughter of Nut, as can Hathor as she is a Solar Goddess and Eye of the Sun. In the New Kingdom there is a new concept of Nut bringing light *"with her face"* which drives away the darkness.[151] Texts on coffins from the 21st dynasty tell how she repulses darkness and brings the dawn. Here the light Nut brings is the birth of the sun. But the phrase *"with her face"* does not suggest birthing the sun. It sounds more like Hathor in her aspect of the sun disc. Does it allude to Nut bringing light in a spiritual sense or just the close association of the two Goddesses?

To an absolute monarch, or an all-important Sun God, the concept of the daily cycle of the birth and the death of the sun was frightening. It meant that they had to relinquish control to an even more powerful Goddess. Little wonder then that the more popular theme became the nightly passage through the underworld which could be viewed as an active process undertaken by the solar hero. The concept of a Heavenly Mother birthing the sun and the same Mother, rather than an Earth Mother, who takes the deceased and resurrects them continued throughout Ancient Egyptian history. The last coffins of the pre-Christian period still depict Nut and with it the hope of resurrection through her power. *"Your ba will live for ever and ever…your ba will live for ever like Orion in the womb of Nut."*[152]

---

[150] The Ancient Egyptian Pyramid Texts, Faulkner, 2007:179 spell 504
[151] Nut: The Goddess of Life in Text and Iconography, Billing, 2002:146
[152] Traversing Eternity, Smith, 2009:187

CHAPTER 6

The Night Sky

"I shall ascend into the space of light, I shall cross the face of the Earth, I shall walk in the light and I shall wait upon the stars."[153]

THE EGYPTIAN ASTRONOMERS

Amenemope, a Ramesside scribe, compiled an onomasticon which is a list of various things he considered significant from *"heaven with its affairs, earth and what is in it"*.[154] He mentions the sun, moon and stars but only lists five of the eleven or so Egyptian constellations. The planets aren't mentioned, neither is Sirius which is very surprising given its connection to the inundation. There are over 600 entries in his list but these are the only ones relating to astronomy. Does this suggest that the sky was of little interest to all but the astronomer priests or just that Amenemope wasn't particularly interested in astronomy? We have 3,000 years of

[153] The Living Wisdom of Ancient Egypt, Jacq, 1999:52
[154] Ancient Egyptian Astronomy, Parker, 1974:51-65

records from Egypt but nothing like the astronomical records of the Babylonians. Was this because the theology had turned its focus from the stars, concentrating instead on the solar and Osirian religions? Professional astronomers would have been attached to temples where the emphasis was on the stars for timekeeping, particularly with regards to important religious festivals.

The astronomer Harkhebi, who lived in the 3rd century BCE, gave details of his professional skills on his statue. This Prince *"observes everything observable in the heavens, skilled in observing the stars with no erring"*.[155] He knew *"the culmination of every star in the sky...announces the rising of Sothis at the beginning of the year and then observes her on her first festival day"*. He also calculated Sirius' *"course at the designated times, observing what she does every day"*.[156] Careful monitoring of Sirius was critical for the temples. A 12-13th dynasty letter to a lector priest from his overseer tells him that *"you should know that the coming forth of Sothis will happen on month 4 of Peret, day 16. Let this be noted by the temple priesthood"*.[157]

There is an underlying assumption that Egyptian astronomy wasn't very advanced compared to that of Babylon and other cultures. There is an absence of mathematical studies and records. Their imagery wasn't adopted by the Greeks so hasn't been absorbed into western culture, and it is further hampered by the fact that there is very little agreement on the identification of the Egyptian constellations. The fact that the astronomical ceilings differ in content and orientation further detract from their scientific accuracy. For the Egyptians knowledge and science were deeply intertwined with religion and the science is hidden beneath the myths.

THE PLANETS

The ancient astronomers only knew the five planets which are visible to the naked eye: Mercury, Venus, Mars, Jupiter and Saturn.

---

[155] Ancient Egyptian Astronomy, Parker, 1974:51-65
[156] Ancient Egyptian Science Volume II: Calendars, Clocks and Astronomy, Clagett, 1995:495
[157] Voices from Ancient Egypt, Parkinson, 1991:89

The Egyptians called them the *"stars that know no rest"*.[158] Our word planet comes from the Greeks who also referred to them as wandering stars. Mercury was aligned with Seth and called *Sbg*. There is often a small figure of Seth added next to the name of the planet. As Mercury is so close to the sun it can only be seen near the horizon in the morning and evening. This may be one reason why Mercury was associated with Seth who *"is in front of the boat of Ra"*.[159] Seth protected the Sun God against Apophis. Despite having a figure of Seth next to the name, possibly acting like a determinative, Mercury isn't depicted as Seth. He has a variety of forms and can be shown as falcon-headed, possibly as a precautionary measure given Seth's temperament. Or it may allude to a composite Horus-Seth persona. One text refers to the planet as Seth in the dusk and a God in the dawn twilight. Perhaps he was considered less malevolent in the morning, having redeemed himself in the battle with Apophis in the underworld. In the *Book of Two Ways* there is reference to *"that district of Nut, to the stairway of Mercury"*.[160] Faulkner translates it as the stairway to the *"barque of Mercury"*. As the spell is for joining the Solar Barque the stairway of Mercury could be seen as a path towards the rising sun.

Both Mercury and Venus never appear far from the sun and both can appear as morning and evening stars. Venus is the brightest object in the night sky after the moon. Venus is named the Crosser, or Star who Crosses, and can also be the Lone Star so named because it is the first to be seen in the evening sky. On some depictions Venus is represented by a heron, the *benu* bird. Its name derives from the word to rise and shine. The *benu* bird was associated with creation and was considered the manifestation of the *ba* of the Sun God and also associated with Osiris.[161] Other epithets for Venus are Morning Divinity and Unique Star.[162] Venus has a variety of depictions; at Edfu it is shown as two Goddesses while at Dendera it appears as a God with two faces and as a falcon-

---

[158] The British Museum Dictionary of Ancient Egypt, Shaw & Nicholson, 2008:46
[159] The Egyptian Calendar, Bomhard, 1999:74
[160] The Ancient Egyptian Book of Two Ways, Lesko, 1977:13 spell 1030
[161] Egyptian Astronomical Texts III: Constellations and Zodiacs, Neugebauer & Parker, 1969:180
[162] The Egyptian Calendar, Bomhard, 1999:74

headed God.[163] The two faces and dual deities may allude to Venus' presence at both the morning and evening. The falcon head aligns it with Horus. One spell in the *Coffin Texts* is to become the Morning Star.

The outer planets are all avatars of Horus. Mars is known as Horus of the Horizon (Horakhty) and in the Greco-Roman Period was called Horus the Red. He is described as he *"who navigates backwards"* alluding to its retrograde motion which is seen every two years.[164] All planets show a retrograde motion, Mars is nothing special in this respect. Mars is usually shown as a falcon-headed God but he can have a human head. Jupiter is Horus who Limits the Two Lands. Other epithets are Horus Mystery of the Two Lands, Follower of the Sky and Horus who Illuminates the Two Lands. The earliest mention of Jupiter is found on an eleventh dynasty coffin. Sometimes he is shown as a falcon-headed God but in later periods he often has a bull's head and at Dendera a human head. Saturn is Horus, Bull of the Sky. He can also be Crosser of the Sky.[165] These three planets do follow the ecliptic, like the sun and moon. Is this one reason why they are depicted as avatars of the Sky God Horus who flew along these paths of Nut?

The planets are also referred to by their position. Jupiter can be the Southern Star. Saturn is the *"western star which crosses the sky"*. Mars is the Star of the Eastern Sky.[166] There is no astronomical explanation for any of these names. All planets move in the ecliptic and outer planets can all be seen in the east and west at varying times of the year. These epithets may refer to their position at a specific point in time which was considered important or related to a myth. Bomhard suggests that certain spells in the *Pyramid* and *Coffin Texts* relating to Seth and Horus may allude to the movements of Mercury and Venus. The fact that both the names of the planets and their depictions vary so much sometimes gives the impression that the astronomers and priests weren't certain exactly who they

---

[163] Egyptian Astronomical Texts III: Constellations and Zodiacs, Neugebauer & Parker, 1969:180

[164] The Egyptian Calendar, Bomhard, 1999:74

[165] Egyptian Astronomical Texts III: Constellations and Zodiacs, Neugebauer & Parker, 1969:177

[166] The Egyptian Calendar, Bomhard, 1999:74

were dealing with, or they were viewed as interchangeable. If they were largely avatars of Horus this is plausible. One rebirth spell in the *Book of the Dead* is addressed to Nut. She tells the deceased that they will live as the Lone Star and that *"blue-eyed Horus"* and *"red-eyed Horus, violent of power"* wait to greet him.[167] Red-eyed Horus will be Mars, blue-eyed Horus might be Venus or an unknown star with a bluish tint.

There is no concept of the planets having any influence on fate and destiny; this was the responsibility of the decan stars (discussed in the following chapter). However, on the *naos* of the Decades there is reference to five wandering demons who follow the orders of Thoth. Some believe that they are connected to the five planets given their description. Thoth is depicted wearing the *hmhm*-crown which is often worn in smiting scenes. Kneeling before him are five knife-wielding genies.

THE STARS

Constellations and asterisms are both groups of stars which appear visually related. The term Asterism is used if the group doesn't belong to one of the recognised constellations. The decans and constellations will be covered in the following chapters. The hieroglyph sign for star (*seba*) is a five-pointed star sometimes with a tiny circle in the centre.[168] This is normally used in the more formal depictions of the night sky. On working documents such as the star clocks and decan tables a variety of figures are used to represent stars including dots and circles. Important stars can be shown within a circle appearing as smaller versions of the solar disc. Wilkinson suggest that the belief that stars were souls of the deceased or of deities predates the Pharaonic Period. Rock art at Wadi Mu'award depicts a boat with a star above the prow which suggests that the boat is heading towards, or following, the star. A rock shelter at Wadi Hammamat depicts a number of boats. The largest boat has a cabin containing two rows of people, possibly the deceased. Again, there is a six-pointed star above the prow.[169] It

---

[167] The Egyptian Book of the Dead, Faulkner & Goelet, 2008:131 spell 177
[168] 100 Hieroglyph: Think Like an Egyptian, Kemp, 2005:111
[169] Genesis of the Pharaohs, Wilkinson, 2003:157

may have been a widely held belief until the kings of the Old Kingdom commandeered it for themselves. Or at least they thought they had done.

Despite the initial importance of stars only Sirius appears to have had an associated deity, Sothis, and a cult. The Pole Star in the Old Kingdom was Thuban (in the constellation of Draco). Given its importance as the fixed pole of the sky it would be expected that it featured in some of the beliefs and mythologies, but the accepted theory is that it didn't.

Research by Hardy (2003) suggests that many prominent stars are reflected in the mythology and have associations with specific deities. His work is based on the New Kingdom Cairo Calendar which contains religious festivals, mythological events and lucky and unlucky days. He looked at multiple mentions of the "*coming forth*" (or the going forth, the terms are used interchangeably) of deities and examined the night skies at the time of the calendar. The phrase "*coming forth*" is used for Sothis which we know has a direct correlation to the heliacal rising of Sirius. The heliacal rising of a star occurs when it is visible just before sunrise having been absent for a period of time. One entry referred to the coming forth of Neith "*when they see her beauty in the night for four and a half hours*". Canopus (in the constellation of Carina) rose in the south-east and set about 5 hours later. Another reference was to her coming forth "*in the presence of the majesty of Atum Ra-Harakhti*". This date coincided with the heliacal rising of Canopus. The third mention was at a time when Canopus wasn't visible because it rose and set during daylight. "*She treads on this day in the flood in order to look for the things of Sobek.*" An observer would have seen Canopus gradually sink below the horizon to the south of the Milky Way, which was very low at that time of year. Sobek, her son, was the Lord of the Winding Waterway. Thoth was aligned with Alphekka, the brightest star in Corona Borealis (the Northern Crown). Its shape may have suggested the crescent moon and lunar crown, aligning it with the God of the Moon. One entry for Thoth refers to his going "*to judge in the presence of Ra*" and that date coincides with the heliacal rising of Alphekka. Hardy suggests that Anubis was aligned with Denebola (in the constellation of Leo), Min with Alpha Centauri,

Shu with Vega (in the constellation of Lyra) and Bastet with Procyon (in the constellation of Canis Minor).[170]

Hardy aligns the confederates of Seth with Sagittarius. Seth himself was aligned with Ursa Major. The calendar refers to the going forth of Seth and his gang to *"the eastern horizon"*. The date coincides with the heliacal rising of Sagittarius. One of the myths tells how they tried to mutilate the body of Osiris but were repulsed. Seth was defeated but his gang *"perish in the west"*.[171] The calendar's date for this coincides with the time that Sagittarius sets at dusk and begins its period of invisibility, or death. At this time Ursa Major is at its lowest point in the sky, an indication of the defeat of Seth.

Some later Greek papyri give calendars which show religious festivals, lucky and unlucky days and astronomical events in a blending of Egyptian religious festivals with the Greek calendar. One dating to about 190 BCE mentions an assembly of Neith at Sais which coincided with the evening rise of Lyra and another with the morning rise of Arcturus. A feast for Horus coincided with the evening rise of the Pleiades.[172] Without accompanying comments similar to those in the Cairo Calendar it is impossible to carry out any investigations into an accurate correlation between asterism and deity.

OTHER CELESTIAL INHABITANTS

Deities are often referenced in specific parts of the sky. In the *Coffin Texts* Wadjet (the Cobra Goddess of Lower Egypt) is referred to as living in the *"starry sky"*. Perhaps this is the Milky Way given its serpentine appearance. One spell in the *Book of the Dead* invokes Horus of the southern sky and *"Thoth in the northern sky who appeases the raging fiery cobra"*.[173] Alongside the deities and souls of the justified deceased were a number of other cosmic dwellers.

---

[170] The Cairo Calendar as a Stellar Almanac, Hardy, 2003:48-63
[171] The Cairo Calendar as a Stellar Almanac, Hardy, 2003:48-63
[172] Remarks on an Egyptian Feast Calendar of Foreign Origin, Spalinger, 1991:349-373
[173] An Ancient Egyptian Book of the Dead, O'Rourke, 2016:144 spell 71

Apophis

The Chaos Serpent Apophis is depicted in the Netherworld Texts trying to destroy the Sun God as he traverses the underworld. Despite being a creature from the *nun* he appears equally at home in the created world. Many of the funerary texts confirm that he isn't confined to the underworld. *"May he not drive me off from the Northern Sky."* One refers to the storm of Apophis *"on the great plain North of the Stretching-the-Bows"*.[174] The seventh hour of the *Amduat* explains that *"the slaughtering of Apophis is done in the Netherworld at this cavern; his place, however, is in the sky"*.[175] The *Book of Gates* describes how *"his sandbank is in heaven"*.[176] In the *Book of the Day* the deceased *"prepare the safe ways of heaven and detour from Apophis"*.[177] He is shown swimming in the *nun* with the Solar Barque sailing above him. There are many references to Apophis in the northern sky and Stemmler-Harding suggests that he is to be found in one of the northern constellations. Unlike Seth who, as the constellation of Ursa Major, is guarded and chained so he can't attack Horus Apophis is free to wander the heavens and endlessly threaten the Solar Barque.

Astral Snakes

Kakosy has studied scenes on temple walls and astronomical ceilings dating to the Greco-Roman Period and has identified what he calls astral snakes who were associated with the inundation. They appear to be identified with the deities or protecting genii of the decans. One is called Senen, another Pecher-Hor. Pecher-Hor is depicted with a distinctive posture. His body coils to form three horizontal loops and his tail is positioned below his head, which is sometimes that of a bird. At the temple of Isis at Philae an inscription describes the king as the son of Sothis and the heir of Pecher-Hor. On the zodiac at the temple of Khnum at Esna Nut holds the hieroglyph sign for sky above her head. Above this is Pecher-Hor and above him are two intertwined snakes with ram's heads. It isn't possible to tell if they are part of the scene or not. At

[174] Devil in Disguise – on the Stellar Mythology of Apophis, Stemmler-Harding, 2016:97
[175] The Egyptian Amduat, Abt & Hornung, 2007:219
[176] The Egyptian Book of Gates, Abt & Hornung, 2014:427
[177] Devil in Disguise – On the Stellar Mythology of Apophis, Stemmler-Harding, 2016:98

90° to Pecher-Hor is a very clear reference to the inundation. Orion stands in a barque with his head turned back to Sothis in the following barque. On the third barque sits an enthroned Goddess, probably Satis or Anukis, who holds two water jars in her hands.[178] These mother and daughter Goddesses are from Southern Egypt, with a cult in Elephantine, and have strong links with the inundation.

The Celestial Serpent

The *Pyramid Texts* refer to the Goddess Kebehwet, known as the Celestial Serpent, who assists the deceased king. Her name is derived from the word for firmament, *kbhw*. One spell refers to her as the *"Daughter of Anubis, who is at the windows of the sky, the companion of Thoth, who is at the uprights of the ladder"*.[179] She appears to be connected with Anubis through her purification role. *"I am bound for the Field of Life, the abode of Re in his firmament, I have found the Celestial Serpent, the daughter of Anubis, who met me with these four nmst-jars of hers...she refreshes therewith my heart for me for life...she cleanses me, she censes me."*[180] She was probably a Pre-dynastic Goddess but we know nothing else about her. Was she once connected with the Milky Way, which does have a serpentine shape, or a long-forgotten constellation? *"The starry sky serves your celestial serpent whom you love."*[181]

THE ROLE OF STARS AND PLANETS IN THE AFTERLIFE

Purification was an essential ritual in the process of rebirth and the stars were strongly associated with purification in the *Pyramid Texts*. *"The Two Enneads have cleansed themselves for me in Ursa Major."*[182] As the celestial expanses were viewed as a watery place the

---

[178] The Astral Snakes of the Nile, Kakosy, 1981:255-260
[179] The Ancient Egyptian Pyramid Texts, Faulkner, 2007:93 utt 304
[180] The Ancient Egyptian Pyramid Texts, Faulkner, 2007:190 utt 515
[181] The Ancient Egyptian Pyramid Texts, Faulkner, 2007:203 utt 535
[182] The Ancient Egyptian Pyramid Texts, Faulkner, 2007:91 utt 302

association with purification is not unexpected. *"I have purified myself in the Lakes of Jackals."*[183]

The stellar aspects of Egyptian religion are very prominent in the *Pyramid Texts*. We know that these were only intended for the king but the other nobles as well as the ordinary people must have had some afterlife beliefs. Did they dare to emulate the king and hope for rebirth as a star? The kings arrogantly expected to enter a very selective afterlife, let us hope that they were disappointed. Nut would not suddenly decide to embrace all of the deceased just because the funerary rituals were no longer the exclusive property of the king. She always has and always will. *"O Great One who came to be in the sky…You have placed this King Pepi…as an indestructible star within you."* An analysis of the headings of the *Pyramid Texts* spells emphasises the astral cult of that period. For example the king becomes a star, the king has authority over the stars and the king is helped by the imperishable stars. *"You have taken each god under your protection, providing for each his skyship to enstar them all amongst the myriad lights, never to be driven away from you among the distant stars."*[184] Kings considered themselves as semi-divine at the very least. Being reborn as a star was a return home to the celestial world after a brief interlude ruling on earth.

The Morning Star and the Lone Star were important concepts in the afterlife. *"You are this Lone Star which comes forth from the east of the sky."*[185] In one *Pyramid Text* spell the king is described as a *"hawk seen in the evening traversing the sky"*.[186] The king is identified with the Morning Star or else it is described as his offspring. The *Coffin Texts* also have the deceased ascend as the Morning Star. One spell describes it as the *"w'3-star of gold"*.[187] In the *Book of the Dead* there is reference to the Morning Star making a path for the deceased just as it clears a path for the ascending Solar Barque. In another spell Nut tells the deceased that she has made a place for them amongst the stars, naming them as the Lone Star. One *Coffin Texts* spell refers to the guard at the gates of the sky as the Lone Star. He is there to

---

183 The Ancient Egyptian Pyramid Texts, Faulkner, 2007:180 utt 504
184 Hymns, Prayers and Songs, Foster, 1995:20
185 The Ancient Egyptian Pyramid Texts, Faulkner, 2007:155 utt 463
186 The Ancient Egyptian Pyramid Texts, Faulkner, 2007:174 utt 488
187 The Ancient Egyptian Coffin Texts Vol II, Faulkner, 2007:274 spell 722

ensure that only the justified deceased and the Solar Barque can pass through the horizon.

The Imperishable Ones were often generic Star Gods who were associated with the circumpolar stars of the northern sky. *"I live beside you, you gods of Lower Sky, the Imperishable Stars, who traverse the land of Libya."*[188] In the *Pyramid Texts* the king becomes the Morning Star who guides the *"wise imperishable ones".*[189] In the *Coffin Texts* the deceased still expect to be stars, as well as to assume a variety of other forms. *"Every man who learns this formula will be a light in the sky...in the matrix of the stars."*[190] Taking the form of a star sounds a much more enviable afterlife than work in the Field of Reeds. The Imperishable Stars occur a lot in the *Coffin Texts.* The deceased state that they will become as a king having authority over them. One spell says the deceased will be brighter than the stars of the horizon and the Lone Star. The desire to be reborn as a star is still present in the *Book of the Dead. "Travel to the sky to the Field of Reeds, make your abode in the Field of Offerings, among the imperishable stars."*[191]

The Unwearying Stars and the deceased follow the Sun God into the *duat* where they are renewed either daily or on a regular basis like the decan stars. Like the Sun God they set in Nut's arms. In the eleventh hour of the *Book of Gates* twelve *"Gods who know no decay"* carry oars to row the Solar Barque. Ra says to them *"receive for you your oars and take a rest in your stars! Your transformation is verily my transformation, your rebirth is my rebirth! My oarsmen, you shall not decay."*[192]

Sothis and Orion play an important part in the afterlife. They are discussed in the following chapter. Very few stars are named, as far as we can tell. One ascension spell from the *Pyramid Texts* includes the phrase *"when Montju is high, I will be high with him; when Montju runs, I will run with him".* This may be the name of a star.[193] Another possible reference to a star is *"I traverse the sky like*

---

[188] The Ancient Egyptian Pyramid Texts, Faulkner, 2007:224 utt 570
[189] The Routledge Dictionary of Egyptian Gods and Goddesses, Hart, 2005:153
[190] The Living Wisdom of Ancient Egypt, Jacq, 1999:69
[191] The Cosmology of the Pyramid Texts, Allen, 1989:6
[192] The Egyptian Book of Gates, Abt & Hornung, 2014:395
[193] The Ancient Egyptian Pyramid Texts, Faulkner, 2007:179 utt 503

Zwntw…and the Cow who traverses the waters prepares my fair roads".[194] One possible asterism is "*you belong to the nhhw-stars which shine in the train of the Morning Star*".[195] The *i3d*-star is referred to in the *Pyramid* and *Coffin Texts* but which star this refers to is not known. The deceased climb or tread this star so it may be associated with a ladder. In one *Coffin Texts* spell the deceased say that they climb the sun-beams as a follower of Hathor so it may allude more to following the light or path of this particular star, or merely to the actual sunbeams from the rising sun. "*The i3d-star is in my hand by means of my twin powers…I have traversed the orbit of the i3d-star*".[196] In one spell from the *Book of the Dead* the deceased state that they were conceived by Sekhmet and that it was "*Shesmetet who bore me, a star brilliant and far-traveling*".[197] This is one of the few references to the deceased as a star in the *Book of the Dead*. Shesmetet is a lioness-headed Goddess who is usually an avatar of Sekhmet.

Star deities are present in the Netherworld Books largely with a timekeeping role, such as the Goddesses of the Hours, and as the decans being reborn and protecting Ra. In the *Book of Gates* the twelve Star Goddesses are called "*the hour goddesses who tow…and guide him on the ways of heaven. It is these goddesses who guide this great god in the Netherworld*".[198] At the twelfth hour in the *Book of Gates* are four Gods "*those who carry stars…they make jubilation with their stars. They go with him to the sky, they rest in the womb of Nut*".[199] The one exception to the timekeeping role is seen in the use of stellar energy in the process of rebirth. Rebirth is highly complex and requires the interplay of various energies; serpentine, earthly, solar, stellar and temporal. In the twelfth hour of the *Book of Gates* are eight Goddesses of the First Light who guide the Solar Barque. Each sits on a tightly coiled serpent and one hand reaches towards the head of the serpent. In their other hand they hold a star. There is no explanatory text so the vignette can only be speculated on. The stars may symbolise a cosmic or stellar energy which they channel into the serpents providing a conduit between the heavenly and earthly

---

[194] The Ancient Egyptian Pyramid Texts, Faulkner, 2007:187 utt 511
[195] The Ancient Egyptian Pyramid Texts, Faulkner, 2007:289 utt 675
[196] The Ancient Egyptian Coffin Texts Vol II, Faulkner, 2007:261 spell 696
[197] The Ancient Egyptian Book of the Dead, Faulkner, 1989:174 spell 174
[198] The Egyptian Book of Gates, Abt & Hornung, 2014:396-397
[199] The Egyptian Book of Gates, Abt & Hornung, 2014:412-413

world allowing the energies to interact. The role of stellar energy is most prominent in the *Enigmatic Book*. It was given this name as it is very hard to interpret as it uses cryptographic hieroglyphs, focusing on the unification of Ra and Osiris.

A number of scenes from the *Enigmatic Book* show an intermingling of energy. One depicts eight mummified Goddesses with solar discs at their feet and stars above their heads. A series of dots show the light flowing from the stars into their heads. The text says that the *"Great god casts his light into the corpses of these goddesses"*.[200] Both a star and a sun disc are used in this book to depict the *"light of Ra"*. We know that the sun is a star but it is unlikely that the Egyptians were of the same opinion. Perhaps it shows the lingering influence of the stellar aspects of the religion. In another scene are six Goddesses who each stand in front of an emerging snake. Light streams from sun discs near their heads and pours from their hands like water onto the heads of the snakes. The Goddesses have a star and sun disc on their lower body. There is no associated text but it may allude to the regenerative womb of Nut who rebirths both sun and star.

THE MEANING OF STARS

Stars have both a functional and a spiritual role. Through the apparently mundane, but essential, role of telling the time and seasons they enabled the keeping of rituals. They held the *bas* of the deities and the deceased and reflected the myths as a constant reminder of the presence and actions of the deities. More importantly they awakened something spiritual in people. A longing hard to put in words, a calling to the soul; as this prayer of *The King as a Star Fading in the Dawn* illustrates.

> *I have come to you, O Nephthys; I have come to you, Sun*
> *Barque of Night;*
> *I have come to you, You Who are Just in the Reddening;*
> *I have come to you, Stars of the Northern Sky – remember me.*
> *Gone is Orion, caught by the underworld, yet cleansed and alive*
> *in the Beyond;*

---

[200] The Ancient Egyptian Netherworld Books, Darnell, 2018:559

Gone is Sothis, caught by the underworld, yet cleansed and alive
in the Beyond;
Gone am I, caught by the underworld, yet cleansed and alive in
the Beyond.[201]

Over the course of their history many cultures have stopped reaching for the stars, rejecting the astral cults to become more introspective. Like astronomy, the stars provide comfort and interest only for a few. Others reject them as too remote and irrelevant. Perhaps this was the same in Egypt but those who follow the Way of Nut know that *"the paths to rebirth are in the Heavens"*.[202] Regardless of their specific destination in the afterlife, the deceased hoped to be transfigured into an *akh*. The word has associations of radiant light or luminosity suggesting that the justified deceased would become beings of light. This course of action, or more realistically, this hope and longing, is backed up by physics. *"To become eternal, you'd need to turn yourself into light."*[203]

---

[201] Ancient Egyptian Literature, Foster, 2001:75
[202] The Living Wisdom of Ancient Egypt, Jacq, 1999:70
[203] The Universe in Your Hand, Galfard, 2015:162

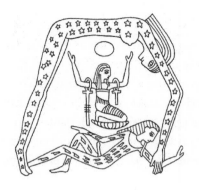

CHAPTER 7

The Decan Stars

"You shall live! You shall rise with Orion in the eastern sky, you shall set with Orion in the western sky."[204]

INTRODUCING THE DECAN STARS

A decan is a group of stars which rise above the horizon at dawn for a period of ten days, after which time they are superseded by another group. Decans were mainly used to mark the hours of the night as a star clock. They divide the year into 36 periods of ten days (hence the name). There are eleven to twelve triangle decans which were used for the five epagomenal days. They were given this name because they were written in a triangular area on the chart. The names and lists of decans vary over the texts. The technical details of the process are given in chapter 12. Despite the extensive records of the decan stars it is not clear which stars they refer to, apart from Sirius and Orion. Some scholars have tried to work this

---

[204] Ancient Egypt, Oakes & Gahlin, 2004:53

out but there is rarely any consensus. Each decan has a specific function and associated deities. The deities are often those from the family of Horus; consisting of Horus and his four sons Damutef, Hapy, Imseti and Qebehsenuf.

The Khonsu cosmography holds the serpent Kematef as the original Creator. He created himself as the serpent Irta who in turn created the deities of the Ogdoad, four snake-headed Goddesses and four frog-headed Gods. These deities completed the work of creation but in the process they were destroyed. They are buried in mounds at Djeme and rites for them were celebrated every ten days. Their death was considered to have created the *bas* of the decan stars.[205]

DEPICTING THE DECANS

The decans are shown in one of two forms; either as a deity or symbol representing each decan or as a list or chart in the more functional form of a star clock. A number of the tombs in the Valley of the Kings have astronomical ceilings and the decan stars form the main component of the southern panel. On the ceiling of the tomb of Sety I (19th dynasty) they are depicted as deities, painted in gold, who march from east to west.[206] On some depictions of the *Book of Nut* the first five decan stars are shown around the feet of Shu as they wait to be reborn at their heliacal rising.

By the New Kingdom lists of decans appear in royal mortuary temples and on the ceilings of tombs. The ceiling from the tomb of Senenmut shows the decans in two groups, the ordinary and the triangle decans. The stars and the decan deities are named and sometimes the deity is depicted. Lists on ceilings differ slightly but the order of the decans is normally constant, not surprisingly as this is their most significant feature. Decans on some of the ceilings are not in the correct order. On the ceiling of the tomb of Sety I the four sons of Horus are sometimes given the wrong depiction. Decans 32-38 are not given in the correct order and decan 31 has

---

[205] The Genesis of the Stars in Ancient Egypt, According to the Naos of the Decades, Bomhard, 2016:130
[206] The Egyptian Calendar, Bomhard, 1999:52

been omitted. The scene is overcrowded and complex in this area. This suggests that it was done by someone inexperienced or careless but it was left as it was too complicated to correct, especially when no-one would be able to see the mistakes from the ground.[207]

The star clocks which were designed to tell the time are shown in a more functional manner with hourly tables and grids. Some coffins from the 9th and 10th dynasty have tables listing the decans and the hours of night painted on the inside of the coffin lid. This enabled the deceased to be integrated into their cycle of rebirth and helped them read the night sky, something they would need during their journey through the afterlife. The 20th dynasty tombs of Rameses VI, VII and IX all have star clocks. These consist of 24 seated figures. A grid is superimposed on them which enables the transit of the decans through the sky to be followed and hence the passing of time to be measured.

The *Naos* of the Decades

A *naos* is a shrine from the inner part of the temple. The *naos* of the Decades comes from a chapel dedicated to Shu by Nectanebo (30th dynasty) at Yat-Nebes in the eastern Delta. It was broken into pieces when Christians destroyed the temple but much has been reassembled. Its name derives from the fact that the external walls are divided into 37 columns which list the decans of the year and those covering the epagomenal days. Shu is depicted in lion form and is viewed as the Creator. The 36 Gods of the decans are described as *"the guides of Rê"* and the *"guarantors of the perennial existence of the sky, of the earth, of the duat and the gods"*. Shu is described as being *"at their head"*.[208] Another *naos*, that of Ismailia, explains how Shu came to rule the decan stars. He once ruled on earth but abdicated following a major conspiracy in the palace and his place

---

[207] Ancient Egyptian Science Volume II: Calendars, Clocks and Astronomy, Clagett, 1995:243
[208] The Genesis of the Stars in Ancient Egypt, According to the Naos of the Decades, Bomhard, 2016:127

was taken by his son Geb. Once back in heaven Shu became closely connected with the planets and stars.[209]

On the *naos* of the Decades the decans are divided into five groups and each decan is represented by a figure. Their position in the year (season, month and day) is given. As the decan stars were believed to be the *bas* of deities they are depicted as *ba*-birds on the *naos*. On their heads they wear a star within a circle, which represents the *duat*. On the base of the *naos* are 37 vultures, one for each decade. The vulture is a symbol of protection and a form of the Goddess Nekhbet. It is associated with motherhood which aligns it with the life cycle of the decan stars.

Another section on the *naos* explains how Ra ordered Thoth to construct a temple for the decans *"in the line of sight from the mound of the jujube-tree"*.[210] The temple is later referred to as the Gate of the Sky and it says that the decan stars *"rise and set towards their temples at Yat-Nebes"*.[211] There are many references to Ra's Headdress and the Headdress House on this and other *naos*. This refers to the point at which the sun rises; when the Sun God emerges from the underworld it is his crown which will appear first. In astronomical terms this is the solar crown or corona, the name given to the luminous halo of light and the fine rays surrounding the sun which are visible just before the sun appears over the horizon. Just above the crown is the rising decan star. On the *naos* of Ismailia the crown of Ra is depicted as a wig with the *uraeus* on top. This corresponds visually to the rising decan which precedes sunrise and the solar corona from the soon to be visible sun.[212]

THE LIFECYCLE OF THE DECAN STARS

The papyrus Carlsberg says that the sun travels *"on the road of the decans"* which implies that the decans are all located on the

---

[209] The Naos with the Decades (Louvre D 37 and the Discovery of Another Fragment, Habachi, 1952:251-263

[210] Genesis of the Stars in Ancient Egypt, According to the Naos of the Decades, Bomhard, 2016:127

[211] Genesis of the Stars in Ancient Egypt, According to the Naos of the Decades, Bomhard, 2016:132

[212] Genesis of the Stars in Ancient Egypt, According to the Naos of the Decades, Bomhard, 2016:133

ecliptic.[213] In the tomb of Sety I there is reference to a book entitled the *Plan of the Movement of the Stars*. The text explains that the decan stars travel *"to the boundaries of the Sky"* at night when they are outside the body of Nut. *"It is within her that they travel in the day when they do not shine and are not seen."*[214]

According to some texts the decans are *"the living souls"* of the Sun God who *"sparkle when he sinks in the evening…they are the hours in their time, the living souls of the gods, those who announce good things"*.[215] They were referred to as "the living" because like us they appeared to be born, to live and to die then they were born again. The annual cycle begins with Sirius and ends with the decan of Orion. Sirius was considered the most important of the decan stars as its heliacal rising heralded the inundation and the start of the new year.

Sirius became the prototype for all decan stars. Astronomical texts explain the theory behind the pattern that the decan stars follow. They spend 80 days in the eastern sky *"before work"*, that is before they are of any use for timekeeping. The next 120 days they can be used and so are referred to as *"doing work"*. After this time they have 90 days in the western sky when they cannot be used before they disappear for 70 days and are considered to be in the *duat*, because they have died and are in the process of being rejuvenated.[216] So at any time there are seven groups of decan stars in the *duat*. This would have been deemed significant given the importance of the number seven. *"They pass the day and they pass the night, they rise and they set and they refresh themselves near the Lake of the North."* It explains that this lake is to the east of Yat-Nebes. *"It is the Duat of Hwt-Khati in Yat-Nebes. The way of the gods to heaven is by this door, when they come to the necropolis in the Duat."*[217]

The Roman Period papyrus Carlsberg has a commentary on the *Book of Nut*. Some versions include what is referred to as the *Dramatic Text* which deals with a quarrel between Nut and Geb over

---

[213] Egyptian Astronomical Texts I: The Early Decans, Neugebauer & Parker, 1960:100

[214] Genesis of the Stars in Ancient Egypt, According to the Naos of the Decades, Bomhard, 2016:129

[215] Genesis of the Stars in Ancient Egypt, According to the Naos of the Decades, Bomhard, 2016:131

[216] Egyptian Astronomical Texts I: The Early Decans, Neugebauer & Parker, 1960:55

[217] The Naos with the Decades (Louvre D 37 and the Discovery of Another Fragment, Habachi, 1952:251-263

her apparently killing her stellar offspring. He calls her the *"Sow who eats her piglets"*. Shu warns Geb not to interfere in a process he has so clearly misunderstood. He tells Geb that Nut protects each star as it goes through its cycle of rebirth. *"Not one among them falls."*[218] He reassures Geb that each star is reborn, like Re, from their mother Nut. Geb has a very earthbound and limited focus, like most of us, and the Way of Nut can appear incomprehensible to those on earth. It is all about your point of view and Geb's misunderstanding is due to his position in space. When viewed from the earth the sun, moon and many stars appear to rise and set – to be born and then die only to be born again after a period of time. An observer in a different position would see a completely different pattern, including the same process occurring to the earth. *"She receives the stars into her mouth and arms of yesterday."*[219]

SIRIUS

Sirius is the alpha star in the constellation of Canis Major, who is one of Orion's hunting dogs, and so Sirius is known as the Dog Star. Sirius is the name of the star and Sothis, or Sopdet, is the Goddess. The reappearance of Sirius after an absence of 70 days was called *peret sepdet*, the *"coming forth of Sopdet"*.[220] Sirius is invisible during this time because it is so close to the sun. At the end of the 70 days Sirius is visible for a short time just above the eastern horizon. At around 3,000 BCE the helical rising of Sirius occurred at the summer solstice. Now it is about 6 weeks later.[221] The annual Nile flood is a result of heavy summer rainfall in the Ethiopian Highlands. The rising water levels were seen at Aswan in late June but it wasn't until September that the highest water level occurred at Cairo. The heliacal rising of Sirius marked the start of the New Year because of the critical importance of the inundation. Sothis is the *"Bringer of the New Year and the Nile flood"*.[222] A decree of Ptolemy III (246-221 BCE) states that *"the day of the appearance of Sothis is called*

[218] My Heart, My Mother, Roberts, 2000:103
[219] Nut: The Goddess of Life in Text and Iconography, Billing, 2002:249
[220] The Egyptian Myths, Shaw, 2014:121
[221] The Egyptian Calendar, Bomhard, 1999:26
[222] The Complete Gods and Goddesses of Ancient Egypt, Wilkinson, 2003:167

the Opening of the year".[223] For the Egyptians the mythical source of the Nile and the inundation was a cave at Elephantine, the place where the water was believed to flow in from the *nun*. "*Sothis who gives the Nile from its cavern*."[224]

Sirius was seen as the embodiment of the Goddess Sothis from Pre-dynastic times when she was depicted as a cow, aligning her with the Cosmic Cow. It has been suggested that stars on the Gerzean palette represent Orion and their presence on and around the cow's head alludes to the rising of Sirius and the arrival of the inundation.[225] The earliest confirmed depiction of Sothis is on a 1st dynasty ivory tablet where she appears as a seated cow with a plant between her horns. It is thought that the plant symbolises the rising of Sirius bringing the inundation and subsequent plant growth.[226] In the later astronomical ceilings, such as at Dendera, she can be represented by a recumbent cow on a barque with a star between her horns.

Sothis can be shown as a woman with a star either on her head or on the top of her crown. Her crown is tall, similar to the White Crown of Upper Egypt, with long horns at the sides probably reflecting her original association with the Cosmic Cow. On Middle Kingdom coffin lids Sothis can be depicted with a thin triangle on her head, this is the hieroglyph sign for thorn (*seped*). Her Egyptian name Sopdet gives a near pun with *seped*. "*Sothis sharp of horns, high of disk*."[227] Priskin suggests that they represent the three stars which form the head of Canis Major.[228] On Senenmut's astronomical ceiling she is depicted as a standing woman who holds an *ankh* and a *was*-sceptre in one hand. Her other hand is raised near her crown which consists of two feathers plus the feather of Maat with a disc above them. Her gesture is unusual. The God Min is depicted in a similar pose. He is associated with the dark and new moon through his fertility aspects both in terms of the growth of crops and the

---

[223] The Egyptian Calendar, Bomhard, 1999:xii
[224] Men and Gods on the Roman Nile, Lindsay, 1968:58
[225] Ancient Goddesses, Goodison & Morris, 1998:110
[226] The British Museum Dictionary of Ancient Egypt, Shaw & Nicholson, 2008:310
[227] The Ancient Egyptian Coffin Texts Vol III, Faulkner, 2007:46 spell 876
[228] The Constellations of Egyptian Astronomical Diagrams, Priskin, 2019:137-180

breeding of animals. Sothis may mimic his pose as a hint at the fertility which the inundation will bring.

By the Late Period Sothis was strongly associated with Isis and, like so many other Goddesses, lost much of her independence. Texts from the temple of Isis in Hathor's Dendera temple equate the birth of Isis with the helical rising of Sirius. "*Ra rises...after she has come forth from the womb*".[229] Isis was not originally a cosmic Goddess but through her close association with Sothis she acquired this important aspect. She was often referred to as Isis-Sothis. "*She is the one who pours out the Inundation.*"[230] In the *aretalogy of Kyme* Isis says "*I am the one who rises in the Dog-star*".[231] At Dendera Isis is referred to as "*Sothis in the sky, Female Ruler of the Stars*".[232] On the astronomical ceiling on the Ramesseum Sirius is depicted, and named, as Isis.[233] In Greek and Roman depictions Isis-Sothis is often shown on the back of a dog. Sirius was called *canicula*, meaning puppy, by the Romans. The appearance of Sirius heralds a hot period, sometimes referred to as the dog days of summer. Plutarch tells us that "*they consider Sirius to be Isis's – as being a water-bringer*".[234] In the Greco-Roman Period it was usually Isis of Behdet who gave "*the king a high Nile*".[235] The other major influence aligning Isis with Sothis was that Orion was associated with Osiris. "*Your sacred image, Orion in heaven, rises and sets every day; I am Sothis who follows him, I will not depart from him!*"[236] Isis is always there to protect Osiris as she is for the deceased. "*You are Orion in the southern sky while I am Sothis acting as your protector.*"[237]

Sothis has important afterlife aspects. In the *Pyramid Texts* she unites with Osiris, or the king. "*Your sister is Sothis, your offspring is the Morning Star.*"[238] She also takes on the role as mother of the deceased. As befits a star she acts as a guide "*Sirius, pure of thrones.*

[229] The Theology of Hathor of Dendera, Richter, 2016:185
[230] Hymns to Isis in Her Temple at Philae, Zabkar, 1988:51
[231] Hymns to Isis in Her Temple at Philae, Zabkar, 1988:140
[232] The Theology of Hathor of Dendera, Richter, 2016:96
[233] Men and Gods on the Roman Nile, Lindsay, 1968:59
[234] Plutarch: Concerning the Mysteries of Isis and Osiris, Mead, 2002:218
[235] Men and Gods on the Roman Nile, Lindsay, 1968: 59
[236] Ancient Egyptian Literature Volume III, Lichtheim, 2006:118
[237] Traversing Eternity, Smith, 2009:189
[238] The Ancient Egyptian Pyramid Texts, Faulkner, 2007:252 utt 609

She is your guide on the goodly paths of heaven, in the Field of Reeds".[239] The deceased ask her to prepare a stairway and their path. Through her association with the waters of the inundation Sothis was associated with purification. "*Sothis goes forth clad in her brightness, she censes the bright ones who are among them.*"[240] Faulkner says the literal translation of the word is 'sharpness' and he suggests that this was an allusion to the brilliance of the star. Does the brightness of Sirius suggest that it has been newly washed hence associating Sothis with purification? By using the word for sharpness it also alludes to her *seped* crown.

Satis (Satet) Lady of Elephantine is the guardian of the border with Nubia and is associated with the inundation and thus with Sothis. Her consort is Khnum, the ram-headed Creator God associated with the Nile cataracts and the rising of the Nile. Their daughter Anukis is also associated with the cataracts and the Nubian border.

An event as critical to survival as the inundation inevitably had many myths associated with it. One such is the *Return of the Distant Goddess* who can be Hathor, Sekhmet or Tefnut. Thoth, or Shu, is despatched to the south to pacify the estranged Eye Goddess and bring her back to Egypt to reunite with her father. This is covered in detail in Jackson (2018) and only the concluding parts are relevant here. An inscription at Philae states that when Tefnut arrived here "*a great flame was around her. She burned the enemies of her father Re. She went up into the sky 10,000 cubits and immediately became peaceful*".[241] The hieroglyph for 10,000 is a finger but this can also be the measure of the width of a finger. Quack suggests that this relates to the rising of Sirius. The text says that Thoth and the Goddess came northwards from the Place of Finding in Nubia (Bigge). From Philae this is the direction in which the heliacal rising of Sirius can be seen. Sirius appears red when it rises due to dust in the atmosphere but returns to a blue-white colour later. This could be interpreted as the Goddess losing her rage as she cooled down. Another reference from Philae regards Sekhmet who "*came forth as*

---

[239] Writings from Ancient Egypt, Wilkinson, 2016:159

[240] The Ancient Egyptian Pyramid Texts, Faulkner, 2007:178 utt 502a

[241] A Goddess Rising 10,000 Cubits into the Air...or Only One Cubit, One Finger? Quack, 2002:284

a fire-serpent into the sky, and so her name 'Sothis' came into being".[242] Quack says that in Mesopotamian astronomy they used the cubit to measure an angular distance of 2°. A finger would measure 0.05° which is the distance Sirius could move before being lost by the rising sun's light. Is this serious astronomy hidden in mythology?

ORION

> *"I am Orion the Great who dwells among the souls of Heliopolis."*[243]

Called Sah by the Egyptians, the constellation of Orion was strongly associated with Osiris. Wilkinson suggests that the God Sah may have been Rigel, the brightest star in Orion, rather than the constellation itself.[244] Orion is described as *"the glorious soul of Osiris".*[245] Isis and Osiris on earth are echoed in the stars by Sothis and Orion. *"I am Orion who treads his land, who precedes the stars of the sky who are on the body of my mother Nut."*[246] In some depictions Orion has one arm raised. *"I have gone up upon the ladder with my foot on Orion and my arm uplifted."*[247] In his other hand he carries the *was*-sceptre, which is a symbol of power. A *Coffin Texts* spell mentions Orion who is standing on the path with his *"staff of rank"*. Like Sothis he is depicted in a boat, as he constantly sails the night sky. There are a number of spells for reaching Orion. The deceased calls to Orion a number of times *"come, Orion, and see me"*. Orion replies *"come, be a spirit, be equipped".*[248]

The barques of Sothis and Orion face each other, Orion often has his back to Sothis and looks over his shoulder at her. *"Isis, Sopdet, she faces Orion."*[249] Facing barques indicates a transition, in this case from the old to the new year. Orion looks behind as the year ends towards Sothis who inaugurates the New Year. Some Middle

---

[242] A Goddess Rising 10,000 Cubits into the Air...or Only One Cubit, One Finger? Quack, 2002:289

[243] Writings from Ancient Egypt, Wilkinson, 2016:169

[244] Writings from Ancient Egypt, Wilkinson, 2016:160

[245] Death in Ancient Egypt, McDermott, 1998:6

[246] How to Read the Egyptian Book of the Dead, Kemp, 2007:90

[247] The Ancient Egyptian Pyramid Texts, Faulkner, 2007:259 utt 625

[248] The Ancient Egyptian Coffin Texts Vol II, Faulkner, 2007:102 spell 469

[249] The Egyptian Calendar, Bomhard, 1999:22

Kingdom coffins have the text *"Orion turn thy head, that thou mayest see Osiris"*.[250] Perhaps it alludes to the fact that Osiris will join with Orion once he has been reborn or that Osiris joins with the full moon. *"He has come as Orion, behold, Osiris has come as Orion."*[251]

The murder of Osiris by Seth may have originated in a myth explaining the regular disappearance and reappearance of the constellation of Orion. He is associated with the renewal of life by his links to the inundation through Sirius and the growth of crops through his identification with Osiris as a Vegetation God. In one *Pyramid Texts* spell the king is *"that Great Star, the Supporter of Orion, traveling through heaven with Orion, navigating the Duat with Osiris"*. Wainwright suggests that the Great Star is actually Sirius. At the latitude of Heliopolis, Orion appears to be lying down when he first rises. Sothis appears under his belt. As the evening progresses Orion becomes upright and Sirius appears behind Orion. This would have been more pronounced in Pharaonic times.[252] This visible raising up of Orion is another good reason to associate Orion with Osiris. The phrase *"supporter of Orion"* may allude to Sirius appearing to raise Orion into an upright position. This is comparable to the funerary rite where the mummy of the deceased is raised before the ritual of opening the mouth for breathing is performed.

The deceased associate with Orion for the same reason that they associate with Osiris, so that they can participate in his regular rebirth. *"You ascend from the east of the sky, being renewed at your due season and rejuvenated at your due time. The sky has born you with Orion."*[253] In the *Pyramid Texts* Osiris is addressed *"in this your name of Dweller in Orion, with a season in the sky and a season in the earth"*.[254] Another spell refers to the king as the companion of Orion who traverses the sky with him. *"You shall reach the sky as Orion, your soul shall be as effective as Sothis."*[255] In the *Coffin Texts* Orion grants the deceased access to

---

[250] Orion and the Great Star, Wainwright, 1936:45-46
[251] The Ancient Egyptian Pyramid Texts, Faulkner, 2007:147 utt 442
[252] Orion and the Great Star, Wainwright, 1936:45-46
[253] The Ancient Egyptian Pyramid Texts, Faulkner, 2007:155 utt 466
[254] The Ancient Egyptian Pyramid Texts, Faulkner, 2007:47 utt 219
[255] The Ancient Egyptian Pyramid Texts, Faulkner, 2007:135 utt 412

the entire sky. *"Go over all the celestial expanses of the gods…you have taken possession of the limits of the horizon."*[256]

Triads, a grouping of three deities, became popular in the New Kingdom. Orion and Sothis form a triad with their son Soped. He was the God of the eastern desert border and one of the Cosmic Falcon Gods which aligns him with Horus the Elder. He was referred to as the one *"of the shining plumes"* and may have been associated with the Lone Star.[257] The triad of Isis, Osiris and their son Horus is thus reflected in the heavens.

THE OVOID

On astronomical ceilings there is an unnamed asterism. It is depicted as three nested ovoid shapes (similar to the body of the ovoid bull mentioned in the following chapter) with a star in the centre and three around it. Could the ovoid shape represent a womb with the star inside it the developing decan? On one of the ceilings of Rameses VI (20th dynasty) it seems to be called the Womb of Nut. The ovoid is repeated later as a fish shape. Piankoff suggests that it represents a constellation called the Womb of Nut, possibly the ovoid asterism in Pisces.[258] Text near to the shape refers to *"the water of the constellation"* but this may refer to a W formation of stars nearby. Priskin suggests that these are the five bright stars of Cassiopeia. They make an open W shape suggestive of the hieroglyph sign for water.[259]

THE TWO TURTLES

The African turtle is large and aggressive with a strong bite. It lives in the mud and was associated with negative feelings such as choking and being trapped. The 9th Dynasty tomb of Ankhtifi at Mo'alla depicts a turtle who inhabits the *nun* and is an enemy of the sun. Two turtles are depicted on the astronomical ceilings where they represent one of the triangle decans used during the

---

[256] The Ancient Egyptian Coffin Texts Vol III, Faulkner, 2007:118 spell 1017
[257] Egyptian Mythology, Pinch, 2002:205
[258] The Tomb of Rameses VI, Piankoff, 1954:384
[259] The Constellations of Egyptian Astronomical Diagrams, Priskin, 2019:137-180

epagomenal days. These were considered dangerous days which may be why they were assigned the turtles. Priskin locates this asterism to the south of Leo and says that at the winter solstice during the New Kingdom the sun rose as the Two Turtles set in the west. The winter solstice is the time when the sun's power fades and then begins to increase again. If the turtles are associated with Apophis then the winter solstice could be seen as the time of a battle for the survival of the sun. One spell to open the doors of the sky in the *Book of the Dead* invokes the cardinal directions and states that "*Re lives, the turtle dies*".[260]

THE SHEEP

The sheep is depicted with straight horns suggesting that it was an ancient asterism. The straight horned sheep was rare by the New Kingdom as it had been replaced by a breed with curled horns. One *Coffin Texts* spell refers to the Waterway of the Two Sheep. Could this be a reference to the constellation? Priskin suggests it covered the constellations of Scorpio, Sagittarius and Capricorn assuming that its position on the ceilings is correctly placed next to the ship.[261]

THE SHIP

The decan lists contain references to specific stars of the ship, such as the Middle of the Ship. Priskin suggests that one of the pieces of rock art from Wadi Mineh reflects this asterism. It consists of the outline of a ship and a figure with upraised arms. The figure is either a deity in their heavenly barque or the deceased journeying to the stars. "*The ship which Greeks call Argo is an image of the bark of Osiris…it sails not far from Orion and Dog.*"[262] The star Canopus (in the constellation of Carina) was considered to be the pilot of the ship. There is no consensus as to which asterism the Ship is. It may indeed tie up with Argo Navis. Priskin suggests that it stretches from Pyxis to Ursa Major.[263] Lull and Belmonte say that

---

[260] The Constellations of Egyptian Astronomical Diagrams, Priskin, 2019:137-180
[261] The Constellations of Egyptian Astronomical Diagrams, Priskin, 2019:137-180
[262] Plutarch: Concerning the Mysteries of Isis and Osiris, Mead, 2002:206
[263] The Constellations of Egyptian Astronomical Diagrams, Priskin, 2019:137-180

it may include the group of decans of the asterism *khent*, the prow or front. They don't come to a consensus. One suggests the Ship is in Capricorn, which has the look of a pre-dynastic boat, with *khent* in Scorpio. The other says that the Ship has its prow from Sagittarius to Libra, where it sails on Milky Way.[264] Antares (in Scorpio) could be identified with the decan called Red One of the Prow.[265]

THE GIANT

The Giant, Nekht, appears to be one of the decans as he is present on the Ramesside star charts. Lull and Belmonte suggest that it is a very large constellation covering Aquila to the Square of Pegasus.[266]

DECANS AND THE AFTERLIFE

The 70 days the decan stars spend in the *duat* was reflected in the 70 days of the formal mummification process. By having a mummification process which lasted 70 days it was easy to align the funerary preparations for each individual to what was happening to the stars. The *Dramatic Text* explains that during their time in the *duat* the decan is purified where "*its evil falls to earth*". Given that the decans were associated with fate and retribution they needed to be purged and purified. It also follows the mummification process where the evil of decay is removed from the corpse. Once purified the stars dissolve into the liquid of the Lake in the Sky and then begin to grow as embryonic stars. "*The life of a star begins in the lake…it begins as a fish. It flies upwards from the Great Green as an image. So the stars live.*"[267] The fish-shaped womb of Nut mentioned earlier may reflect this interim form of the rejuvenating decan stars.

The decans, and some stellar deities, are prominent in the Netherworld Texts in their role as timekeepers. Time and its passing is important, especially for the complex and critical alchemical process of rebirth. The decans protect Ra at the same

---

[264] The Constellations of Ancient Egypt, Lull & Belmonte, 2009:170
[265] The Egyptian Calendar, Bomhard, 1999:54
[266] The Constellations of Ancient Egypt, Lull & Belmonte, 2009:162
[267] My Heart, My Mother, Roberts, 2000:102

time as they go through the process of rebirth. In the seventh hour of the *Amduat* Horus is responsible for the progress of the decans. "*May your flesh be in order, may your forms come into being that you may rest in your stars.*" He has to "*make the star-gods move and to set the positions of the hours in the netherworld*".[268]

FEAR OF THE STARS

It wasn't the constellations and planets which the Egyptians studied to determine the future but the decan stars who had a major influence on their life. The *naos* of the Decades describes some of these. "*They rise and they set in their abodes...causing the going forth of the inundation...It is they who give the wind, it is they who are the protectors of heaven, dismissing the clouds.*"[269] As Shu is the God of air it is appropriate that his emissaries generated the weather. It appears strange that clouds were seen as the enemy of the sky. In such a hot country it might be expected that clouds would be more appreciated. The action of covering the sun and sky was seen as an insult and threat to the Sun God, even though it might have beneficial consequences for people.

Other duties assigned to the decan stars were those of "*all life, all death, all massacre*" so it is no surprise that they were feared.[270] An amulet from the 21st dynasty asks for protection from "*the seven stars of the Great Bear, from a star that falls from the sky, and from the decan stars*".[271] The very recognisable seven-star asterism of the Plough is part of Ursa Major. These seven stars may have been associated with the seven demon emissaries of Sekhmet who brought disease and disaster. At Esna it says that people live or die depending on the whims of the decans and so "*everybody trembles when they rise*".[272] Texts from the *naos* of the Decades refer to the "*duat of their temple*" of one group of slaughtering genies which appears to correspond

---

[268] The Egyptian Amduat, Abt & Hornung, 2007:237-238

[269] The Naos with the Decades (Louvre D 37 and the Discovery of Another Fragment, Habachi, 1952:251-263

[270] The Genesis of the Stars in Ancient Egypt, According to the Naos of the Decades, Bomhard, 2016:127

[271] The Secret Lore of Egypt, Hornung, 2001:28

[272] The Genesis of the Stars in Ancient Egypt, According to the Naos of the Decades, Bomhard, 2016:133

to a lake in the north-east of Yat-Nebes. The slaughtering genies are frequently depicted in association with snakes to emphasise their dangerous nature. The first vignette on the *naos* of the Decades depicts a *ba*-bird in a barque which is supported by a snake.[273]

The *naos* of the Decades does explain that it is Shu who makes the decisions that the decans carry out. The original concept was that the decans had power over the enemies of *maat* who threatened the stability of creation and the Sun God. They acted as his bodyguards who cleared his path across the heavens. The roles of Shu and Thoth overlap in some areas. Thoth is the defender of *maat* and a judge and sometimes the decans are referred to as his emissaries. On the *naos* an enthroned Thoth is depicted with his writing palette, perhaps writing the orders for the decans to carry out. He is called Master of the Books; the books alluded to being those of the *"calamities of him who destroys the lifetime"*.[274] The epagomenal days were especially feared because they were days out of time. They also coincided with the period before the inundation arrived when water and food supplies were very low and pests and disease were rampant. In the section describing the 37th decan the king is shown offering to Shu and his decan emissaries to *"protect the land from calamity"*.[275] In the chapel of Ptolemy VIII (170-116 BCE) at Deir el-Bahri the decans are shown as 36 stars in an oval receiving offerings. The decans were also protective. In the tomb of Osorkon II (22nd dynasty) at Tanis the decans are depicted as lion-headed snakes. An armband from this tomb depicts them in the same form alongside Osiris, Horus, Thoth, Isis and Nephthys. They also had an influence on specific parts of the body.[276]

THE UNWEARYING STARS

With the exception of Sirius and Orion, we only know the decans as a method of telling the time. Most we cannot locate in

[273] The Genesis of the Stars in Ancient Egypt, According to the Naos of the Decades, Bomhard, 2016:135

[274] The Genesis of the Stars in Ancient Egypt, According to the Naos of the Decades, Bomhard, 2016:134

[275] The Naos with the Decades (Louvre D 37 and the Discovery of Another Fragment, Habachi, 1952:251-263

[276] The Secret Lore of Egypt, Hornung, 2001:229

the night sky. There were probably mythologies associated with each one, or group, which we are unlikely ever to uncover. As they were still being incorporated into tombs and ceilings in the Greco-Roman Period they were obviously an important symbol for the Egyptians. Despite their longevity there is debate as to whether the decan stars were a practical method of telling the time especially in the later periods when the lists appear confused as well as out of date. It is possible that the scribes in later periods didn't understand the original texts which were over a thousand years old making it easier to make mistakes which were not spotted. They may have used different documents which we don't have. It is more likely though that the decan lists were included as a funerary motif because they were so old, which made them intrinsically important, rather than because they were useful. Their life cycle of perpetual regeneration was one the deceased wanted to emulate.

CHAPTER 8

The Northern Constellations

"As for this Thigh of Seth, it is in the Northern sky,
attached to two flint stakes by a golden chain. It is entrusted to
Isis, who guards it in the form of a female hippopotamus."[277]

THE CONSTELLATIONS AND THEIR STORIES

It is likely that the majority of the Egyptian constellations were well established by the end of the Pre-dynastic. Storytelling is an important part of human culture especially during periods when we are forced to be inactive. Sitting around the fire at night there are few distractions so the visual focus is on either the fire, the moon or the stars. Directing the listeners' attention to a particular group of stars gives the narrator a point of reference, for example that was where the attack took place, as well as giving the listeners a reminder of that particular story for another night. Anyone looking at the stars can wonder what they are, what are they doing, what do

---

[277] Egyptian Mysteries: New Light on Ancient Knowledge, Lamy, 1986:59

the patterns mean and how do we fit into their story? The search for patterns and order is deeply embedded in our brain and we are particularly adept at seeing faces. This is an essential inherited skill to keep us alive but also it acts as an impulse for storytelling. We may see forms and faces in clouds and trees but when it comes to the named constellations it is sometimes hard to find one that looks like its name. Their naming seems to have arisen partly from the desire to fix important symbols and deities in the sky.

IDENTIFYING THE CONSTELLATIONS

The Egyptian constellations are noticeably different to the Classical ones we are familiar with and a number of scholars have tried to locate the Egyptian constellations in the night sky with reference to our constellations. On the astronomical ceilings red dots are present on the bodies of the figures. These will represent stars but don't appear to be much help in identifying the constellations. The astronomical ceilings differ considerably and they were never intended to be an accurate star chart. There is very little agreement with the suggestions. Identifying pictures in the stars is very much open to interpretation and there is always the risk that you will see what you want to see not what the Egyptians saw. Given the number of stars in the sky it is easy to join the dots to make a picture. This is not to belittle the work done by scholars trying to identify the Egyptian constellations but just to warn that it is often impossible to prove with our current information. Lull and Belmonte worked together to do this but even they weren't able to agree on a number of interpretations. Only a few of the Egyptian constellations have been identified and accepted by the majority of scholars, most identifications are controversial.

THE EGYPTIAN CONSTELLATIONS

The Onomasticon of Amenemope lists five constellations; Orion, Meskhetyu (Seth as the Foreleg), the Ape, the Giant and the

Hippo. [278] The Hippo, Orion and Meskhetyu appear on the astronomical ceilings. The Giant is one of the decans but the Ape (*T'n*) is unknown. Etz splits the astronomical ceilings into two types: the Sety I (19th dynasty) version and the Pedamenope version. Pedamenope was a 25th dynasty lector priest. Both depict the majority of the constellations discussed here but some are in different positions or have different forms. Figures can be arranged differently to fit the available space and sometimes contain elements from the other type. Each ceiling will have been bespoke so people could have asked for any specific figures which were significant for them.

The Female Hippo

Hippos are dangerous and destructive animals both on land and in the water. The male was associated with Seth but surprisingly the female, who was more dangerous when she had young, was considered a benign Goddess who was well disposed to ordinary people. She was protective and sympathetic, especially towards mothers and children. As there were three Hippo Goddesses (Ipy, Reret and Taweret) in the Old Kingdom it is probably safe to say that the hippo would have been an important Pre-dynastic Goddess. All three are depicted in a similar fashion and they can be seen as aspects of each other. They take the form of a standing hippo with pendulous breasts and a swollen stomach. While looking basically like a hippo they have the legs and paws of a lion and the back and tail of a crocodile. Using leonine legs and paws rather than a hippo's looked more elegant, especially as they stand upright and hold onto objects.

The Great Ipy (or Ipet) was important in Thebes where she was said to have given birth to Osiris, which links her to Nut. In the *Pyramid Texts* she nurses the king. She was Mistress of Magical Protection and depictions of her were often used for apotropaic purposes. Reret was the Great Sow, the Egyptians viewed the hippo as a water pig. She was also Mistress of the Horizon, Nebet-akhet. She often has a star on her chest or upper arm which is thought by some to represent Thuban, the pole star at that time. In other

---

[278] Ancient Egyptian Astronomy, Parker, 1974:51-65

depictions her front paws rest on the hieroglyph sign for *sa* and the *ankh*. *Sa* means protection and the symbol is a sheaf of reeds folded over and tied. Reret was closely associated with Hathor and her epithet of Great Sow aligns her to Nut. In the *mammisi* at Dendera there is a Hippo Goddess referred to as Shepet who has the head of a crocodile. She is thought to be a variation of Reret. Taweret, the Great One, was a very popular domestic Goddess and she appears on amulets from the Old Kingdom. She is frequently associated with Hathor. In one vignette for the *Book of the Dead* spell 186, which address Hathor, Taweret stands in front of the deceased with the Hathor Cow behind her. In this vignette her long wig continues to form a plaited cloak which becomes a crocodile tail. This looks very much like the stylized crocodile cloak worn on some constellation depictions. She was also associated with Isis and referred to as Isis-Djamet.

The constellation of the Hippo is the largest in the ceilings which emphasises her importance. Why was she so important? Is it just because she restrains Meskhetyu who represents Seth? Perhaps the Hippo constellation was an important part of Pre-dynastic astronomical myth which was never discarded. Was she a remnant of an ancient Mother Goddess, or an avatar of Nut, who forever looked down from the skies to offer her protection and support?

The Hippo stands upright with her front paws resting on either mooring posts or on a small crocodile and a mooring post. A chain or cord is sometimes stretched from the post to Meskhetyu. In the papyrus Jumilhac it says that Meskhetyu is kept in the northern sky by Reret so that *"it cannot travel among the gods"*.[279] The male hippo was considered a manifestation of Seth so it was appropriate that his severed leg was guarded by a Hippo Goddess. She is shown either with a crocodile on her back or with a thick cloak which looks like a stylised crocodile body with the tail of a crocodile. Why would she have a crocodile on her back whether stylised or not? Is the crocodile attacking her or is its position behind her deemed as protective? Protective deities are often pictured directly behind the one they are protecting. A crocodile determinative is used in words such as aggression so is this a way of emphasising her ferocity? The

---

Hippo Goddess is often shown in a composite form so this may allude to the crocodile component, perhaps in terms of strength, stealth and ferocity. It could be a way of either humiliating a defeated crocodile or a shamanic method of acquiring his power. Perhaps it alludes to a mythic event which we are unaware of. Crocodiles were not considered in a totally negative light. Their habit of basking on sandbanks and facing east into the morning sunlight was seen as greeting Ra.

What is the difference in meaning when the Hippo is shown without the crocodile on her back? Is it merely the preference of the artist or the person who commissioned the ceiling? Does it depict a different part of a myth or was it done in areas, or for people, where the crocodile was viewed differently? Is the object on her back something other than a cloak? If so what? On the Pedamenope ceiling her cloak has seven stars on it which are split into groups of four, two and one. Does this tie up with a significant asterism?

On some Middle Kingdom coffins there is a plan of the Field of Offerings, taken from one of the *Coffin Texts* spells. It includes the "*Waterway of the White Hippopotamus*" which is described as being devoid of fish and snakes. It is 1000 *schoeni* long and of undetermined width. [280] The *schoeni* was an Egyptian measure, meaning river-length, but its precise length isn't known. It is thought to be in the region of 9-11km. Reret may be the White Hippo as she has a more celestial nature but all the Hippo Goddesses can be viewed as avatars of each other. The funerary texts refer to other seemingly less benevolent hippos in the heavens. One *Coffin Texts* spell refers to the deceased harpooning a hippo in the Winding Waterway, alluding to Seth who took the form of a hippo in one of his battles with Horus.

There is no agreement as to which constellation the Hippo is aligned with. Priskin suggests that she is located roughly parallel to the ecliptic from Serpens and Ophiuchus to Cepheus, Andromeda and Pegasus.[281] Lull and Belmonte suggest that the Hippo is a large area near the pole star stretching from Lyra to Bootes. Her head is

[280] The Ancient Egyptian Coffin Texts Vol II, Faulkner, 2007:93 spell 466
[281] The Constellations of Egyptian Astronomical Diagrams, Priskin, 2019:137-180

near the head of Draco. Such a large area of the sky would emphasise her mythic importance. The crocodile on her back is the area of Serpens Caput.[282] Another suggestion is Auriga plus parts of neighbouring constellations. Three of the major stars of Auriga form a line which points to the place where the ecliptic intersects the galactic equator which may form the Mooring Post.[283]

Meskhetyu – the Foreleg and the Bull

The main difference between the two ceiling types is in the depiction of this constellation. Ursa Major is the largest Classical constellation in the northern sky. Its seven brightest stars form the asterism known as the Plough. This is one of the most easily identifiable asterisms as well as having the symbolically significant seven stars and so is associated with myths in many cultures. This constellation is depicted either as the foreleg of a bull or as a bull and it can refer to either Ursa Major or the Plough. The Egyptians saw the Plough as the hind leg of a bull and called it the Bull's Foreleg, Meskhetyu. In the *Book of the Day* it refers to Meskhetyu as "*this thigh of Seth*".[284] During one of their endless battles Horus hacked off Seth's leg and threw it into the sky where it formed Meskhetyu. Isis used magical chains to tether it in place so that it could not wander about the heavens and cause further havoc. The *Pyramid Texts* refer to Horus "*who presides over his thigh-offerings*".[285] Some Middle Kingdom coffin lids show four figures; Nut, Orion, Sirius and Meskhetyu as a Foreleg. This has seven stars on it, in a similar arrangement to those of the Plough, and is called "*mshtyw in the northern sky*".[286] Plutarch says that "*the soul of Isis is called Dog by the Greeks, but Sothis by the Egyptians, while the soul of Horus is called Orion, and Typhon's Bear*".[287]

Why is Meskhetyu so prominent given Seth's disruptive nature? Priskin suggests that Meskhetyu was the most important constellation as it was used in foundation rituals. If so, it seems

---

[282] The Constellations of Ancient Egypt, Lull & Belmonte, 2009:162
[283] A New Look at the Constellation Figures in the Celestial Diagram, Etz, 1997:143-161
[284] The Tomb of Rameses VI, Piankoff, 1954:400
[285] The Ancient Egyptian Pyramid Texts, Faulkner, 2007:145 utt 437
[286] A New Look at the Constellation Figures in the Celestial Diagram, Etz, 1997:143-161
[287] Plutarch: Concerning the Mysteries of Isis and Osiris, Mead, 2002:205

surprising that the constellation was associated with Seth. Would it be wise to align a temple to the Chaos God, unless it was his temple? The original use of the constellation for temple alignment may have predated its identification with Seth, or dated to a period when he was less maligned. He wasn't always a chaotic and untrustworthy God. He was associated with the unification of Egypt and is shown with Horus binding together the symbols of Upper and Lower Egypt in a motif called the *sema-tawy*.

Orion, Sothis and Meskhetyu are mentioned together in a number of *Pyramid* and *Coffin Texts* spells where Seth acts in a beneficial way towards the deceased. "*It is Orion who has given me his warrant; it is the Great Bear which has made a path for me to the western horizon; it is Sothis who greats me.*"[288] He works with Horus to help the deceased ascend to heaven. "*Horus lifts me up; Seth raises me.*" The deceased then says "*I will propitiate the two gods who are contented and propitiate the two gods who are discontented*".[289] From the New Kingdom onwards Seth was increasingly demonised. Regardless of his deteriorating nature, Seth is essential in the battle against Apophis. "*Orion binds him in the southern heaven, the Great Bear overturns him in the northern heaven, those who are in the starry firmament fetter him.*"[290]

Seth was said to have torn his way out of Nut's womb in his impatience to be born. Did the Egyptians see the rip in her side, the instrument he used or even his leg bursting out when they viewed the Plough? The shape of the Plough is similar to depictions of the adze used in the opening of the mouth ritual which enabled the deceased to breathe in the afterlife. The hieroglyph of an adze was used as the determinative for the constellation in the *Pyramid* and *Coffin Texts*. At that time the only iron available in Egypt was meteoric "*iron which issued from Seth*". The magically endowed adze can "*split open*" the mouth of the deceased the same way as it did for the "*mouths of the gods*" and split open the sky for Seth.[291] Meskhetyu was seen as a place of purification, like the Milky Way in general. For Seth to be so clearly associated with a constellation directly

[288] The Ancient Egyptian Coffin Texts Vol II, Faulkner, 2007:127 spell 482
[289] The Ancient Egyptian Pyramid Texts, Faulkner, 2007:187 utt 510
[290] The Bremner-Rhind Papyrus III: The Book of Overthrowing Apep, Faulkner, 1937:166-185
[291] The Ancient Egyptian Pyramid Texts, Faulkner, 2007:4 utt 21

linked with rebirth (purification and opening the mouth for breathing) highlights his original importance and character compared to his reduced and demonised persona in the Greco-Roman Period.

Meskhetyu can be depicted as a normal bull, as a bull with an ovoid body and tiny legs, as a foreleg with a bull's head or as a foreleg. Hieroglyphs giving the bull's name (a vulture, disc and fox skin) usually appear inside the body of the ovoid bull and above the depiction of the normal bull. On the Sety I versions of the astronomical ceilings Meskhetyu is depicted as a normal bull. His head always faces away from the Hippo. When a bull is shown it is always depicted restrained or being attacked. This is because there is magical power in words and art and this carries the risk that the Bull of Seth, or his influence, might manifest either in the temple or in the sky and cause havoc and the disruption of cosmic *maat*.

The ovoid bull on the Pedamenope versions doesn't look very Egyptian in style. It is similar to the ovoid in the southern sky, which represents the Womb of Nut, shown on ceilings such as the tomb of Rameses VI. Did it depict the bull as a foetus and refer to Seth bursting out of Nut's side unwilling to wait to be born? On Middle Kingdom coffins and Late Period monuments the constellation is always depicted as a bull's foreleg. Etz suggests that the Foreleg and the Bull both relate to Seth but are from different sources. He proposes that the Foreleg refers to the dismemberment of Seth and only occurs in later texts. The Bull alludes to Seth as Lord of the Northern Sky who is associated with a different Hippo Goddess. Priskin suggests that the ovoid bull isn't the Plough but is Bootes, which does have an ovoid shape. Sometimes the ovoid bull has three stars on his body and three where the tail should be. The red star in a circle could be Vega (the brightest star in the constellation of Lyra). He suggests that the Foreleg and the ovoid bull had been conflated by the New Kingdom but were originally separate entities.

The festival of Meskhetyu is listed in the Cairo papyrus with the advice "*do not do anything on it*". The timing of this festival, 13 days after the heliacal rising of Sirius, marked the lowest culmination of the Plough.[292] Was the Plough interpreted differently when it was in different positions in the sky over the year? Priskin suggests that when the handle pointed south it could be seen as the Foreleg but when it pointed north it was the man with a spear. These movements, as well as those of other asterisms, could be viewed as telling an annual story. If the man is viewed as Horus and the Foreleg as Seth it may reflect the ambiguity of both Gods as a single entity.

In the eleventh hour of the *Book of Gates* is a God with the heads of both Horus and Seth who is called His Two Faces. The two Gods are reconciled and use their power to fight Apophis rather than each other. Some of the astronomical ceilings depict a Horus-Seth composite figure. Is this in part a reflection of the human psyche containing both good and evil in varying proportions? A lot of the Egyptian myths use the theme of mutilation leading to transformation just as death is a prerequisite to rebirth. Is the slaying and mutilation of Seth alluding to the rejection or controlling of the dangerous Sethian aspects within an individual? The symbols of destruction, the rip in the sky and the severed leg, become the symbols of salvation and rebirth in the adze which grants the breath of life to the deceased and in the constellation which purifies the deceased and guides the alignment of temples.

The Mooring Post

Various texts describe Isis, or Reret, tethering Meskhetyu to the Mooring Post so he can't wander "*into the southern sky towards the water of the gods born of Osiris, which is beyond Orion*".[293] The trio of the Hippo, Meskhetyu and the Mooring Post are frequently mentioned in the *Pyramid* and *Coffin Texts* but a lot less in the New Kingdom funerary texts. Ursa Minor and Draco are one suggestion for the constellation. Another is in the area of Bootes including the star Arcturus.[294]

---

[292] The Mythological Importance of the Constellation Msḫtjw in Mortuary Representations, Nemes, 13:1-61
[293] Egyptian Mysteries: New Light on Ancient Knowledge, Lamy, 1986:59
[294] The Constellations of Ancient Egypt, Lull & Belmonte, 2009:165

Anu – the Falcon-headed God

The name Anu ('Anw or 'An) hasn't been identified or related to any known God. He is probably an avatar of Horus given his falcon head. In some of the ceilings a hieroglyph is added to the end of his name. This is a man with a spear which faces away from the rest of the name. On one ceiling Anu is given the epithet "*the one who turns back*".[295] Does he look back to check for other enemies or does it indicate that he was interrupted while traveling in a different direction? Mars is called Horus "*who navigates backwards*". Is Anu somehow related to Mars? Is this why Mars is sometimes absent in astronomical ceilings, because he is elsewhere fighting or restraining Meskhetyu?

On the Pedamenope-type ceilings Anu spears the ovoid bull but on the Sety I version it is a more complex composition. The bull stands on a platform which has a bulge in the middle. Anu holds what looks like a staff which bends down at the front end and is attached to the bull's platform. Some refer to it as a harpoon and Horus did use a harpoon in one of his battles with Seth. Personally I can't see it as a harpoon and it is not in the shape of the hieroglyph for harpoon. Does the bulge in the platform refer to a hobble? The hieroglyph sign for hobble is an inverted U. It also looks a bit like a stylised yoke. Anu could be holding a goad or whip. Alluding to the domestication of the Bull of Seth, treating him like an ox, would be a pointed insult as well as a way controlling his powers.

Suggestions as to the relevant constellations vary. Etz suggests it may be Lynx and part of Ursa Major but admits it isn't ideal.[296] Lull and Belmonte say Anu is a large area from parts of Canes Venatici to Lynx.[297]

The Gesticulating Man

This figure, who is never named, is only found on the Sety I-type ceilings. He sometimes has a very similar stance to Anu despite not holding a spear. If the spear was present it would be aimed at the crocodile next to him. Priskin proposes that the two men are

---

[295] The Constellations of Egyptian Astronomical Diagrams, Priskin, 2019:137-180
[296] A New Look at the Constellation Figures in the Celestial Diagram, Etz, 1997:143-161
[297] The Constellations of Ancient Egypt, Lull & Belmonte, 2009:162

both Horus and represent his duality. Anu's epithet *"the one who turns back"* may hint at this. Does he turn away from the bull to counter the threat of the crocodile? On the Sety I ceiling he appears to be pointing at the crocodile and up towards the bull. His finger points into, or has caused, the bulge in the bull's platform. Is he connecting the two in some way, giving hand signals or pointing the way? Is he reminding us that the bull and the crocodile are one and the same entity? Gemini is a popular suggestion for his constellation while Priskin suggests he is part of Ursa Major.

The Man Holding a Rope

This man is only found on Sety I-type ceilings. He grasps a double rope which is attached to the bull's rump and the Mooring Post. Priskin says his name is shepherd but shouldn't that be oxherd under the circumstances? One *Coffin Texts* spell refers to the *"Ox-herd who is on his pool"* which may have some relevance.[298] The man has a disc on his head which Priskin suggests is a bright star in or near Capricorn. He suggests that this constellation is roughly parallel to the ecliptic in the area of Capricorn, Aquarius, Aquila and Pegasus. For the rope he suggests from Scorpius through Ophiucus, Aquila, Delphinus, Pegasus, Lacerta and Cephu to Draco. This covers a huge expanse of the sky. Such a large constellation suggests importance but is it really the case here?[299]

The Crocodile

The large crocodile, Hetep-Redwy, is shown recumbent with a straight tail. His name translates as *"restful of feet"* or *"lying on his feet"*. This name suggests that he isn't going to wander, probably to minimise his threat. This is also an epithet of the Crocodile God Sobek. Despite the justifiable terror crocodiles inspired Sobek was revered, though still feared, at various places in Egypt. He was an ancient God, probably Pre-dynastic in origin, who was associated with the inundation and the growth of vegetation through his obvious association with the Nile. He could be associated with a number of Gods including Osiris, Min (a fertility God), Horus and

---

[298] The Ancient Egyptian Coffin Texts Vol II, Faulkner, 2007:205 spell 622
[299] The Constellations of Egyptian Astronomical Diagrams, Priskin, 2019:137-180

Ra. The shared epithet doesn't prove that Hetep-Redwy was Sobek as this epithet was used for other minor crocodile deities. There are a number of *Coffin Texts* spells to become Sobek, the deceased assume the identity of a number of powerful deities during their journey through the afterlife. Spell 268 has a particularly riverine element referencing marshes, creeks and riverbanks – all good crocodile habitat. Sobek is described as the Lord of the Winding Waterway. If the Milky Way was similar to the Nile, and as dangerous, then a crocodile spirit is a good shape to assume. This may be the reason for the predominance of crocodile and hippo constellations.

Sobek wasn't universally worshipped, in Dendera and Edfu he was associated with Seth. One myth tells how Seth was transformed into a crocodile by Geb after he had murdered Osiris.[300] Regardless of who the Crocodile is, the celestial afterlife appears to have been plagued by crocodiles. In the *Pyramid* and *Coffin Texts* there is reference to the Crocodile of the North who lives on the unwearying stars. Another spell refers to one "*living in the twilight in the midst of the distant stars*".[301] One spell in the *Book of the Dead* is to drive away a crocodile who tries to steal magic from the deceased.

On some of the ceilings Hetep-Redwy is shown next to the Gesticulating Man who is often described as spearing him. He has the correct posture for this action but is without a spear. A God like Sobek was unlikely to be depicted being attacked but is the crocodile actually being attacked? Does the man's pose indicate something else? One hand points at the Crocodile, the other upwards to the Bull. Is it the man who is the threat? In depictions the sting is removed from the scorpion to render it harmless, was the spear removed from the man for the same reason?

Stemmler-Harding suggests that the Crocodile represents Apophis when he dwells in the heavens. He is normally depicted as a snake so why would he be depicted as a crocodile on astronomical ceilings? Apophis could be aligned with the turtle. In the Late Period tomb of Petosiris a man is shown spearing a turtle. In the late New Kingdom the name of Apophis was written using the

---

[300] The Routledge Dictionary of Egyptian Gods and Goddesses, Hart, 2005:145
[301] Devil in Disguise – on the Stellar Mythology of Apophis, Stemmler-Harding, 2016:109

turtle determinative. All three reptiles are dangerous and considered unpleasant to look at (by most people). They have staring eyes and scaly skin and very fast reactions. Crocodiles and turtles are aggressive towards people, most other dangerous animals prefer to avoid people. All are associated with dark and dangerous water as well as basking on sandbanks. Apophis was the most dangerous and threatening monster the Egyptians conceived of and by combining all three reptiles they could emphasise his worst aspects. Alternatively they might have been fearful of depicting Apophis in what might be considered his 'true form' on a representation of the night sky in case they fixed it in reality. In the *Book of Gates* Apophis is shown being attacked. He is depicted in the usual manner of a long coiling snake. Above him is a crocodile, Shesses, which faces in the opposite direction. The rearing head of a snake emerges from the crocodile's tail. The text refers to "*this serpent*" which infers that the two beings are one.

Stemmler-Harding believes that the Crocodile is the constellation of Hydra and that the myths are influenced by the movements of Hydra throughout the year. Apophis' epithet of the Wanderer could refer to this. Hydra is a very large constellation, taking six hours to rise and set, but it has few bright stars. It does have a serpentine appearance. It is difficult to see clearly and it could be that the Egyptians saw the shape of a crocodile in asterisms close to Hydra. If Alphard, the brightest star, is taken as his eye then the surrounding stars could form his open jaws. Given the size of the constellation this crocodile represents a huge threat. This might be why he was depicted a lot smaller on astronomical ceilings. Stemmler-Harding discovered that at the Egyptian New Year (about 2222 BCE) Hydra paralleled the ecliptic but it was particularly prominent, and thus threatening, during the winter when the sun is at its weakest. Perhaps the rituals against Apophis were related to the positions of Hydra throughout the year as well as at different hours of the night. Hetep-Redwy is usually in a distinct group near the Lion, the Small Crocodile with the curved tail and Serket. Is there a myth linking them and sometimes the Gesticulating Man? Many scholars agree that the Crocodile is Hydra, but not all. Priskin suggests that it is Leo Minor through Leo to Hydra. He also says that this constellation overlaps his suggestion for Two Turtles so the man can be seen as attacking them as well.[302]

Neighbouring cultures were more comfortable referring to Hydra as the serpent constellation. Hydra is the Greek name for the Babylonian Serpent constellation. Alphard was derived from its Arabic name *"the Solitary one in the Serpent"*.[303] The snake is a very common form of deity and symbol in Egyptian religion; from the *uraeus* and Cobra Goddesses to the Time Serpents and the mysterious Mehen who protects the Sun God in the netherworld. It is interesting then that the Egyptians appeared to place crocodiles in areas of the sky where the Classical and Babylonian astronomers placed serpentine creatures; Hydra, Serpens and Draco.[304] As serpents are everywhere else in Egypt why are there no serpent constellations or asterisms?

The Crocodile with a Curved Tail

This small figure is an enigma. He is called Hequ, Plunderer, on Senenmut's ceiling which suggests that he was viewed as a threat.[305] Why is he placed so far away, next to the name of Serket, when the ovoid bull is depicted on the Pedamenope versions? Does this allude to his actual position in the sky? What does the curved tail mean? Females will lie in a semi-circle with a curved tail around their eggs so this may hint at protection and a warning but the crocodile appears to be male from the grammar. Sometimes his name is given as Saq. The hieroglyph of a crocodile with a curved tail was used in words such as *sak*, which means to collect or gather together. This does suggest that he was somehow the link connecting the Hetep-Redwy group together. Both Etz and Lull and Bellmonte suggest Leo Minor. Another suggestion is Virgo and Bootes.[306]

---

[302] The Constellations of Egyptian Astronomical Diagrams, Priskin, 2019:137-180
[303] Devil in Disguise – on the Stellar Mythology of Apophis, Stemmler-Harding, 2016:104
[304] The Constellations of Ancient Egypt, Lull & Belmonte, 2009:166
[305] The Sky at Night: Astronomical Knowledge in the New Kingdom, Bastijns, 2017:24-30
[306] The Constellations of Egyptian Astronomical Diagrams, Priskin, 2019:137-180

The Divine Lion

The Lion is shown recumbent and sometimes has a thick crocodile tail. He is referred to as the *"divine lion that is between the two of them"*.[307] 'Them' presumably are the crocodiles. Is he controlling them? In some depictions he has many stars along his head, back and tail. One spell in the *Book of the Dead* invokes a Lion of Re in the sky who eats the Foreleg. In another there is reference to a lion who went out with his bow. The rest of the text explaining who or what he intends to shoot is missing but it may well have been Seth. *"I am the Lion who has gone forth with the bow. He has shot, he has netted, he is the Eye of Horus."*[308] Shu has a lion form, as does Thoth through his association with Shu and the Distant Goddess. He was the *"living lion who repels the rebels"*.[309] The references to netting and the Eye of Horus suggest that the lion may well be either Shu or Thoth. The constellation of Leo, or incorporating it, is a popular and obvious choice for the Divine Lion. He is often depicted with a star at the end of his tail. Etz says this is Velorum (in the constellation of Vela).[310] Lull and Belmonte say that if the Lion is Leo it is most logical to have crocodile in Hydra and smaller crocodile in the area of Leo Minor.[311] Priskin suggests it is Leo Major through Crater to Vela.

The Raptor

On some Sety I-type ceilings a bird, probably a raptor, is positioned next to the Lion and the Crocodile with a curved tail. The bird is referred to as a black bird who *"issued from Ursa Major"*. Lull and Belmonte suggest Corvus or Triangulum and Perseus.[312]

Serket (Selkis)

The Scorpion Goddess Serket is usually depicted as a woman wearing a scorpion as a crown, shown without its tail or sting for

---

[307] The Constellations of Egyptian Astronomical Diagrams, Priskin, 2019:137-180
[308] The Egyptian Book of the Dead, Allen, 2010:217 spell 132
[309] Sekhmet and Bastet: the Feline Powers of Egypt, 2018:99
[310] A New Look at the Constellation Figures in the Celestial Diagram, Etz, 1997:143-161
[311] The Constellations of Ancient Egypt, Lull & Belmonte, 2009:166
[312] The Constellations of Ancient Egypt, Lull & Belmonte, 2009:162

safety reasons. *"Serket the great, the Divine Mother."*[313] She is an ancient Goddess who was present from at least the 1st dynasty and may have been more prominent in the earlier periods. Serket is nurse to the king and the *Pyramid Texts* refer to the king as the son *"of the sky-goddess who dwells in the Mansion of Selket"*.[314] She is one of the four Goddesses (with Neith, Isis and Nephthys) who guard the coffin and canopic jars. Serket was considered a protector against snakes and scorpions and was invoked to heal their bites and stings. *"Words spoken by Selkis...the noble and the powerful one, who came forth from the primeval water, the noble serpent, great of awe, who heals every snake bite."*[315] The fact that she is depicted on the astronomical ceilings emphasises her importance in the celestial sphere. In the *Book of Two Ways* she guards a bend in the river and in the *Book of Gates* she fights against Apophis and helps bind him.

> *"Serket, the great one, mistress of the ropes of the god of magic."*[316]

Knotting is important in Egyptian magic and medicine, as it is in many cultures. Just as in practical use there are a variety of knots for specific purposes, in magical usage the act of tying and untying creates different outcomes. One spell against scorpion venom invokes the seven Hathors who each tie seven knots. The tail of a scorpion has seven sections. Serket is not the only deity associated with knotting. Nut, Seth and Ra are invoked in one *Book of the Dead* spell. *"A knot was knotted around me by Nut in the primeval period."*[317] Their knots connect the deceased to heaven and open a connection from our world to the divine. Serket was closely allied with Isis. When Isis, while pregnant with Horus, escaped from Seth and went to the marshes to hide she was accompanied by Serket in the guise of seven scorpions.

Serket is positioned at 90° to the Hippo. Her position on the ceilings varies depending upon how Meskhetyu is depicted. When shown as a normal bull Serket is placed to the left edge of the group

---

[313] The Routledge Dictionary of Egyptian Gods and Goddesses, Hart, 2005:142
[314] The Ancient Egyptian Pyramid Texts, Faulkner, 2007:226 utt 571
[315] The Canopic Box of NS-'3-RWD (BM EA 8539), Ouda, 2017:127-138
[316] The Litany of Re, Piankoff, 1964:54
[317] Entangled, Connected or Protected? The Power of Knots in Ancient Egypt, Wendrich, 2006:256

but when the bull has an ovoid form she is depicted above him and slightly apart, holding his chain. This must reflect differing mythologies, perhaps the ovoid bull is more dangerous or she was more important in that version of the myth. The two men included on the Sety I-type ceilings might have more relevance to another version of the myth and so were placed in a more central position. Or does it reflect the night skies at a different time of year when different powers were at play?

There are a number of suggestions for the constellation she represents and this is complicated by her two different positions. Lull and Belmonte suggest Ursa Minor or Virgo.[318] Etz says Ursa Minor and part of Draco.[319]

SACRED SEVENS

Like many cultures, the Egyptians viewed seven to be a potent and magical number. It is thought to be associated with concepts of perfection and effectiveness as it embodies the values of three (plurality) and four (totality and completeness). It is a potent number in magic where spells are recited seven times and seven knots are tied. Hathor has a seven-fold aspect as does Sekhmet with her seven demons and Serket has her seven scorpions who accompanied Isis.

Were some, or all, of these seven-fold aspects of Goddesses identified with seven star asterisms in the sky? As Serket appears as a constellation it would be easy to assign her seven-fold aspect to an asterism. The Pleiades (sometimes called the Seven Sisters) is a prominent seven star asterism. Could the scorpions be seen here? The problem is that with so many stars in the sky it is possible to find many seven star asterisms so that is just an unsubstantiated guess. The only decan or Egyptian constellation that I am aware of which has been associated with the Pleiades is the Star of Thousands as the star Alcyone.[320]

---

318 The Constellations of Ancient Egypt, Lull & Belmonte, 2009:163
319 A New Look at the Constellation Figures in the Celestial Diagram, Etz, 1997:143-161
320 A New Look at the Constellation Figures in the Celestial Diagram, Etz, 1997:143-161

"I have established myself among you, you six Imperishable Stars."[321] Is this a reference to a seven star asterism or constellation with the deceased forming the seventh star? From the New Kingdom the four sons of Horus formed part of a group of seven Star Gods who helped Anubis protect the body of Osiris.[322]

SOME POSSIBLE CONSTELLATIONS

In the funerary texts there are a number of references which might allude to constellations or asterisms such as the Lake of Two Knives in the northern sky which the deceased crosses. Is the Lake of Jackals, or the Jackals, a constellation? One *Coffin Texts* spell refers to the unwearying stars trembling at the sight of the deceased in the Solar Barque *"within the Jackals"*.[323] Another contains a number of references to what might be constellations or asterisms. After being lifted up by Orion the deceased will *"shine in the plumes of Sopd...sit in the Ship of God"*.[324] The *"great plain North of the Stretching-the-Bows"* mentioned previously may refer to one or two asterisms.[325] An ascension spell from the *Pyramid Texts* refers to the Mountain of the *zhzh*-bird. Another similar avian reference is found in a *Coffin Texts* spell where the deceased ascend from the valley of the Mountain of the *sehseh*-bird. These might refer to the same type of bird, but might it also allude to the Raptor depicted on the astronomical ceilings?

READING THE NIGHT SKY

There is no reason for the Egyptian constellations to tell just one story. Each of the Classical constellations has its own story but few are linked together. For the Greeks, and other cultures, the constellations formed a picture book highlighting some of the characters from their myths. It was never intended to be read as a single story. Perhaps the Egyptians viewed their constellations in the same way. Meskhetyu, the Hippo and the Mooring Post are

---

[321] The Ancient Egyptian Coffin Texts Vol II, Faulkner, 2007:308 spell 786
[322] Egyptian Mythology, Pinch, 2002:204
[323] The Ancient Egyptian Coffin Texts Vol I, Faulkner, 2007:243 spell 317
[324] The Ancient Egyptian Coffin Texts Vol I, Faulkner, 2007:56 spell 61
[325] Devil in Disguise – on the Stellar Mythology of Apophis, Stemmler-Harding, 2016:97

connected in reference to Seth. If we exclude the decans of Sirius and Orion, who are identified with Isis and Osiris, the other major players in the background religion and mythology are not present and there is no surviving mythology for the other constellations. This suggests that we are missing some key parts of the puzzle. There is a preponderance of crocodiles which may reflect the fact that the Milky Way was considered a Celestial River so would be populated with riverine fauna. This may be part of the reason why the dominant Goddess is depicted as a hippo. The sky changes nightly as well as over the seasons. It is perfectly possible that the Egyptians treated this as a moving narrative but we can only see the story at one point in time as captured on the astronomical ceilings.

CHAPTER 9

The Uniting Moon

"It is Thoth, it is the secret of the full moon, and it is what
you have learned in the house of the night".[326]

THE REALM OF THOTH

Although usually thought of as nocturnal the moon divides its time between the day and the night, linking the nocturnal realm of Nut with the diurnal realm of Hathor. The deceased align themselves with the moon for that reason, so they can be free to travel the sky at any time.

The Egyptians viewed the moon with affection and appreciation. Its constant cycle of waxing and waning acted as a timekeeper and illustrated the concept of the eternal cycle of rebirth. The full moon brought the gift of light during the night and was the moment of triumph when the sun and moon, the Two Bulls of the Sky, were united and the sacred balance was restored. *"On the*

---

[326] The Ancient Egyptian Book of the Moon: Coffin Texts Spells 154-160, Priskin, 2019:74

15th day of the month the right eye is full and the left eye is ip and their rays unite."[327] The word *ip* has the meaning of complete or filled. The Egyptians had none of the western paranoia about full moons, madness and werewolves. Their view of the moon was the complete opposite to that of the west. They viewed it as a regulator, timekeeper and stabiliser and its chief God was wise and kind. Compare this to the Lunar Goddesses of Classical civilisation and the moon's descent into something sinister and unstable. Worship of the moon was universal in early societies and although there is no evidence it is probably safe to say that there was some kind of lunar cult from the Pre-dynastic period. *"He who enlightens the darkness, who shines in the extreme limits of the world in the dark, who traverses the four limits of the sky."*[328]

SOME LUNAR SCIENCE

In the Solar System, our moon is the largest in comparison to the size of its planet. It is also relatively close and both these factors give it a strong influence both in terms of physics and also psychology. The fact that it is at just the right distance to appear the same size as the sun is either a happy coincidence or divine planning depending upon your point of view. A smaller moon would make a total eclipse of the sun impossible and partial eclipses a minor event. The fact that both bodies are the same size made it easy for the Egyptians to align them with the eyes of a Sky God.

What is more important for life on Earth is less obvious. Because the moon is large and close it acts as a stabiliser giving the Earth a stable spin angle of 23° within a tolerance of 1-2°. Without the moon, or if it was just 10% further away, there would be nothing to stabilise the spin of the Earth. As a result it could easily tip over producing catastrophic and fluctuating climate change.[329] By acting as a celestial stabiliser the moon brings *maat* to the earth and so it is very fitting that the Egyptians made Thoth, the Lord of Maat, its divine protector.

---

[327] Thoth or the Hermes of Egypt, Boylan, 1922:69
[328] Of Min and Moon, Altmann-Wendling, 2017:10
[329] Book of the Moon, Aderin-Pocock, 2018:133

LUNAR NUMBERS

Lunar numbers have found their way into mythologies across the world. 33 is considered the number of the Solar Hero as it takes 33 solar years to complete 34 lunar years.[330] It takes 19 years for the sun and moon to return to the same places in the sky, this is called the metonic cycle.[331] While these cycles were no doubt noticed by the Egyptians did they have any influence? As yet I haven't found any. The synodic lunar month is measured from one identical phase of the moon to the next. The sidereal lunar month is the time the moon takes to complete one full revolution around the Earth with respect to the background stars. There are 13.37 sidereal months and 12.37 synodic months in a year – giving a 12:13 rhythm.[332] Thirteen is the number strongly associated with the moon and Goddesses, and as such it is often a victim of superstition. It doesn't appear to have had any significance for the Egyptians.

An average lunar synodic month is 29.5 days but the actual time from one new moon to the next varies from 29.3 to 29.8 days.[333] Ideally there are 30 days in a lunar month but sometimes the mathematics gives us a 29 day month as it is not possible to have a portion of a day. Thus we have a full lunar month of 30 days and a diminished or hollow lunar month of 29 days. For the *maat*-loving Egyptians this was not ideal and needed an explanation especially as critical rituals were timed according to the lunar calendar. This is alluded to in one spell where Anubis *"gives you incense at all seasons, and there is no deduction therefrom at the festival of the New Moon"*.[334] This suggests that the deceased still receive the full offerings even when the lunar month is shorter. 28 days is sometimes quoted as a lunar cycle number. It has the advantage of being divisible by the significant number seven. Sometimes the mathematics has to be made to fit the mythology. As mentioned earlier, Thoth created the five epagomenal days using some of the moon's light. Plutarch refers to *"each of the lights"*. The calculation of $1/70^{th}$ using the 30 day month or the 28 day month produces a value of 5.1 or 4.8,

---

[330] Sun, Moon & Earth, Heath, 2006:40
[331] Sun, Moon & Earth, Heath, 2006:28
[332] Sun, Moon & Earth, Heath, 2006:14
[333] Egyptian Festival Dating and the Moon, Spalinger, 2002:382
[334] The Ancient Egyptian Coffin Texts Vol I, Faulkner, 2007:39 spell 45

either of which is adequate for the myth. If the moon is invisible for two days this would give 28 days of the moon's light and it is in this context that Plutarch refers to it.

LUNAR GODS

Iah

Iah personified the moon, the word for moon is interchangeable with his name and he has no other aspects. In the *Pyramid Texts* the deceased king claims family ties to Iah either as his father or his brother. The focus changes in the *Coffin Texts* when Iah is associated with the light of the moon. "*I am Iah, I have swallowed the darkness.*"[335] In the New Kingdom tomb of Maya and Meryt one inscription refers to "*Iah, who is in the new moon, whose brilliance illumes the Silent Land*".[336] The *Book of the Dead* associates Iah with the lunar cycles. "*I have entered with the sun-disk, I have come out with Iah*".[337] In the New Kingdom Iah is merged with Thoth and depicted as ibis-headed. "*I have made provision for Thoth in the house of Iooh.*" Seshat says to Sety I (19th dynasty) "*thou shalt renew thy youth, thou shalt flourish again like Iooh-Thoth when he is a child*".[338] (The Goddess Seshat is covered in chapter 12.)

There is no evidence for a cult of Iah until the New Kingdom when there are references to his temple staff, possibly as a consequence of being merged with Thoth. An 18th dynasty *stele* refers to the "*First prophet of Iah*" and a walking stick of the same date is inscribed "*Chief of the workmen of Iah*". A number of other inscriptions refer to Iah-Thoth. "*Guardian of the temple of Iah-Thoth in Memphis.*" There was a 19th dynasty temple of Thoth in Memphis. Names with Iah as a component became popular for both men and women, such as Iahmes (born of the moon) and Iahhotep (peace of the moon).[339] Iah became popular again in the 2nd Intermediate Period when the Hykos rulers equated him with Sin, their Lunar

---

[335] The Moon God Iah in Ancient Egyptian Religion, Garcia-Fernandez, 2017:222
[336] The Tomb of Maya and Meryt I, Martin, 2012:31
[337] The Moon God Iah in Ancient Egyptian Religion, Garcia-Fernandez, 2017:223
[338] Thoth or the Hermes of Egypt, Boylan, 1922:63
[339] The Moon God Iah in Ancient Egyptian Religion, Garcia-Fernandez, 2017:224-225

God. There are amulets and statues of Iah as a man wearing the lunar crown.

Isden (Isdes)

Isden is an aspect of Thoth but its usage is not very common. At Dendera the king is depicted offering to Hathor to pacify her. *"He is like Isden who provisions the Udjat Eye, who makes shine the Shining Eye with its parts."*[340] One suggestion is that Isden is used when referring specifically to Thoth's afterlife judgment aspects another that it refers to a syncretised Thoth-Anubis. A *Coffin Texts* spell refers to the souls of the new moon as Osiris, Anubis and Isden. In the Greco-Roman *Books of Breathing* Osiris is referred to as the *"living ba of Isden"*.[341] Spell 17 in the *Book of the Dead* refers to Seth and Isden as Lords of Justice. Another reference to Seth in a more positive light.

Khonsu

The name Khonsu means Wanderer or Traveller and in funerary spells the deceased express the hope that they will be free to travel like Khonsu. He can be depicted as a young man in a tight garment or as a child with a side-lock of hair. His crown is the lunar disc supported on a crescent and he often carries the crook and flail of Osiris. He has a falcon-headed form where he appears similar to the other Falcon Gods. This suggests that Khonsu was one of the original Falcon Gods of the early Dynastic or Pre-dynastic. If the Sky God Horus the Elder was a falcon and the Sun God had a falcon form, as Ra-Horakhty, then it is logical to have a Lunar God with a falcon form.

In the Old Kingdom Khonsu is depicted as a bloodthirsty aggressive God, the *"angry one of the gods"*.[342] The *Cannibal Hymn* from the *Pyramid Texts* describes how he helps the king kill and devour minor deities so that he can absorb their powers. The rising sun obliterates the stars, often with a rosy glow, in effect killing the star deities. Was Khonsu identified with the sickle-shaped crescent

---

[340] The Theology of Hathor of Dendera, Richter, 2016:146
[341] Traversing Eternity, Smith, 2009:118
[342] Egyptian Mythology, Pinch, 2002:155

moon which rises just before sunrise? Was he the lunar equivalent of the Angry Eye of the Sun God? Earlier texts describe him as living on hearts. In the New Kingdom Khonsu formed part of a triad with Mut and Amun as their son. As Amun is a Creator God and Mut can be a Solar Eye Goddess the inclusion of Khonsu brought a lunar balance to the triad. In northern Egypt he was considered the son of Sekhmet and Ptah while at Kom Ombo, where Sobek had a cult centre, he was the son of Hathor and Sobek. Khonsu provides a similar lunar balance for Hathor and Sekhmet as Solar Eye Goddesses and for Sobek who could be linked to the Sun God as Sobek-Ra. By the New Kingdom Khonsu has become a benevolent God, probably as a consequence of joining the Theban triad.

Both sides of his nature are present in the *Coffin Texts*. He is still referred to as living on hearts and burning with anger. One spell gives him the epithet Ruler of Provisions, possibly a reference to the fertility aspects of the moon. Like Thoth, he will open the doors of the netherworld and the horizon for the deceased. A number of *Coffin Texts* spells refer to a path that the deceased use. Here they will meet Khonsu either standing on the path or on his way to Punt. The land of Punt lay to the south-east, the direction of the rising sun which is where the last crescent of the waning moon can be seen just before dawn. Khonsu was invoked in spells against demons because of his aggressive nature. He takes a baboon form when associated with Thoth. In this aspect he was the Keeper of the Books of the Year, which listed all those who would die that year. He was appealed to, probably euphemistically, as *"Khonsu the Merciful"* by those hoping to alter their fate. He was particularly venerated at Thebes and his temple at Karnak is well preserved. Here he was considered a Creator who, in the form of a snake, fertilised the cosmic egg.

Thoth

"Hail to thee Lunar-Thoth, thou self-engendered, the unknown." [343] Thoth is a God with a wide range of aspects, wisdom and justice being prominent ones. He is a Lunar God both as the Moon and as

---

[343] Thoth or the Hermes of Egypt, Boylan, 1922:63

its protector. The importance of his lunar aspect is emphasised by his crown – the lunar disc on a crescent moon. He can be depicted as an ibis, an ibis-headed man or a baboon. Plutarch said the Egyptians linked Thoth, whom he equates with Hermes, with the moon *"for the revolutions of the moon resemble the works of reason and super-abundant wisdom"*.[344]

The *Book of the Heavenly Cow* explains how Thoth became the moon and why it is seen during the day and at night. The Sun God became fed up with human behaviour and retreated into the heavens on the back of Nut in her form of the Cosmic Cow. He nominated Thoth as his deputy and said *"I shall cause you to encompass both the heavens with your perfection and with your brightness. And so the Moon of Thoth came into being"*. In an acknowledgment of the importance of the lunar cult the Sun God adds *"the eyes of all who look at you are opened through you, and everyone thanks you"*.[345] Thoth becomes the Silver Sun.[346] In the *Book of the Dead* he is called *"Thoth, the herald of Re in the sky"*[347] and *"Re that shines in the night"*. The deceased *"traverses the heaven like Re and speeds through it like Thoth"*.[348] The moon moves quickly, it takes an hour to cover an angular distance equal to its own diameter. During the New Kingdom Thoth seems to have had a particularly strong association with the moon. There are a large number of *stelae* from this period which are dedicated to Thoth in his lunar aspect referring to him as Lunar-Thoth and the Lord of Heaven. A *stele* of Pashed, Draftsman in the Palace of Truth, reads *"Thanksgiving to Lunar-Thoth. Veneration to the stars of heaven"*. Another refers to *"when Thoth and the stars are visible"*.[349]

One of Thoth's roles is that of psychopomp, a guide for the deceased through the dangerous afterworld. As the moon who traverses the Winding Waterway he is excellently placed to do this and sometimes acts as the ferryman. In one ferryman text the deceased summons the Celestial Ferryman and ends by stating *"if*

---

[344] Plutarch: Concerning the Mysteries of Isis and Osiris, Mead, 2002:222
[345] The Literature of Ancient Egypt, Simpson, 2003:295
[346] Thoth or the Hermes of Egypt, Boylan, 1922:65
[347] The Book of the Dead or Going Forth by Day, Allen, 1974:177 spell 169i
[348] Thoth or the Hermes of Egypt, Boylan, 1922:63
[349] Thoth or the Hermes of Egypt, Boylan, 1922:64

you do not ferry me over, I will leap up and put myself on the wing of Thoth and he will ferry me over to yonder side".[350] Thoth's most important lunar role is his protection and healing of the Lunar Eye. He is the Physician of the Eye of Horus who "*makes full the eye*".[351] Although he is not a God like Osiris who goes through a death-rebirth cycle one spell in the *Book of the Dead* refers to him as "*Thoth, born regularly*" a clear reference to the lunar cycles.[352]

The Sacred Ibis was closely associated with Thoth. It has black and white plumage and a curved bill. Classical writers pointed out the lunar symbolism of the ibis. Its curved bill represented the crescent moon and its plumage symbolised the phases of the moon. "*The variegated and admixture of its black with its white feathers suggest the gibbous moon.*"[353] Aelian said that the ibis "*knows when the moon is waxing and when waning...The bird is sacred to the moon. At any rate it hatches its eggs in the same number of days that the goddess takes to wax and to wane, and never leaves Egypt*".[354] He also reported that during a lunar eclipse "*it closes its eyes until the goddess shines out again*".[355]

Anubis as the Moon

Anubis is a Funerary God, responsible for mummification and acting as a guide for the deceased. He is depicted as a jackal or as a jackal-headed man. His funerary role is to purify, preserve and reassemble the body through the mummification process then raise the mummy and enable the deceased to breathe again. The ever-renewing moon has a direct link with the cycle of rebirth. This concept became increasingly important when Osiris was identified with the moon, which appears to have begun during the New Kingdom. In the *Book of the Dead* there are references to "*repeating of births like the moon*" and being "*rejuvenated like the moon*".[356] It is through this concept that Anubis takes on a lunar aspect.

---

[350] The Ancient Egyptian Pyramid Texts, Faulkner, 2007:78 utt 270
[351] Thoth or the Hermes of Egypt, Boylan, 1922:72
[352] The Book of the Dead or Going Forth by Day, Allen, 1974:103 spell 127
[353] Plutarch: Concerning the Mysteries of Isis and Osiris, Mead, 2002:249
[354] On the Characteristics of Animals Vol 1, Aelian & Schofield, 1957:133-135
[355] On the Characteristics of Animals Vol 1, Aelian & Schofield, 1957:325
[356] Anubis and the Lunar Disc, Ritner, 1985:149-155

At Deir el-Bahri, in a relief relating to the divine birth of Hatshepsut, Anubis is depicted bending over a large lunar disc. Similar scenes occur in the *mammisi* of Nectanebo I (30th dynasty) at Dendera and it appears to have been a regular feature in Greco-Roman *mammisi*, occurring for example at Edfu and Philae. The *mammisi* was a temple dedicated to the birth of child Gods. Anubis has the same posture with the lunar disc as he has when he attends Osiris on the bier; his body bending forward and his arms outstretched. At Dendera there is a decorative rim around the lunar disc which depicts the phases of the moon. Anubis says *"I have formed his limbs in life and stability, they being rejuvenated like the moon in the month"*.[357] He gives the new-born child the gift of constant regeneration and rebirth. Greco-Roman depictions of Anubis often show him wearing a lunar disc, sometimes it is positioned behind his head to form a halo. These occur on wall paintings and other reliefs where he attends Osiris on his bier. In the Roman Period Anubis was closely connected to the cult of Isis and she has a strong lunar component. A Roman statue of Anubis from Anzio (Italy), now in the Vatican Museum, depicts his crown as a small lunar disc on a crescent. Anubis is present on the underside of the feet of Roman Period mummies from Meir. Here he lifts the lunar disc above his head and in doing so lifts the mummy upright as a prelude to the rebirth process and their journey to the afterlife.[358]

Min and the Moon

Min is an ancient God of fertility and sexual procreativity so is depicted as ithyphallic. His crown consists of two long plumes and he carries a flail. He is associated with the moon through his fertility aspect which results in the birth of the moon and the growth of vegetation. He is normally connected to the dark moon and the new crescent. *"Lord of Akhim, who opens the month, having appeared as Iah."* On the last day of the lunar month Min was thought to impregnate the next cycle. He is often described as a bull *"who impregnates the cows"*. There is a lot of emphasis on Min appearing at the *"right moment"* because this is an essential requirement for the constancy

---

[357] Anubis and the Lunar Disc, Ritner, 1985:149-155
[358] Anubis and the Lunar Disc, Ritner, 1985:149-155

of the heavens and the continuation of cosmic *maat*. At Athribis Min is called *"He who rejuvenates at his right moment, who becomes young at his right time, who makes himself a child at the beginning of the 30 days"*.[359]

A calendar from Medinet Habu describes a feast of Min *"celebrated on the going forth of the protector of the Moon"*.[360] Spell 162 in the *Book of the Dead* addresses the Lord of Might, identified as Min because he is called Lord of the Phallus and it refers to his tall plumes and flail. He is described as protecting and hiding the Sacred Eye until its birth. At Philae there is a relief depicting the offering of the *wedjat* eye to Min.

Osiris as the Moon

"I will cause you to enter the left eye so that you become the moon."[361] While not directly a Lunar God, Osiris is strongly linked to the cycles of the moon. When Osiris dies Isis conceives a son through him and so Osiris can be viewed as being reborn as his son Horus, in the same way as the old moon is reborn as the new. A *stele* of Ramesses IV (20th dynasty) to Osiris says *"you are the moon in the sky; you rejuvenate yourself according to your desire and become old when you wish"*.[362] An inscription from Dendera says that Osiris *"awakes from sleep and he flies like the benu bird and he makes his place in the sky as the moon"*. Another states that Horus is *"the old child…the circulating one…the Moon is thy name"*. [363] The Egyptians didn't see a contradiction in having three basic views about rebirth and the afterlife. They were trying to describe what no one had actually experienced after all. The options were to live as a star, to follow the daily life-cycle of the sun or to follow the lunar cycle. *"I will see Osiris every day with Thoth."*[364] A number of bronze statues of Osiris, dating to the Late Period, address him as Osiris-Iah. As Iah is generally used to denote the moon, a more accurate translation may be Osiris-Thoth. On one of the statues he wears a composite crown consisting of a lunar disc on a crescent and an *atef*-crown with an

---

[359] Of Min and Moon, Altmann-Wendling, 2017:9-10

[360] Egyptian Festival Dating and the Moon, Spalinger, 2002:386

[361] Traversing Eternity, Smith, 2009:189

[362] Anubis and the Lunar Disc, Ritner, 1985:149-155

[363] The Moon: Myth and Image, Cashford, 2003:36

[364] The Ancient Egyptian Book of Two Ways, Lesko, 1977:56 spell 1164

ibis head projecting from the centre. A *wedjat* eye is inscribed in the disc.[365]

The light of the waxing moon is associated with the growth of vegetation in many cultures. *"The moon, in that its light is generative and moistening, is favourable both for breeding of animals and sprouting of plants."* Osiris was a Vegetation God and the seasonally dying-resurrected Gods such as Osiris are easily linked to the moon. Plutarch reported that at the rituals of the Burial of Osiris *"they cut the tree-trunk and make it into a crescent-shaped coffin, because the Moon, when it approaches the Sun, becomes crescent-shaped and hides itself away"*.[366]

A text from the temple of Hathor at Dendera says that *"Osiris enters into the left eye on the 15th"*.[367] By associating Osiris with the full moon it removes any reference to his death, the waning and dark moon, and the subsequent need for his rebirth. He enters the moon at the most important part of its cycle and he is fully restored to glory. *"Receive the Eye...in thy name of Osiris-Iooh-Thoth, that thou mayest illuminate the Two Lands, and make full the Eye on the 15th."*[368] A *Coffin Texts* spell for empowering the soul of the deceased alludes to Osiris ascending to join the moon on the 15th, accompanied by the justified deceased. *"When Ra rises, when the hidden spirits ascend, when the Lord of the spirits ascends in his primordial shape and the moon shines."*[369] Referring to Osiris' primordial shape hints at an ancient connection with the moon. The pig, especially the boar, has a negative association for the moon. Plutarch says that Seth *"when pursuing pig towards full-moon found the wooden coffin in which the body of Osiris lay dead, and scattered it into pieces"*. He explains that is why the Egyptians have an annual feast *"sacrificing and eating pig at full-moon"*.[370] The pig is also an enemy of the Eye of Horus.

Plutarch describes the association of Osiris with lunar numbers. *"The death of Osiris took place on the seventeenth, when the full-moon is most conspicuously at the full."* He says that Osiris either lived, or reigned,

---

[365] Osiris and the Moon in Iconography, Griffiths, 1976:153-159
[366] Plutarch: Concerning the Mysteries of Isis and Osiris, Mead, 2002:221-222
[367] Thoth or the Hermes of Egypt, Boylan, 1922:69
[368] Thoth or the Hermes of Egypt, Boylan; 1922:65
[369] The Moon god Iah in ancient Egyptian Religion, Garcia-Fernandez, 2017:222
[370] Plutarch: Concerning the Mysteries of Isis and Osiris, Mead, 2002:189

for 28 years "*for this is the number of the lights of the Moon*".[371] His body was cut into fourteen pieces by Seth. "*Typhon, taking his dogs out by night towards the moon, came upon it and recognising the body, tore it into fourteen pieces, and scattered them abroad.*"[372] Plutarch explains that this is how the Egyptians "*refer enigmatically to the days in which the luminary wanes after full-moon up to new-moon*".[373] As mentioned earlier, seven was one of the most symbolic numbers for the Egyptians so multiples of seven are important. Cutting the body of Osiris into fourteen pieces gives seven for Upper Egypt and seven for Lower Egypt. Fourteen cubits was considered the minimum level of the inundation that would give an acceptable harvest. The lunar association doesn't mean that Osiris lost his connection to Orion. Isis says that she will "*cause his ba to appear in the sky as the disc of the moon, illuminate his corpse as Orion in the womb of Nut*".[374]

LUNAR GODDESSES

The gender of words was significant for the Egyptians and as the word for eye was a feminine noun there is reason to assume that it would be associated with a Goddess. The Eye of the Sun was considered female and so a Goddess but for some reason the Eye of the Moon was considered male and had a God. Perhaps the energy or cycle of the moon was perceived as masculine and this was more important than the gender of the word. It might be that the cool male Lunar Eye balanced the hot female Solar Eye, balance being an important concept for the Egyptians. They were not alone in having a Lunar God. Their neighbours in Sumer, Assyria and Babylon all had Lunar Gods. The Greeks and Romans viewed the moon as female and a Goddess and this view is often strongly held today. Western culture tends to have a resistance to a Lunar God. When the Greeks and Romans came to Egypt they were unable to lose their cultural conditioning and either assumed that the Egyptian Goddesses were lunar or just imposed it upon them.

---

[371] Plutarch: Concerning the Mysteries of Isis and Osiris, Mead, 2002:221
[372] Plutarch: Concerning the Mysteries of Isis and Osiris, Mead, 2002:200
[373] Plutarch: Concerning the Mysteries of Isis and Osiris, Mead, 2002:223
[374] Traversing Eternity, Smith, 2009:469

Tefnut was associated with fire and the Solar Eye because she was one of the daughters of Ra but she does have a dual aspect. Even in the Pharaonic Period Tefnut was sometimes equated with the moon. *"Thy right eye is Shu, thy left eye is Tefnut."*[375] Shu and Tefnut were often depicted as twins, they appear as the twin lion Ruty, as two cats and two *ba*-birds. On a Roman Period votive statue two children stand within the coils of a snake (either Isis-Thermouthis or Serapis-Agathos Daimon). There is no inscription so their identification is open to debate. It has been suggested that they represent Shu and Tefnut. The boy wears a solar disc inscribed with the right *wedjat* eye whilst the girl wears a lunar disc inscribed with the left *wedjat* eye.[376]

Bastet was another of the Solar Eye Goddess. She was originally a lioness-headed Goddess but she became strongly associated with the cat in later periods. As she did her character became more benign. In the Greco-Roman Period she was sometimes aligned with the Eye of the Moon. To the Egyptians the cat was a solar creature associated with the Sun God Ra and with Bastet. The Greeks viewed cats as lunar creatures because of their association with Bastet and Isis. Of all the Egyptian Goddesses it is Isis who is most strongly associated with the moon but this was entirely due to the Greek influence on her character. *"There are those...who declare Isis to be no other than Moon."*[377] It was particularly pronounced in the cult of Isis in Greece and the Roman Empire. Here she was transformed into a largely Hellenic Goddess with a strong lunar connection. The Greeks associated her with their Goddess Selene (the Roman Luna). In a complete reversal and misunderstanding they assigned Osiris to the sun and Isis to the moon. Her cow-horn sun-disc crown was reinterpreted as a crescent moon and lunar disc. When Apuleius, in the *Golden Ass*, calls upon Isis in his wretched despair she appears out of the sea. *"Above her brow was a flat disc resembling a mirror, or rather the orb of the moon, which emitted a glittering light."* He says *"the supreme goddess wielded her power with exceeding*

---

[375] The Litany of Re, Piankoff, 1964:52
[376] A Greco-Roman Group Statue of Unusual Character from Dendera, Abdala, 1991:189-193
[377] Plutarch: Concerning the Mysteries of Isis and Osiris, Mead, 2002:231

majesty...that the bodies of earth, sea and sky now increased at her waxing, and now diminished in deference to her waning".[378]

FOLLOWING LUNAR THOTH

Lunar components are found in varying quantities throughout the various funerary texts but it is during the Middle Kingdom that we find the strongest lunar themes. Those from the *Coffin Texts* are discussed in chapter 11. A variation on the *Coffin Texts* is the *Book of Two Ways*, named for the map on the base of the coffin. They all come from the area around Hermopolis which was the cult centre of Thoth. Ra and Osiris dominate but Lunar Thoth is present accompanied in the night sky by the deceased in the form of stars. All three Gods are a goal for the deceased. There are three variants in the *Book of Two Ways*, the two later ones being *"propaganda for the cult of Ra"* according to Lesko. He believes, and I fully agree, that the priests of Ra superimposed their solar religion upon the cults of Osiris and Thoth. The priests of the major cults were in competition, not to impose monotheism, but for power and wealth. As the Sun God was backed by royalty there is no surprise that they were successful. Section VI of the *Book of Two Ways* is a local tradition of Hermopolis which makes Thoth, and his home in the sky, the goal for the deceased. *"Your way, O Thoth, is toward the house of Maat. I shall be in the suite of Thoth at night."*[379] Thoth is present in the Lunar Barque and the deceased wish to join him there. *"Cause that I be brought to you, O Thoth."*[380] Some versions call him Bull of the Constellations. Other sections refer to Re and Thoth as the Two Companions – those who cross the sky sometimes close together at other times apart.

"I am in the suite of Thoth, and I am joyful because of all he has done." Two spells in the *Book of the Dead* emphasise the overall importance of Thoth. One is for worshipping Osiris but ends with the deceased assuming the role of Thoth who then recites an *aretalogy*. *"I am Thoth, the skilled scribe whose hands are pure".*[381] The other focuses on Thoth

---

[378] The Golden Ass, Apuleius & Walsh, 1994:218-219
[379] The Ancient Egyptian Book of Two Ways, Lesko, 1977:94 spell 1093
[380] The Ancient Egyptian Book of Two Ways, Lesko, 1977:94 spell 1089
[381] The Ancient Egyptian Book of the Dead, Faulkner, 1989:184 spell 183

giving a similar but longer *aretalogy* including his role in the resurrection of Osiris as well as the pacification of Horus and Seth. "*I am Thoth, the favoured of Re…I have come and have washed away the blood, I have calmed the tumult.*"[382] These may have been specifically selected by followers of Thoth but they may just acknowledge the critical part played by Thoth in the resurrection of Osiris and the maintenance of cosmic *maat*.

THE MYSTERIOUS MOON

The one place you might expect to find strong lunar symbolism and mysteries is in the *Book of Thoth*. This is a Ptolemaic work which incorporates some Pharaonic components. It is presented as a dialogue between Thoth and his pupil and instructs the initiate in a wide range of scribal, scholarly and mystical knowledge. The place of learning is treated as a symbolic place in the "*darkness of twilight*".[383] Secret knowledge is hidden and must be searched for away from all earthly distractions. It is also a reference to the illuminating wisdom of Thoth which is always available to those who are diligent and worthy. "*As for his (the god's) beloved, he being in complete darkness, the teacher will light for him a torch.*"[384] Apart from that there doesn't appear to be a significant lunar or stellar component. Or perhaps it is just too well hidden.

---

[382] The Ancient Egyptian Book of the Dead, Faulkner, 1989:181 spell 182
[383] The Ancient Egyptian Book of Thoth, Jasnow & Zauzich, 2005:35
[384] The Ancient Egyptian Book of Thoth, Jasnow & Zauzich, 2005:5

CHAPTER 10

The Eyes of Heaven

"Hermopolis is open...O Thoth, the Eye of Horus is excellent. The Eye of Horus saves me."[385]

THE SOLAR AND LUNAR EYES

The sun and moon were considered the eyes of Horus the Elder or one of the Creator Gods such as Amun. The sun could also be the Right Eye of the Sun God while the moon was the Left Eye of Horus, the son of Isis and Osiris. However, the symbolism is fluid. In the *Litany of Ra* it says that *"thy right eye is Shu, thy left eye is Tefnut"*. [386] As with all Egyptian religious thought it wasn't considered contradictory to refer to the moon as different deities and different symbolic objects either at the same time or consecutively. It was perceived as adding nuances to the meaning, helping to explain a complex concept in a more complete manner.

---

[385] An Ancient Egyptian Book of the Dead, O'Rourke, 2016:157 spell 8B
[386] The Litany of Re, Piankoff, 1964:52

The Eye myths played a central role in Egyptian religion. The Eye of Horus is injured in many of the battles between Horus and Seth and it is healed by Thoth. The injuring and healing of the Eye follows the moon and its waxing and waning cycles.

The *Wedjat* Eye

The symbol of the *wedjat* eye is a combination of a human eye with the facial markings of a falcon. It represents the healed Lunar Eye of Horus and is a symbol of healing and wholeness. Thoth presented the original healed Eye to either Ra or Horus and this act became the precedent for offerings to deities. Most offering scenes include the king or a deity offering the *wedjat* eye to another deity. At Edfu the ritual for entering the shrine includes "*I break the seal. I bring the eye to its lord. I am Thoth who brings the Eye to its lord*".[387] At Dendera Shu offers the *wedjat* eye to Hathor. "*Take the Udjat Eye, whole in its form.*"[388]

The components of the *wedjat* eye were used to represent the fractions of 1/2, 1/4, 1/8, 1/16, 1/32 and 1/64. Each stroke making up the symbol of the *wedjat* eye was used to notate one of these fractions. They were used to work out relative proportions when mixing medicines which further aligned the physician with the healing powers of Thoth. "*The dbh-measure with which Horus measured his eye — so that it was examined and found alive prosperous and healthy.*"[389] These components are also called the Horus Eye fractions. They sum to 63/64 which does not represent wholeness. Only Thoth can provide the missing 1/64th. This mathematical imperfection also reflects the fact that the lunar month is not a precise number of days. The average lunar month is 29.5 days compared to the ideal of 30 days. 1/64th of 30 days is 0.47 which gives us the missing part to fill the eye as it adds up to 29.9. There are six components of the *wedjat* eye. When Thoth completes the eye by providing the missing 1/64th he gives it its seventh component turning the *wedjat* eye into a discrete but important symbol of seven.

---

[387] Thoth or the Hermes of Egypt, Boylan, 1922:73
[388] The Theology of Hathor of Dendera, Richter, 2016:26
[389] Ancient Egyptian Magical Texts, Borghouts, 1978:48

Thoth is referred to as *"the ba that fills the eye"*.[390] To do this he uses both his magic and his mathematical and scientific knowledge. Spells in the *Coffin Texts* and *Book of the Dead* say that Thoth healed or filled the eye *"with his fingers"*. This may refer to the application of ointment, cleansing or the use of magical gestures. A hand with either a thumb and finger or two fingers outstretched was a protective gesture. Depictions of the ritual of anointing a statue show two fingers being used. Counting was often referenced in connection with the healing of the Lunar Eye. *"I am Thoth...I have come to search for the Eye of Horus...I have brought it and numbered it. I have found it so that it is now completely numbered and intact."*[391] Fingers are associated with counting and allude to Thoth's mathematical skill and the associated rituals involved. In one long ferryboat spell the ferryman asks the deceased to count their fingers which they do. *"Take one; take the second; quench it; remove it; give it to me; be friendly toward me; do not let go of it; have no pity on it; make the Eye bright; give the Eye to me."*[392] Was this a counting rhyme for a lunar ritual? A mnemonic for recalling the order or content of a lunar ritual? In a ferryboat spell from the *Pyramid Texts* the deceased says *"I am seeking the endangered eye of Horus, I am bound for the numbering of fingers"*.[393]

The *wedjat* eye could represent the Eye of the Sun as well as the moon. A right-facing *wedjat* eye is likely to be a Solar Eye as is one made of carnelian. It is not always clear which Eye is referenced but some *wedjat* eyes are definitely solar as they incorporate a *uraeus* and solar disc.[394]

THE MYTHS OF THE EYES OF HEAVEN

There are three basic forms to the Eye myths, two of which are solar. The Angry Eye explains the creation of the *uraeus* and is discussed in detail in Jackson (2018). The myth of the Distant Goddess is covered below. The myths of the Eye of Horus are the ones which involve the lunar cycle. Eyes are of vital importance to

---

[390] Thoth or the Hermes of Egypt, Boylan, 1922:72
[391] Seth, God of Confusion, te Velde, 1967:48 spell 249
[392] The Ancient Egyptian Book of the Dead, Faulkner, 1989:95 spell 99
[393] The Ancient Egyptian Pyramid Texts, Faulkner, 2007:116 utt 359
[394] Egyptian Myth: A Very Short Introduction, Pinch, 2004:90

us. They are also very vulnerable to disease and damage. This was a particular problem in Egypt due to working conditions, dust, snake venom, flies and parasites. The Ebers medicinal papyrus lists over 30 treatments for eye diseases. It is little wonder that the healing of the damaged Eyes of Heaven were so prominent in the myths and medicine.

Horus and Seth have endless battles and it is always the Eye of Horus which is injured in some way. In the various battles Seth devours, scratches or gouges out one or both of Horus' eyes. At other times the Eye flees from the battle. *"The Eye of Horus leapt up on yonder side of the Winding Waterway and fell on Thoth's wing."* [395] Plutarch reports, *"they say that Typhon at one time strikes the Eye of Horus, and at another takes it out and swallows it. By "striking" they refer enigmatically to the monthly diminution of the moon".* [396]

In the *Contendings of Horus and Seth* the pair transform into hippos to fight. Isis intervenes and refuses to kill her brother Seth because it would disrupt *maat*. Furious at this apparent betrayal Horus decapitates his mother who turns into a headless flint statue. Thoth then gives her the cow-head of Hathor. In revenge Seth *"removed his two eyes from their places and buried them on the mountain".* [397] Overnight they grew into lotuses. Another injury to the Eye was caused by Seth who had transformed into a black boar. Like the hippo, the boar was considered hostile and the sow maternal and more benign. Horus becomes unwell whenever he sees a black boar. The fact that the boar is black alludes to the waning of the moon making it increasingly black. The *Book of Gates* has one reference to the boar of Seth trying to attack the Eye of Horus. The fifth Gate depicts the Judgment Hall where Osiris sits on his throne. To the right of this scene is a barque in which one or two baboons drive away or beat a pig with a stick. The baboon *"protects the eye"* and *"causes what was swallowed to be spat out".* [398]

In the *Pyramid Texts* there are references to the mutilation of both the Eye of Horus and the testicles of Seth. Some of the myths

---

[395] The Ancient Egyptian Pyramid Texts, Faulkner, 2007:116 utt 359
[396] Plutarch: Concerning the Mysteries of Isis and Osiris, Mead, 2002:233
[397] Ancient Egyptian Literature Volume II, Lichtheim, 2006:219
[398] The Egyptian Book of Gates, Abt & Hornung, 2014:188-189

involve homosexual abuse and rape of Horus by Seth. The *Contendings of Horus and Seth* gives a detailed description. Horus catches Seth's semen in his hands and goes to see Isis. She cuts off his hands and throws them in the river, using her magic to replace them. Then she puts some of Horus' semen on a lettuce. The next day it is eaten by Seth. This aligns Seth with Min whose sacred plant it was. The Egyptian lettuce is vaguely phallic-shaped and has a milky white sap. In a trial before the Ennead Thoth commands the semen of Seth to emerge and it comes from Seth's head as "*a golden sun-disk*" which Thoth takes and places on his head.[399] Why would Thoth take a sun-disc when he is a Lunar God? Perhaps because he is the Deputy of Ra, it also acknowledges the role of the sun in illuminating the moon. The full moon can have a golden tinge at times. Does it also allude to Horus being assigned to the waxing phase of the moon and Seth to the waning while Thoth is the arbitrator in the eternal battle?

Both mutilations of the combatants are healed to ensure a return to balance. In almost all cases it is Thoth who heals the Eye. This is a frequent theme in the funerary texts where the deceased align themselves with Thoth by carrying out his tasks. They remove the bleariness from the eye, clean the injured eye, save it from Seth and return it to Horus. Sometimes the word filling is used instead of healing alluding to the fact that an increasing amount of light occurs with the waxing moon and also to the fractions of the *wedjat* eye. The *wedjat* eye is "*distinguished in its parts. There are no requirements absent from it*".[400] The moon is a self-healing physician. The full moon is the injured moon healed so its healing light and cycles can be used to heal others. This is one of the repeating motifs in the *Pyramid Texts* although the injured Eye is never explicitly related to the moon, probably to ensure that the injuries to the Eye cannot become permanent. Writing something would fix it in reality as long as the writing existed. By the Middle Kingdom the healing of the Eye is included in texts relating to the lunar festivals. "*It is filled with the monthly festival*" and "*the sight is cleared because of it in the monthly*

---

[399] Ancient Egyptian Literature Volume II, Lichtheim, 2006:220
[400] The Theology of Hathor of Dendera, Richter, 2016:218

festival and half moon festival.[401] Many healing spells relating to eye conditions allude to the healing of the Eye of Horus where the healer takes the role of Thoth. *"I am Thoth, that physician of the Eye of Horus."*[402]

It is Hathor who finds Horus after Seth had gouged out his eyes and buried them. She takes the milk of a gazelle and applies it to his eye sockets and heals them. The gazelle is associated with Hathor in her role as Mistress of the Desert and also because Hathor was aligned with the Goddess Anukis whose sacred animal is the gazelle. As a desert dweller the gazelle was also connected to Seth. Using one of Seth's sacred animals would have been an appropriate antidote to the damage that he had caused. In another variation of the myth the eyes are buried by Anubis and Isis waters them and they grow into the first grape vines. The Eye of Horus was closely connected with ritual wine offerings. One offering text says *"may all the vineyards prosper as you wish, may the inundation rejoice at what is in it. I fill for you the Eye of Horus with wine"*. Wine was sometimes referred to as the *"Green Horus Eye"*. Green refers to the papyrus with its association with freshness and plant growth rather than to the colour of the wine.[403] The growth of lotus and vines from Horus' eyes is comparable to the growth of barley and wheat from the body of his father Osiris. It also emphasises the regenerative effect that the moon has on vegetation. Despite being a Lunar God Thoth doesn't have a vegetation aspect, which is probably why it is Isis and Hathor who are involved in the healing in these particular myths.

Horus was sometimes worshipped as a dual God; Horus-with-eyes and Horus-without-eyes. While Horus is normally a benevolent God Horus-without-eyes was malevolent and seeking vengeance.[404] Blindness is a terrible condition and when it is inflicted on purpose there is little wonder that Horus-without-eyes turned malevolent and wanted revenge. He personified a probably unspoken but deeply felt fear of blindness and the worry that the

---

[401] Monthly Lunar Festivals in the Mortuary Realm: Historical Patterns and Symbolic Motifs, Eaton, 2011:229-245
[402] Ancient Egyptian Magical Texts, Borghouts, 1978:49
[403] Wine and Wine Offering in the Religion of Ancient Egypt, Poo, 1995:82
[404] Egyptian Myth: A Very Short Introduction, Pinch, 2004:96

blindness of an individual might be reflected in heaven. The loss of both the sun and moon would mean the loss of creation and the total triumph of chaos. The Eye of Ra is not immune to damage. In one spell from the *Book of Two Ways* the deceased say they will *"repel bleariness"* and *"spit on the wounds of Re"*.[405] The Solar Eye is wounded after an attack by Apophis which was equated to dust storms, heavy clouds or solar eclipses.

Throughout the Eye myths there is a very clear pairing sequence. A few examples are; Seth as a boar swallows the Eye of Horus and Nut as a sow swallows the Eye of the Sun. The Eye of Ra retrieves Shu and Tefnut then Shu retrieves Tefnut in her role as the Eye of the Sun. Seth wounds the Eye of Horus and Horus tears off the testicles of Seth. Both Horus and Ra lose their Eye and regain it. Thoth returns the Eye of the Sun and restores the Eye of the Moon. Running through these myths is a theme of transformation. Cyclical change is integral to both the solar and lunar cycles. Transformation occurs as a natural unfolding, such as the growth of the lotus and vines, and as a strategy or deceit, for example, Seth as the boar and the two Gods fighting as hippos. It is also a process of growth as a result of trial. The assimilation of Hathor by Isis is illustrated in one of these myths. The beheaded Isis turns into a flint statue, flint was considered a celestial substance and was associated with Hathor in her aspect of Sky Goddess. Isis gains the powers of Hathor because Thoth replaces her head with the cow-head of Hathor.

The Eye myths often get entangled. The Distant Goddess can explain the north-south wandering of the sun, the disappearance and reappearance of Sirius and the inundation. At the temple of Hathor at Dendera it also gets entwined with the retrieval of the lost and damaged Eye of Horus. Cosmic harmony and ordered time are restored when the sun and moon are in their proper places. As a consequence of the rituals and offerings, as well as the efforts of the deities, the Eye Goddess is reunited with her father and the Eye of Horus is retrieved and healed.

At Dendera Hathor, the estranged Distant Goddess, reunites with the *uraeus* on the head of Ra making the Sun complete. The

---

[405] The Ancient Egyptian Book of Two Ways, Lesko, 1977:94 spell 1089

sun can then unite with the Lunar Eye making it full. Hathor is described as *"uniting with the Left Eye, brightening the Banks"*.[406] This solar-lunar interaction is seen when Hathor heals the eyes of Horus and the gouged-out eyes regrow as the lotus which will birth the sun. In the sanctuary at Dendera there are a number of paired depictions on east and west walls alluding to the critical event of the safe return of both Eyes. Mirrors are one of Hathor's cult objects. Their shape is similar to that of the solar or lunar disc and when paired could represent the Divine Eyes of Heaven. Another reason for their cultic importance might be because a mirror reflects light, just as the moon shines by the sun's reflected light. In one paired scene the king offers a mirror to Hathor on the western wall and to Isis on the eastern wall, symbolising the return of both Eyes. In another area Thoth and Ihy (the son of Hathor) present the *wedjat* eye to Hathor whilst on the opposite eastern wall Shu offers the *wedjat* eye to Hathor. The accompanying text says *"I give you the Healthy Eyes fast in their place"*.[407] The importance of the two eyes in their rightful places is emphasised by the use of sign play in the text. The word *wedjat* is written by a left and right *wedjat* eye next to each other. In a dual scene the king offers *maat* (in the form of a statute of the Goddess Maat) to Hathor and to Isis. He wears the White Crown when offering to Hathor and the Red Crown when offering to Isis.

In another scene Hathor is adored by the king and the deities of the Ogdoad. One of the Goddesses, Nunet, says *"I have adored your face at the extreme limits"*.[408] That is, as far as the sun's light can travel. Like Nut, Hathor has become the Great One in Heaven. Unlike Nut though, the sun and moon have now become Hathor's eyes rather than those of the Cosmic Horus. As this temple is dedicated to Hathor her aspects and importance are naturally elevated as much as possible. Why are the sun and moon never considered to be the eyes of Nut or the Cosmic Cow? Perhaps she was thought of as more encompassing than the Cosmic Horus or

---

[406] The Theology of Hathor of Dendera, Richter, 2016:147
[407] The Theology of Hathor of Dendera, Richter, 2016:158
[408] The Theology of Hathor of Dendera, Richter, 2016:168

Hathor as the diurnal sky. She held both of these deities within herself.

THE ESSENTIAL SETH?

Despite his usually malign and chaotic aspect Seth does display positive attributes although these get increasingly discarded in the later periods. Horus and Seth waste their time and energy fighting each other rather than directing their combined force against the real enemy, Apophis. Blinded by hatred and rage each God seeks to annihilate the other. Te Velde suggests that their battles need to be seen in terms of misdirected divine energy. The result of this is seen in the constant wax and wane of the moon as first one God then the other overpowers their opponent. Thoth has to constantly stabilise the pair. If either one should destroy the other then cosmic *maat* would be disrupted and creation imperilled. The damage to the Eye of Horus and the testicles of Seth together with the sexual abuse and the tale of the semen of Horus and Seth demonstrates the loss of vitality and energy of the pair. In what now might be considered a sexist and homophobic comment, te Velde says that the semen and vitality of the two Gods that should have been used to generate new life has been misused. *"Cosmic powers have been wasted."*[409]

Seth represents otherness; the foreigner with strange customs, the desert dweller and the trickster. His energy is different to that of the other deities and this can be used to instigate change. The Egyptians certainly didn't like change for its own sake but accepted that stasis and too much rigidity couldn't accommodate the eternal cycles of the cosmos. Seth has always attacked the Eye of Horus so it is surprising to find a reference in the *Pyramid Texts* to *"the finger of Seth, that causes the clear eye of Horus to see"*. Has Thoth discovered a way to harness Seth's energy to provide the missing $1/64^{th}$ of the Eye? The existing 63 components need a final injection of energy to enable them to combine and reform as the healed and completed Eye. Rather than trying to ignore or deny the negative and chaotic forces present in creation, Thoth uses his wisdom and skill to

---

[409] Seth, God of Confusion, te Velde, 1967:42

reconstruct the Eye using part of the power which damaged it. In doing so he creates "*a new image of reality which takes into account the existence of Seth*".[410]

Is this the mysterious missing part which was too dangerous a secret to be revealed? The destructive and chaotic forces in society had to be controlled if *maat* was to be honoured and maintained. The fact that they might be useful or even essential was not something that most people should be permitted to hear or even think about. Despite the intense and imaginative curses and spells against Apophis, and to a lesser extent Seth, the Egyptians' world view remained dualistic and realistic. They understood the world as a number of pairs of opposing powers and wisdom lies in accepting and integrating them.

THE LUNAR AND SOLAR BALANCE

Duality, unity and balance were very important to the Egyptians and were seen as a visible manifestation of *maat*. A balance in heaven and the regularity of celestial cycles was seen as confirmation of the underlying harmony of creation. It showed that *maat* was present in heaven and what happened in heaven had a direct impact on affairs on earth. The fact that the Egyptians celebrated the full moon as the uniting of the sun and moon underlines this.

The Solar Eye was seen as volatile and quick to anger, a suitable attribute of a Solar Goddess. In the myth of the Distant Goddess she quarrels with Ra and leaves him to roam the desert where her rage increases. Ra is left lonely and vulnerable so he sends Thoth to pacify her and bring her back so that they can be reunited. When Tefnut took the role of the Distant Goddess it was Shu who was sent to pacify his sister-wife. Although Shu is not considered a Lunar God he was often aligned with Thoth and Khonsu. It is not by chance that a Lunar God is sent to pacify the Solar Goddess and persuade her to return to Egypt and her father. Balance is achieved between the female, fiery and angry Solar Eye and the cool, calming and male Lunar Eye. If the lunar-solar balance was so important

---

[410] Seth, God of Confusion, te Velde, 1967:46-48

why did the religion become increasingly solar? The fact that kings aligned themselves with the Sun Gods and the great power of the priests of Amun and Ra is the main reason. Perhaps the lunar cult was always more secretive and more contemplative in line with the moon. *"Thoth is in the secret places."*[411]

LUNAR AND SOLAR CONFLICT

Where there is balance there is the potential for disharmony. There are infinitely more ways of being out of balance than there are of being in balance. The most obvious conflict is seen in the solar eclipse which is discussed in chapter 12.

In both the *Coffin Texts* and the *Book of the Dead* Re argues with a snake named either Who Dwells in his Consuming Fire or Who is in his Fire. During the conflict Ra is bitten on the mouth. The text then explains *"that is how the reduction of the monthly festival came about"*.[412] The spell infers that the crescent moon has injured the Sun God. There is no snake associated with the moon but was the dark moon sometimes aligned with Apophis? The name of the snake can be understood as the one who dwells in Ra's consuming fire. The moon is so close to the sun that it appears to be within its flames. This in itself was a potential threat as the moon is obviously not harmed by the sun's heat. Only something very powerful could get that close to the sun without being injured or killed. This is the only time in the lunar cycle that a solar eclipse can occur so it is not surprising that the moon at this stage of the cycle was viewed as threatening.

Was the dispute over the length of the lunar month? When Ra refused to let Nut give birth at any time of the year Thoth created five extra days from the lights of the moon. The moon had to sacrifice some of its light because of Ra's jealousy and nastiness. Was the moon seen as forever trying to reclaim this lost light back from the sun so it no longer had diminished months? The hostility between Ra and the moon at this time might reflect the solar cult's

---

[411] The Ancient Egyptian Book of the Dead, Faulkner, 1989:119 spell 130
[412] Monthly Lunar Festivals in the Mortuary Realm: Historical Patterns and Symbolic Motifs, Eaton, 2011:229-245

concern that the lunar cult was becoming too important or powerful which would threaten the status and the income of the solar cult. In the earlier *Pyramid Texts* the injuries to the mouth of Ra were not associated with lunar cycles. The dispute between Ra and the snake was *"concerning the division of Heliopolis"*.[413] Joergensen suggests that the dispute was about control of the lunar cycle. Ra brought the moon to full with his light but Apophis stole this light resulting in the waning cycle. The crescent moon was not associated with Apophis but was in the form of a crescent because of his actions.

THE EYES IN THE FUNERARY TEXTS

There are references to the Eye of Horus in the *Pyramid Texts* but these are largely in connection with offerings. *"The perfume of the Eye of Horus is diffused over you – incense and fire."*[414] There are some references to the Eye *"which he rescued from Seth"* and other variations of the myth. The Eye becomes increasingly important in the *Coffin Texts* and the *Book of the Dead*. *"This is Thoth who is in the sky; the Eye of Horus is on his hands in the Mansion of the Moon."*[415] The deceased take on the role of Thoth looking after the Eye of Horus. *"I am the one who brought the dazzling sound eye. I am the one who removed bleariness from the injured eye...I have come to you in this your suite of the night...I am the one who rescued the sound eye, who has cleansed the injured eye."* The spell ends *"I have not opposed you, O Thoth, at night"*.[416] One spell refers to Seth *"who made the dark eye"*.[417]

In the *Book of the Dead* there are many references to the Eye of Horus being healed or being unblemished. One spell says that the Eye escapes from Seth and goes to the eastern side of the sky. This is similar to *Pyramid Texts* spells. Seth, as the constellation Meskhetyu, is tethered in the northern part of the sky so he cannot chase the escaping Eye. The east is the direction of sun and moon rise, a place where both are refreshed and reborn. The deceased

---

[413] Secrets, Knowledge and Experience in Ancient Egyptian Religion, Joergensen, 2006:19
[414] The Ancient Egyptian Pyramid Texts, Faulkner, 2007:5 utt 25
[415] The Ancient Egyptian Coffin Texts Vol III, Faulkner, 2007:152 spell 1096
[416] The Ancient Egyptian Book of Two Ways, Lesko, 1977:96 spell 1094
[417] The Ancient Egyptian Book of Two Ways, Lesko, 1977:31 spell 1138

emphasise their ability to heal the Eye, aligning themselves with Thoth. *"The Eye of Horus which is in my possession serves me in the entourage of Thoth."*[418] By claiming the Eye of Horus they hold a very powerful symbol of rebirth and regeneration. The full moon is alluded to in two spells for torches. One refers to the bright and shining Eye of Horus and driving off Seth. The other version states that *"the Eye of Horus is your protection"* and that it *"comes intact and shining like Re in the horizon"*.[419] The White Crown is linked to the Eye of Horus. The deceased king *"wears the White Crown, the Eye of Horus"*.[420] Its colour is an immediate link with the moon, the Red Crown can be aligned with the sun and the Double Crown symbolises the uniting of both celestial bodies as well as the Two Lands. Knowledge of lunar festivals is important in the *Book of the Dead*. In one spell the deceased say they have celebrated the new moon festival and witnessed the full moon festival.

In the second hour of the *Book of the Amduat* the Solar Barque sails in procession behind four other barques. *"Behold me – I go behind my brilliant eye, and I proceed behind my left eye."*[421] The barque carrying the Solar Eye contains a large Hathor Head. In her role as the Eye Goddess Hathor is the visible sun disc. She is flanked by two Goddesses, probably Isis and Nephthys, and a scarab on the prow. The other barque carries a crescent moon and lunar disc upon a pedestal. A kneeling God supports the feather of Maat. The tenth hour shows the regeneration of the Solar and Lunar Eyes. Two enthroned Goddesses, wearing the Red and White Crowns, are placed either side of a pair of entwined rearing snakes who support a red disc. Next to this scene is another pair of enthroned Goddesses who hold a smaller red disc on a staff. *"The left eye it goes forth from the double coiled; the right eye it goes forth from the wrapped staff."*[422]

A Symbol of Power and Hope

From the moon, with its constant waxing and waning, the Egyptians were inspired to create the *wedjat* eye. In a few elegant

---

[418] An Ancient Egyptian Book of the Dead, O'Rourke, 2016:91 spell 149
[419] The Ancient Egyptian Book of the Dead, Faulkner, 1989:127 spell 137a
[420] The Ancient Egyptian Pyramid Texts, Faulkner, 2007:196 utt 524
[421] The Egyptian Amduat, Abt & Hornung, 2007:73
[422] The Egyptian Amduat, Abt & Hornung, 2007:304-305

strokes they created a rich and distinctive symbol which summarised the Eye myths. A symbol of healing and balance, of cosmic harmony and rebirth. It gave physicians a way of measuring proportions of ingredients which was both practical and magical, aligning their powers with those of Thoth as he completed the damaged Eye, recreating what had been irretrievably lost. In the *Book of the Dead* the deceased express their wish to join the Two Companions, Re and Thoth, in their barques as they traverse the sky. It is pedantic to say that the deceased can't be in both the Lunar and Solar Barques. The lunar and solar cycles are entwined and can be viewed as two parts of one cycle.[423]

---

[423] The Ancient Egyptian Book of the Dead, Faulkner, 1989:176 spell 178

CHAPTER 11

Lunar Cycles

"How beautiful is your appearance at the right moment.
The country shines with your love, heaven and earth are flooded
with your perfection."[424]

THE PHASES OF THE MOON

Like the stars and the planets, the moon shows a cycle full of
order and meaning for those who study it. The presence of the
Goddess Maat and the actions of the Moon Gods are encoded in
these patterns. Studying, or merely actively observing, the ever-
changing yet constant lunar cycle is one way of bringing you closer
to these deities. As the moon orbits the earth the sun will illuminate
different portions of it and these appear to us as the different
phases of the moon. The new moon appears as a sliver (reverse C
shape) to the left of the setting sun. During its waxing phase it trails
the sun and is increasingly seen in the night sky until at full moon

---

[424] Of Min and Moon, Altmann-Wendling, 2017:10

it rises in the east as the sun sets in the west. This is the only time that it is truly nocturnal, being in opposition to the sun. The waning moon is increasingly seen in the daytime sky as it leads the sun in decreasing amounts. It becomes a sliver again, this time as a C shape. When it is at its closest to the sun it becomes lost in the sun's light. *"The moon, guardian of darkness, who replaces the Bright One at nightfall hiding its position in the sky at the time of its appearance. People adore its light."*[425]

UNDERSTANDING THE LUNAR CYCLE

The astronomer priests studied the moon in detail, largely for timekeeping purposes. One 26th dynasty astronomer priest knew *"the movements of the two disks"*. On one wall at the temple of Horus at Edfu is inscribed a list of books held in the library. This includes one which gives *"information about the regular appearance of the two stars and the periodical return of the other stars"*.[426] The 'two stars' are the sun and moon. The Egyptians will have been aware of the science behind the cycles but to explain and illustrate them, and to give a deeper spiritual understanding, they turned to mythology. *"Khonsu-Ioh, light of the night, image of the left Eye…who rises in the east while the sun is in the west…the left Eye receives the light of the right Eye."*[427]

The absence of the crescent moon in the eastern horizon marked the first day of the lunar month, called the *"new one"*. The second day was the *"beginning of the new crescent"* with the sighting of the crescent moon on the horizon. The moon was considered to arrive on the third day. The waxing moon was a time of growth and it is the cycle most often depicted. *"Thou shalt flourish again like the Moon-Thoth when he is a child."*[428] The full moon was the Union of the Two Bulls and an auspicious time. In the solar chapel at Abu Simbel are two statues of a baboon and a scarab which some interpret as alluding to the full moon. Texts from the temple of Khonsu at Karnak say that the moon *"is conceived on psdntyw, he is*

---

[425] The Depictions of the Entire Lunar Cycle in Graeco-Roman Temples, Priskin, 2016:111-144
[426] The House of Horus at Edfu, Watterson, 1998:69
[427] Egyptian Mysteries: New Light on Ancient Knowledge, Lamy, 1986:44
[428] The Moon: Myth and Image, Cashford, 2003:338

born in 3bd, he grows old after smdt".[429] These are the first, second and fifteenth days respectively.

The 28th day was considered the end of the cycle and was the *"day of the jubilee of Nut"*. Another one of her eternal cycles had been completed and was already in the process of restarting. It wasn't clear whether the 29th day would be the end of the cycle or not so it was a day of uncertainty. It was called the *"station of the guardian"*.[430] The moon at conjunction was referred to as *"appearing in glory with Re"*.[431]

The waxing moon is viewed as a bringer of fertility and growth in many cultures. A text from the temple of Khonsu at Karnak refers to this. *"The moon is his form. As soon as he has rejuvenated himself he is a heated bull. When he is old he is an ox...his waxing moon brings light...brings the cows to calf, and causes the egg to grow in the body."*[432] This gives a very different image of Khonsu as the moon compared to that of Thoth who is the regulator of the moon and the restorer the Lunar Eye. With Khonsu the waxing of the moon is associated with growth in terms of vegetation and fertility. The reference to the ox, a castrated bull, also reflects the damage to the testicles of Seth in his battles with Horus.

THE BOOK OF THE MOON

This is the name that Priskin gives to *Coffin Texts* spells 154 to 160. He proposes that they are a distinct sub-set of spells referring to the moon. They cover the lunar cycle, lunar invisibility, the waxing moon, the full moon, the waning moon and the last crescent. A solar eclipse is referred to in spell 160. All but one of these spells are found in a similar form in the *Book of the Dead*. These spells all have titles relating to knowledge of the *bas* of various deities. The deceased, or their relatives, specified what they wanted on the coffin so those with a particular affiliation, or who were in a specific cult, would be able to request any relevant spells. Some may have been reserved and even kept secret from all but higher cult

[429] The Egyptian Calendar: keeping Ma'at on Earth, Belmonte, 2009:116
[430] Egyptian Festival Dating and the Moon, Spalinger, 2002:386
[431] The Ancient Egyptian Coffin Texts Vol I, Faulkner, 2007:151 spell 176
[432] Hathor Rising, Roberts, 1995:78

members. There were also local traditions which would have been followed. Many of the spells emphasised different concepts and were multi-layered. The use of specific hieroglyphs could alter the emphasis of the phrase so changing the nuance of the spell. If the priests and priestesses were concealing hidden teachings they had to make them obscure so that the scribes who worked on the coffin, or any subsequent reader, couldn't access these teachings.

The Lunar Cycle

Spell 154 is titled knowing the *bas* of Heliopolis, joining with these *bas* and gaining Thoth's knowledge of healing spells. At the end of the spell the *bas* of Heliopolis are revealed as Ra, Shu and Tefnut. The deceased say they know how to heal the injured Lunar Eye and remove bleariness from the Solar Eye. They claim specialist and secret knowledge that even the great priests and physicians don't have as it requires special initiation. Priskin's translation says that this secret teaching was obtained yesterday. This may refer to the onset of lunar invisibility. The Egyptian day started at sunrise. When the last crescent was no longer visible at sunrise the observer knew that the exact moment of lunar visibility was yesterday. The deceased say they know how the diminished month comes about, through the argument with the snake.

Shu and Tefnut are referred to as the Eyes of the Sun God, or of the Sky God Horus the Elder. Priskin suggests that Shu might specifically allude to the invisible moon as his name puns with the word for being empty or lacking.[433] I think that these three deities emphasise the fact that the two individual Eyes are part of the whole (the eyes of the Sky God or Creator God) and part of the same cycle.

Lunar Invisibility

Spell 155 is to know the *bas* of the new moon who are Isden, Anubis and Osiris and to enter into the temple of Osiris. This is a very clear connection of this part of the cycle with Osiris, even though he is normally just associated with the full moon. The

---

[433] The Ancient Egyptian Book of the Moon: Coffin Texts Spells 154-160, Priskin, 2019:39

presence of Anubis alludes to the death of Osiris. The rebirth of the deceased is forever tied to the rebirth of the moon and Osiris. There are references to lunar rituals including the counting of the Eye and what is missing on the day when the parts are counted. This is the part that Thoth has to supply. Perhaps the secret teachings explained how he did this. The spell also references the fifth part of an entire half. 1/5th of 15 (half of a full lunar month) is 3 which is the maximum number of days the moon is invisible.

"*Open to me, the bas of the moon's invisibility, for I am the one who completes the eye.*"[434] The deceased claim to know more that the embalmer of the temple, namely Anubis, which links the embalming rituals to the moon. By the New Kingdom the word for new moon was written with a horizontal line dividing a circle. This represented the "*moon within the sun*".[435] One part of the spell refers to the slaughterer coming out of the slaughter house. This could allude to the fact that the moon is no longer being cut into smaller and smaller pieces. As in many spells the deceased say they have been initiated into this secret knowledge and that they won't disclose it to anyone else.

The Waxing Moon

Spell 156 is for knowing the *bas* of Hermopolis, which was the cult centre of Thoth. The initiate understands that Thoth is both the moon and the power behind its cycles. "*What is small in the full month and great in the half-month, that is Thoth.*"[436] The first crescent of the new moon is usually seen on the evening on the second day but about 30% of the time it is not visible until the evening of the third day. "*The feather is thrust into the shoulder and the Red Crown rises in the mentjat-bowl.*"[437] The new crescent moon can be seen as a feather floating in the air. Despite being the same shape as the last crescent it is referred to in more positive terms than a knife. The waning moon suggests diminution and dissection as does a knife. A feather alludes to air which is aligned with breathing especially that of the

---

[434] The Ancient Egyptian Book of the Moon: Coffin Texts Spells 154-160, Priskin, 2019:58
[435] Monthly Lunar Festivals in the Mortuary Realm: Historical Patterns and Symbolic Motifs, Eaton, 2011:229-245
[436] The Ancient Egyptian Coffin Texts Vol I, Faulkner, 2007:134 spell 156
[437] The Ancient Egyptian Book of the Moon: Coffin Texts Spells 154-160, Priskin, 2019:73

deceased. But whose shoulder is it thrust into? Could it be the shoulder of Orion, the star Betelgeuse? On some coffins from Asyut, and in spell 114 in the *Book of the Dead*, it says that the feather is thrust into the shoulder of Osiris. The word thrust implies force and aggression. Perhaps a better word would be attached or even planted. Later on the spell refers to the deceased enabling the feather to grow. As the moon waxes the growth of the feather, seen as the increasing whiteness of the moon, is reflected in the growth of crops in bare soil – all evidence of the generative power of the moon's light. As the cycle progresses the moon moves towards full and the *"feather has grown and the Red Crown is whole, so now there is rejoicing over what has had to be counted has been counted"*.[438]

As mentioned previously the White Crown of Egypt was identified with the moon, as in this hymn to the White Crown of Upper Egypt. *"Praise to thee, thou Eye of Horus, white, great, over whose beauty the Ennead of gods rejoices, when it riseth in the eastern horizon."*[439] However this spell appears to align the Red Crown with the moon. The full moon can have a reddish tint as it rises on the horizon suggesting the Red Crown. The White Crown could then be the risen full moon. The deceased say that they have made the Red Crown whole in the *mentjat*-bowl. From depictions on coffins we know that the *mentjat*-bowl is a shallow bowl with a wide rim which was placed on a cylindrical stand. It probably held water offerings. Was it placed outside to capture the light of the full moon and then used in rituals? The rising moon may have been watched in the *mentjat*-bowl rather than in the sky. Focusing on this image in a meditative or trance state could have been used to allow it to act as a portal so that the participants could have joined in, or observed, the divine processes which brought the moon to full and raised it into the sky.

The Full Moon

Spell 157 is for knowing the *bas* of Pe. The spell explains that Pe was given to Horus as *"recompense for the injury to his eyes"*.[440] Pe

---

[438] The Ancient Egyptian Book of the Moon: Coffin Texts Spells 154-160, Priskin, 2019:73
[439] *Ancient Egyptian Poetry and Prose*, Erman, 1995:11
[440] The Egyptian Book of the Dead, Allen, 2010:187

and Dep were two cities who merged to form Buto. They are usually paired with the *bas* of Nekhen (Hierakonpolis) to represent the north and south of the country. The *bas* of Pe are given as Horus, Imsety and Hapy. The latter two are sons of Horus. On a depiction of the lunar cycle on a ceiling at Dendera the *bas* of Pe and Nekhen are shown as falcon-headed and jackal-headed men respectively. They surround the barque carrying Isis, Nephthys and Osiris. The text refers to Osiris entering the moon on the fifteenth day. It also addresses the *"ones belonging to the ba of the night"*.[441]

Surprisingly in a text celebrating the full moon is reference to injuring the Eye of Horus, giving a foretaste of things to come. Given the Egyptians' respect for the power of words it might be expected that this would be omitted. The spell refers to two injuries to the Eye in the battle between Horus and Seth. In the first instance Ra examines the Eye and Horus says that he sees it as *"altogether white"* and *"this is how the oryx came into being"*.[442] There is a pun between the phrase *"altogether white"* and the word for oryx. As a desert animal the oryx is allied with Seth. It is shown being sacrificed in a relief at the temple of Edfu. The spell references the sacrifice of an oryx as the *wedjat* eye is built up. The oryx has a cream body and black horns so can allude to the full moon starting to wane as the black edge begins to form. The horns of the oryx are long and straight and could represent the first and last crescent. They can also be likened with two fingers, giving the oryx a connection with the fingers that healed the Eye and the last two fingers that are counted in spell 99 of the *Book of the Dead*. Priskin suggests that this alludes to a lunar eclipse which can only occur at the full moon. The Eye is injured, seen as it changes colour, but it remains full and hence white.

The second injury to the Eye was inflicted by Seth as a black boar and caused the waning, and blackening, of the moon eventually resulting in its death at invisibility. Re tells Horus to look at a black pig. Horus looks and suffers extreme pain in his eyes, the same as *"it did at that blow which Seth struck at my Eye"*.[443] The spell

---

[441] The Ancient Egyptian Book of the Moon: Coffin Texts Spells 154-160, Priskin, 2019:95
[442] The Ancient Egyptian Book of the Moon: Coffin Texts Spells 154-160, Priskin, 2019:101
[443] The Egyptian Book of the Dead, Allen, 2010:187

says that the pig was Horus' sacrificial animal when he was a child. Did the Horus child take power from Seth enabling him to grow into adulthood at the full moon? By this time Seth had regained his strength so was able to attack Horus and absorb his energy resulting in the waning moon.

The spell ends with the mention of Horus on his pillar. The deity of the seventeenth day of the lunar month is Horus on his papyrus column. The papyrus was associated with concepts such as flourishing, growth and health; very appropriate for the waxing cycle. Plutarch says Osiris was killed on the seventeenth day so Horus would inherit his throne on that day. Here Horus is called the counter of eternity. The word used for eternity is *neheh*, cyclical time. The moon embodies such time with its repetition of cycles and time.

The Waning Moon

Spell 158 starts in a similar way to the previous one as it is knowing the *bas* and mystery of Nekhen. The *bas* of Nekhen are given as Horus, Duamutef and Kebhsenuf the other two sons of Horus. The rubric says it must not be recited whilst eating pig, as it was the boar of Seth who caused the waning of the moon.

The spell starts by referencing the hands of Horus which Isis threw into the Nile. Sobek tries to retrieve them but they evade him and slip away. Eventually he catches them in a fish-trap or basket. Re refers to the mysterious secret of this basket. The captured hands of Horus are "*exposed to view only on new-crescent day and midmonth day*".[444] The basket alludes to protection as well as hiding their light until the basket is brought to the surface but the exposure of the hands cannot refer to the light of the moon as it is seen constantly during this period. It may allude to the mysteries of regeneration which start and end the waxing cycle. As a Crocodile God Sobek is well suited to the task of retrieving the hands from the water. The spell may contain a reference to the constellation of the Crocodile, but if it does it is not obvious. As the moon wanes its light slips slowly back into the waters of the *nun*. In the *Book of Nut* the decan

---

[444] The Egyptian Book of the Dead, Allen, 2010:188

stars are first reborn as fishes, the regenerating hands of Horus may have gone through a similar process.

The Last Crescent – the Moon on the eastern horizon

Spell 159 is entitled knowing the *bas* of the Easterners and going out from the eastern gates of the sky. The *bas* of the Easterners are Horakhty (Horus of the Horizon), the Solar Calf and the Morning Star. Ra is "*a calf of gold born of the sky*".[445] This is a rare reference to Ra assuming the form of his mother Nut as the Cosmic Cow. The deceased then show their knowledge about the locations of sunrise. It refers to the middle gate where Re rises. In the south it is the Lake of Waterfowl and in the north it is the Waters of the Geese. The actual position of sunrise, or the gate of the horizon, moves north and south over the year. The moon in this phase rises very close to the sun so it is invisible. There is little obvious lunar reference in this spell.

While this collection of spells clearly references aspects of the lunar cycle, there must be a deeper layer of lunar mysteries either buried within them or pertaining to the lunar cult. The intricacies of the lunar cycle are fairly basic astronomical knowledge available to anyone who takes the time and effort to study the moon but any other wisdom is well hidden.

OTHER *COFFIN TEXTS* SPELLS

The above spells are not the only ones which refer to the lunar cycle. Spell 6 focuses on the rebirth of the deceased. It starts by stating the importance of the New Moon festival. "*The finger is removed from upon you…you have planted the plume at the horizon.*" The finger may allude to the moon being restrained when it is too close to the sun or to the fingers used to heal the moon. The spell then says that the feather is planted where there are "*those who know you*".[446] Does this allude to the astronomers who knew exactly where to look for the new moon?

---

445 The Ancient Egyptian Pyramid Texts, Faulkner, 2007:172 utt 485A
446 The Ancient Egyptian Coffin Texts Vol I, Faulkner, 2007:3 spell 6

The invisible moon is hinted at in another spell, that of entering into and coming forth from the fire. "*I am this one invisible of form in the midst of sunshine.*" The moon is now so close to the sun that it is invisible. The deceased say that they travel around "*her who is opposite me*" who is probably the Solar Eye Goddess. The deceased also reference their knife "*which cuts down him who is in the hand of Thoth*".[447] This could be the flint knife seen as both the waning moon and the knife which slices off the portions of the moon. As protector of the moon Thoth will carry the moon in his hand or his barque.

BOOK OF THE MOON REMNANTS IN THE BOOK OF THE DEAD

In the *Book of the Dead* there are some spells which are similar to those in the Book of the Moon. Knowledge of the lunar cycle and the *bas* of Heliopolis appears in spell 115. Spell 114 refers to the *bas* of Hermopolis and the waxing of the moon. The *bas* of Pe and the full moon are covered in spell 112 and spell 113 gives the *bas* of Nekhen and the waning moon. What is noticeably absent is a descendant of *Coffin Texts* spell 155 relating to lunar invisibility or the new moon. By the New Kingdom the influence of the lunar cult and of the priests of Hermopolis had declined so less emphasis on the lunar cycle might be expected. The fact that all but one of these spells are present in some form shows that knowledge of the lunar cycle was still important. The absence of a spell for lunar invisibility is unexpected. Perhaps there was now a taboo over referencing it for some reason. Was it seen as dangerous or restricted knowledge in the New Kingdom? The *Book of the Dead* was compiled by priests in Thebes. Perhaps it wasn't understood, or trusted, by them and the influence of Hermopolis and Thoth was far away. With Osiris increasingly associated with the full moon at this time it is possible that reference to lunar invisibility might have been too strong a reference to his death.

---

[447] The Ancient Egyptian Coffin Texts Vol I, Faulkner, 2007:192 spell 246

DEPICTING THE LUNAR CYCLE

There are a number of methods the Egyptians used to depict all or part of the lunar cycle. Some are straightforward while others are more complex with a composition of deities, Lunar and Solar Barques, and multiple depictions of the moon.

Processions

A common way of depicting the waxing or entire cycle was with a procession of deities, either in one line or on either side of the lunar symbol. They always face the lunar symbol as it would be highly disrespectful to turn your back on such an important symbol and God. They are sometimes shown on a staircase alluding to the increasing size of the moon. The deities unite with, or bring their power and offerings to, the moon as it waxes until it is full. As the deities depart they take their light and power with them. Such processions were probably re-enacted in temple rituals. A symbol of the full moon, a lunar disc or the *wedjat* eye, is placed after the fifteenth deity. At the Temple of Khonsu at Karnak the entire cycle is shown with its 30 deities. The moon is represented by a disc sat on a crescent moon. Fifteen deities walk towards the moon from the right and the text describes them as entering the Left Eye. The fifteen that are shown walking from the left are described as leaving the Glorious Eye. They are not shown walking away from the moon so without the text the meaning of the scene could be misinterpreted. Each deity contributes light to the moon but as they leave they take back their share of the light.[448]

Another example comes from the Osirian Roof Chapel at the Temple of Hathor at Dendera. On either side of a netting of the *wedjat* eye vignette is a procession of deities who hold a plant and a vessel in each hand. These are offerings to the moon but there is no indication exactly what they are. They will have had lunar connections and were probably used in rituals carried out during the waxing or full moon. The offerings may allude to the fertilising and growth aspects of the waxing moon and represent food crops.

---

[448] The Depictions of the Entire Lunar Cycle in Graeco-Roman Temples, Priskin, 2016:111-144

One of the rituals for Osiris involved sowing grain seeds into effigies of Osiris, the sprouting grains alluding to his rebirth. In a similar fertility reference, in the ninth hour of the *Book of the Amduat* the nine Gods of the Fields of the Netherworld are depicted. They carry either palm branches or stalks of grain as a staff. It is they who *"cause all the trees and all the plants of this place to grow"*.[449]

Netting the *Wedjat* Eye

Sokar is the falcon-headed God of the Memphis necropolis. He was associated with Osiris. His chapel at Dendera shows Thoth and Shu holding the *wedjat* eye in a net. Texts in the Sokar chapel say that Thoth puts a net around the rising moon at the start of the month.[450] The net appears to be needed to protect the young moon or assist in his rising. The hands of Horus were caught in a fish trap in order to retrieve them, this may be a similar concept with the newborn moon being lifted out of the waters of the *nun*.

Shu & Thoth netting the moon

---

[449] The Egyptian Amduat, Abt & Hornung, 2007:293
[450] The Depictions of the Entire Lunar Cycle in Graeco-Roman Temples, Priskin, 2016:111-144

Beneath the net are two ibises emphasising the presence and power of Thoth. Behind each God is a lotus pillar. A baboon sits on the column behind Shu and a falcon perches on the column behind Thoth. Shu represents the Right Eye but he is shown next to a lunar symbol while Thoth is next to a solar symbol. This enhances the mingling and uniting of the two powers and deities. Above this scene is the hieroglyph of the sky. Directly above the baboon is the lunar disc on a crescent. Next to the falcon is a scarab pushing the sun disc towards the sky hieroglyph. The presence of the scarab suggests dawn but the new moon is seen at sunset. Bomhard suggests that it represents the rising full moon, but this isn't associated with the rising sun symbolised by the scarab either. Whatever the reading Thoth and Shu work together to rejuvenate the old moon. There is no reason why the scene should depict only one point in the lunar cycle. It can combine the critical parts of the cycle in one depiction. A similar vignette is found in the Osirian chapel at Dendera and on the walls of the pronoas at Edfu. Here, Thoth and Shu stand in the Lunar Barque and lift the lunar disc inscribed with the *wedjat* eye. The inscription says *"building up the wedjet eye, rejuvenating the glorious eye, netting its pupil and putting it in its place"*.[451] The pupil symbolises protection as it is at the centre of the eye surrounded by the iris. Osiris is referred to as *"the great one in the midst of his eye"*.[452] The pupil was often associated with the Eye of the Sun where it was viewed as comparable to the womb. A child is sometimes depicted within the pupil of the Solar Eye to represent the Solar Child.

A net is made from a series of knots and as knots are magical in themselves this increases and reinforces the magical power of a net. The root of the word for 'knot' is the same as that for the word used for 'raise' or 'lift'.[453] The use of a net by Shu and Thoth to hold the rising moon emphasises the magical power of the net by the word play of knots. The *Book of Thoth* contains references to the *"house of the Fish-net"* which appears to be a temple or sacred precinct

---

[451] The Depictions of the Entire Lunar Cycle in Graeco-Roman Temples, Priskin, 2016:111-144

[452] The Egyptian Book of the Dead, Allen, 2010:214

[453] Entangled, Connected or Protected? The Power of Knots in Ancient Egypt, Wendrich, 2006:248

within Hermopolis.[454] It was said that a net was preserved and venerated at this temple. This may be the net used by Thoth and Shu to lift the moon. The net may be aligned with the basket or fish-trap used by Sobek to retrieve the hands of Horus. It appears that the waxing moon needs the assistance of the other deities to start and complete its cycle. The net is also the equivalent of the protective enclosure of Osiris and the deceased by Nut, as seen in the net placed over some mummies in the Late and Ptolemaic Periods. The word play on knot applies equally to Nut raising the deceased to heaven as it does on Thoth and Shu raising the moon.

The Waning Phase

Some scholars believe that there was a reluctance to depict the waning moon due to its negative connotations and references to the death of Osiris. Others disagree suggesting that the waning phases have been misinterpreted.

The largely Roman Period temple of Khnum at Esna was destroyed in medieval times but the pronaos survived. Part of the ceiling shows a representation of the lunar cycle. Fourteen deities stand above lunar discs on either side of a barque containing Thoth and Horus Khentykhety who flank Khepri inside a solar disc. (Khentykhety is a local version of Horus from Athribis.) Recent cleaning and conservation work revealed that each disc was engraved with varying proportions of the *wedjat* eye to show the phases of the moon. The discs under the deities representing the waning phase are inscribed with decreasing portions of the *wedjat* eye while the discs showing the waxing phase have increasing parts of the *wedjat* eye.[455]

The eastern wall on the pronaos at Edfu shows a long Lunar Barque carrying the lunar disc which is engraved with the *wedjat* eye and fourteen squatting figures. Such a posture demonstrates a lack of energy suitable for the waning phase. Next to the lunar disc Thoth, Isis and Horus present the *wedjat* eye to a baboon-headed God. At the stern are five falcons. Priskin suggests that the five falcons are associated with lunar invisibility and represent the fifth

---

[454] The Ancient Egyptian Book of Thoth, Jasnow & Zauzich, 2005:10
[455] The Ancient Colours of Esna Return, el-Leithy et al, 2019:20-23

part as discussed in *Coffin Texts* spell 155. The *bas* of the full moon, depicted as three falcon-headed deities, stand behind the Lunar Barque and appear to say farewell. *"Glorifying the wedjet eye as it renews its cycle on the fifteenth day."* This is one way of referring obliquely to the waning phase. It continues by saying that they will follow him *"in his form of a child until he comes to his strength when he is borne by Nut by placing him on the mountain of Bakhu while his father, Re, is beside Manu".*[456]

Lunar Invisibility

There is an astronomical frieze on the northern wall of the pronaos of the temple of Horus at Edfu. In the Solar Barque is what looks like a burial mound. A disc sits on top of this enclosing the squatting ram-headed Sun God. The mound and the ram-headed Sun God alludes to the *ba* of the Sun God uniting with Osiris in the underworld and his subsequent rebirth. This scene depicting the 'death' of the Sun God and the moon is firmly connected to the full moon, the culmination of the rebirth and growth of the moon. A horizontal line comes out of the mound to form a step and then a dais which abuts a pillar. On the dais is a small figure of Thoth who stands and worships the *wedjat* eye sitting on a lunar crescent on the top of the pillar. At the far side of this are fourteen steps. At the foot of the steps is a procession of deities. The leading one lifts his foot ready to begin the climb showing the continuous cycle of rebirth and growth.

SOME OTHER LUNAR DEPICTIONS

Lunar motifs are not confined to astronomical ceilings and temples walls, the importance of the lunar cycle and in particular the symbolism of the Eye of Horus making them very popular. One pectoral of Tutankhamun shows a winged scarab lifting up the Lunar Barque. On it a *wedjat* eye is protected by two *uraeus* cobras. A lunar crescent and disc sits on top of the *wedjat* eye. The king is depicted on the disc wearing a lunar disc and crescent flanked by

---

[456] The Depictions of the Entire Lunar Cycle in Graeco-Roman Temples, Priskin, 2016:111-144

Thoth with his lunar disc and Ra-Horakhty with his solar disc. Another necklace has a lunar pectoral. A lunar disc and crescent sits on a gold Lunar Barque. The barque is supported by lotus flowers which grow from the celestial waters depicted by the hieroglyph sign for sky made of lapis lazuli. The New Kingdom *stele* of Neferenpet depicts an ibis-headed Thoth sitting in a crescent-shaped Lunar Barque. He wears the Lunar Crown and is presented with the *wedjat* eye by his alter-ego a baboon. The stern of the barque is a curling notched palm rib – the hieroglyph sign for year. The barque sits above the hieroglyph sign for sky and has a drift net at the prow. Boats often used a drift net when travelling downstream and a sail when going against the current. This emphasises that the Lunar Barque is sailing with the celestial currents.[457]

WORKING WITH THE LUNAR CYCLE

> *"The sky holding her secret image rejoices. The left eye is received by the right eye, the moon keeps to its time, none of its festivals or rituals have any irregularities upon its rising or setting."*[458]

The lunar cycle is the cycle of transformation of humans, animals and vegetation: of birth, growth, decline, death and rebirth. It is the image of eternal cyclical renewal and of time. The cycle shows duality in its light-dark phases and reminds us that they are points on a spectrum not irreconcilable opposites. No doubt the Egyptians worked with the lunar cycle and carried out specific tasks according to its phases. We do not know if they carried out agricultural activities this way but there are references to magic and medical procedures carried out at specific times in the lunar cycle. One restraining spell was carried out when *"the moon stands in opposition to the sun"*. Another protective spell requested of the moon includes *"I now adjure you by this potent night, in which your light is last to fade away"*.[459]

---

[457] The Moon: Myth and Image, Cashford, 2003:46
[458] The Depictions of the Entire Lunar Cycle in Graeco-Roman Temples, Priskin, 2016:111-144
[459] The Greek Magical Papyri in Translation, Betz, 1996:77-78

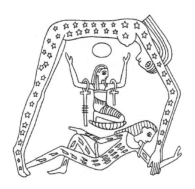

CHAPTER 12

Cycles, Clocks and Calendars

"A star travels in accordance with the existing order of the traveling of stars."[460]

THE SEARCH FOR ORDER

We have always searched for patterns in the passing of time, the changing seasons and the sky. Bones notched with lunar cycles have been found dating from 40,000 BCE. Cosmic patterns are important because what happens in heaven is reflected on earth. The deities were either responsible for the cycles or were found within them so measuring and recording what was happening in both the day and night sky was important. On a more practical level these cycles allow us to position and orientate ourselves temporally in the same way that location and direction position us geographically. They also provide comfort in an often precarious and uncertain world. The sun will rise tomorrow and everything is working as it should

---

[460] Ancient Egyptian Science Volume II: Calendars, Clocks and Astronomy, Clagett, 1995:372

be. *"There are few things you can rely on but the phases of the Moon are one of them."*[461]

The majority of Egyptians would not have been unduly concerned about times and dates. Agricultural cycles and religious feasts were the main drivers in their lives. Time was more likely to be measured by the changing seasons and by distinct events such as sunrise, milking time or the next full moon. For the king and administrators it was more important and to the priests it was essential. Ceremonies had to be performed at the correct time otherwise they would be out of step with heaven.

THE DIVINE TIMEKEEPERS

Thoth and Seshat were considered to be the creators and keepers of clocks and calendars and they oversaw the work of those who devised and regulated them. Thoth is the Lord of Time, Scribe of Time and the Divider of Time. He is the *"Moon in the night, ruler of the stars, who distinguishes seasons, months and years. He commeth ever-living, rising and setting".*[462] Time and its recording is allocated to Thoth because of his lunar aspect as well those of wisdom and writing. He is also a devoted upholder of *maat*. An inscription in the Ramesseum at Karnak depicts the annual astronomical cycle. The vertical axis shows Sothis as the pivotal moment which begins and ends each year. The axis is supported by the baboon form of Thoth who symbolises the precision and durability of the calendar.[463] Strabo explains that *"it is due to these priests also that people reckon the days, not by the moon, but by the sun, adding to the twelve months of thirty days each five days each year...They attribute to Hermes all wisdom of this particular kind".*[464]

Seshat is an ancient Pre-dynastic Goddess and was referred to as *"the Original One".*[465] Her name means female scribe and she was often associated with Thoth either as a consort or as a colleague. As the Foremost in the Library, Seshat was associated with libraries

---

[461] Book of the Moon, Aderin-Pocock, 2018:6
[462] Thoth or the Hermes of Egypt, Boylan, 1922:83-84
[463] The Egyptian Calendar, Bomhard, 1999:84-85
[464] Geography Vol VIII, Strabo & Jones, 1932:125
[465] Seshat and the Pharaoh, Wainwright, 1939:30-40

and all types of writing, notation and calculation.[466] She was the Goddess of scribes, architects, builders and astronomers. Seshat is shown carving notches into a palm rib to mark the passing years. A notched palm rib is the hieroglyph symbol for year and represents recorded time. She recorded the length of each king's reign on the leaves of the sacred persea tree. Seshat has an afterlife role, sometimes equated to or working alongside Nephthys. "*Nephthys has collected all your members for you in this her name of Seshat, Lady of Builders.*"[467] Her roles made her more of an official Goddess and there is no evidence of her presence in popular religion. She often wears a leopard-skin garment. This is a very ancient style of costume and after the Old Kingdom it was only worn by the *sem*-priests who officiated at funerary rites. The rosette pattern on the leopard skin hints at the patterns of stars. Details of Seshat's dress are clearly visible in a relief of her in the temple of Amun at Luxor. It is decorated with circles containing the five-pointed star sign.

The Goddess Maat is order on a cosmic scale. She is responsible for, and personifies, the harmony of the universe with its regular cycles. Through this she represents the divine order of the created universe. Through her power, and the assistance of various deities, the seasons and the stars follow their appointed paths and timings. The phrase "*as long as lasts the sky*" was frequently used to mean forever and alluded to the eternal cycles of heaven.[468] When Isis became the All-Goddess in the Greco-Roman Period she acquired this role. In the *aretalogy* of Kyme she says "*I showed the paths of the stars, I regulated the course of the sun and the moon*".[469] Lucius, in his prayer to Isis says "*for thee the constellations move, for thee the seasons return*".[470] Her role is more like Maat's, ensuring that the cosmic cycles work properly rather than being involved in explaining the details and recording them as Seshat does.

---

[466] The Routledge Dictionary of Egyptian Gods and Goddesses, Hart, 2005:142
[467] The Ancient Egyptian Pyramid Texts, Faulkner, 2007:119 utt 364
[468] The Egyptian Calendar, Bomhard, 1999:2
[469] Hymns to Isis in Her Temple at Philae, Zabkar, 1988:140
[470] Hymns to Isis in Her Temple at Philae, Zabkar, 1988:144

COSMIC CYCLES

There is an infinity of cycles in nature. Some like the daily solar cycle are self-evident others can only be determined over millennia of extensive record keeping. Ones that stretch over months and years form the basis of the calendars. The problem for us is that they are all of different lengths and never add up to a full number of days. The whole area of calendars and cycles is a specialist subject and can get very involved and mathematical so I have only given a high-level summary avoiding technical details.

The daily solar cycle was imagined and recorded in great detail in the Netherworld funerary texts. Its annual cycle with solstices and equinoxes appears to have been less important to the Egyptians. The myth of the Distant Goddess may have, amongst other things, alluded to the north-south wandering of the sun. When she quarrels with her father, the Eye Goddess goes south and terrorises the desert lands. Once pacified she returns north to Egypt. Like the sun, the moon rises and sets within a north-south band. This is not an annual occurrence, it takes 9.3 years for the moon to move from its major standstill (where it has its widest range) to its minor standstill (where it has its narrowest range). This gives a full cycle of approximately 18.6 years. Was this something that the Egyptians observed or celebrated? It would appear not from the evidence we have.

The lunar cycle has the perceived advantage that is easy for everyone to follow and record. Given clear skies we can all recognise its key phases without having to resort to a written calendar. The priests would have kept records of the lunar cycle which would be needed if the sky was obscured by dust or clouds. A major exception is the accurate sighting of the first crescent moon and similarly when the waning crescent could no longer be seen. Spalinger reports that about 15% of naked eye sightings of the new crescent are anticipatory rather than actual.[471] People have a tendency to see what they want or expect to see and the fine sliver of the moon is easily obscured by dust or light on the horizon. There is nothing to suggest that the Egyptians were any different.

---

[471] Egyptian Festival Dating and the Moon, Spalinger, 2002:379

Any slight mismatch between the anticipated time of an astronomical event and its actual occurrence could be ascribed to the fact that the deities have the final say and may have other business to attend to. They are not at the call of our timekeeping.

The Sothic year is the time between two heliacal rises of Sirius at the same latitude. Around 3,000 BCE this occurred at the summer solstice today, at the same latitude, it occurs about 40 days later.[472] The heliacal rising of Sirius officially marked the start of the year, often referred to as the Opening of the Year. The Canopus Decree states that *"the day of which the star of Isis heliacally rises is regarded in sacred writings to be a new year"*. An inscription from Dendera states that *"years are reckoned from her shining forth"*.[473] Latitude is important when referencing the rise of Sirius. There is a difference of seven days between its rise in the far north compared to that in the far south of Egypt. Similarly the inundation at Buto arrived twelve days later than it did at Elephantine. How was this handled? The inundation could be celebrated when it arrived at each cult centre as this was obvious. The New Year was probably taken to be the time of the helical rising of Sirius at whichever cult centre was dominant at the time.

As mentioned earlier, a letter informs the Chief Lector Priest when the helical rising of Sirius will occur. There is a suggestion that the date of the feast of the heliacal rising of Sirius was predicted rather than actually observed. This makes sense as such a major festival would have required a lot of organisation. There is also the problem of what was to be done if viewing conditions were poor over the critical period.

THE LUNAR AND CIVIL CALENDARS

According to the civil calendar the year began on the first day of the first month of *Akhet* (Inundation) with the feast of *wpt rnpt*.[474] The Goddess Renpet personified the year. She wore the hieroglyph

---

472 The Egyptian Calendar, Bomhard, 1999:26
473 The Egyptian Calendar: keeping Ma'at on Earth, Belmonte, 2009:111
474 The Egyptian Calendar: keeping Ma'at on Earth, Belmonte, 2009:77

sign for year, a notched palm branch, on her head. She is depicted with Maat in a relief at the temple of Sety I at Abydos.

The civil calendar, one that was suitable for administration, was developed using the annual helical rising of Sirius at Memphis which was the political capital during the Old Kingdom. The Sothic cycle doesn't coincide exactly with the solar year and one day is lost every four years. After about 1465 years they will synchronise again at the change of the Sothic cycle. Having two calendars would have been a nuisance in some areas but the majority of Egyptians wouldn't have been affected by it. To keep the lunar calendar in step with the civil an extra lunar month was added every three years and dedicated to Thoth who rebalanced the calendars. This made the lunar calendar impractical for legal and fiscal purposes. The New Kingdom Ebers medical papyrus gives a table of corresponding lunar and Sothic dates. The physicians needed this if they were prescribing treatment according to the lunar calendar.[475] The lunar calendar was preeminent in the religious sphere where it coincided with and was reflected in many of the myths. Herodotus was complimentary about the Egyptian calendar. *"In my opinion their method of calculation is better than the Greek…and every year intercalate five additional days."*[476]

Even after the introduction of the five epagomenal days, bringing the year to 365 days there was a discrepancy between this and the real solar year which was about six hours longer. The concept of a leap year was introduced by Ptolemy III (246-221 BCE) and it was recorded in the Decree of Canopus. *"In order to have the seasons follow an absolute rule, that the days of certain solemn feasts to celebrate in winter should never fall into summer because of the displacement of the rise of Sothis…a day shall be added…every fourth year to the five epagomenoi before the New Year."*[477]

---

[475] Defining Time, Franci, 2016:140-142
[476] The Histories, Herodotus & Selincourt, 2003:96
[477] The Egyptian Calendar, Bomhard, 1999:29

TELLING THE TIME

The smallest measurement of time used by the Egyptians was the hour, anything of shorter duration was just called *3t*. There were considered to be twelve hours of day and twelve hours of night. The night was divided into twelve hours because there were twelve visible decans that could be used during the hours of darkness. Such a division causes a problem because the length of daylight varies over the year. A Ramesside papyrus gives the actual hours of the day and night at various months of the year. The first month of *Akhet* has sixteen hours of day and eight of night while the first month of *Shemu* has twelve hours of each.[478] The first hour of the night was referred to as evening, the second to fourth were early night. Middle night was the fifth to eighth hours, noticeably different from our concept of midnight. Late night was the ninth to eleventh hour whilst the twelfth was last darkness.[479]

Measuring the hours proved difficult. Accurate time-keeping was considered essential for rituals carried out at specific times of the day and night. During the day the Egyptians used shadow clocks which had to be calibrated to specific locations because latitude affects the length of the shadow as well as the time of the year. Water-clocks (*clepsydrae*) were also used. These are V-shaped vessels with a spout at the base. Internal markings allow the hours to be read from the depth of the water. Some water-clocks have the baboon of Thoth above the drip hole. One New Kingdom example from Karnack has the spout in the shape of a baboon. Around the top of the container is a register depicting the twelve Gods who represent the months. The baboon acts as the thirteenth month of the epagomenal days.[480] The rest of the water-clock is decorated in a similar way to some of the astronomical ceilings. It has three registers which depict the decans and planets, the northern constellations and lunar deities and then the deities of the months.

---

[478] Egyptian Astronomical Texts I: The Early Decans, Neugebauer & Parker, 1960:119
[479] Egyptian Astronomical Texts I: The Early Decans, Neugebauer & Parker, 1960:35
[480] Timekeeping in Ancient Egypt, Wernick, 2009:29-32

THE STAR CLOCKS

The star clocks date to the Middle Kingdom. They are the earliest known Egyptian astronomical texts and appear on the inside of coffin lids. The basis of the star clocks is the rising of specific decan stars at hourly intervals during the night. For ten days the same star appears to rise at the same time before the drift becomes noticeable. After ten days another star takes its place. The theory is sound but in practice it is very difficult to find a star at exactly the right place in the sky without using modern equipment. The star clocks are displayed in a grid. The rows give the reading for each hour of the night and the columns give the names of the decans at their positions throughout the year. Many believe that it was never a very practical way of measuring time.

In the New Kingdom a different method of telling the time by stars was devised and depicted on the 20th dynasty tomb ceilings of Rameses VI, VII and IX in the Valley of the Kings. The date and time given for the culmination of Sirius suggests that the ones depicted were produced about 1500 BCE. There are 24 tables giving details for each half month. Within each table is a seated figure and above him an eight by thirteen grid in which one star is marked in each row. The text explains how the system works. For example; the head of the giant corresponds to the beginning of the night and his pedestal corresponds to the fourth hour. The grid gives the altitude and east-west position. It was developed from the earlier system but Toomer says it was a very crude system although it would work *"after a fashion"*.[481] The astronomers who watched the sky every night over the years would gain experience and understanding of the patterns and cycles of heaven. They probably could have made fairly accurate estimates of the hours of the night. Perhaps they learned practical time-keeping first rather than trying to work from the star charts. Without the need for modern timekeeping accuracy it was good enough for what the priests wanted. The deities had no need for millisecond accuracy. Such star clocks would have to be revised about every hundred years.

---

[481] Mathematics and Astronomy, Toomer, 1988: 49-51

The only calculating and measuring instrument we know of is the *merkhet* whose name was derived from the word for 'knowing'. It was an all-purpose instrument used for land surveying and astronomical measurements. One part was the rib of a palm leaf with a slot in the top which acted as a sight. The other was a plumb square. One belonging to Hor, an astronomer priest of the 26th dynasty, was inscribed "*be vigilant about regular hours…I know the path of the solar disc, each star, placed according to their position*".[482] One from the 18th dynasty was inscribed "*pointer to determine the beginning of a season and to put all people in their hours*".[483]

To tell the time during the night needed two observers on a temple roof and, obviously, a clear sky. They sat on a north-south axis at a predetermined distance and one acted as a point of reference. The observer located the relevant decanal stars using the *merkhet* and used a papyrus table to determine which hour of the night it was. The sighting stick was held close to the eye and the plumb square held at arm's length. The observer then looked at his assistant. The hours were counted when the specified star crossed the plumb line which was aligned to various parts of the assistant's body. "*When the star Sar is above the right eye, it is the fifth hour…when the star Orion is above the left eye, it is the seventh hour. When the star that follows Sothis is above the left eye, it is the eighth hour.*"[484] This does seem a rather vague technique but it was deemed sufficient. I am no surveyor so perhaps issues like the size of the assistant's body and accurately locating his left eye in the darkness caused a negligible error in the overall calculation.

Precise observation of when a star rises is difficult as it can easily be obscured by dust and haze. The new system which was developed in the Ramesside Period used the meridian transit of the stars, which is the highest point on their course. This caused other problems. Two stars which cross the horizon an hour apart may reach their highest elevation at different times depending upon their declination (how far above the celestial equator they rise). The 70 days the decan is invisible is an approximation and the brightness

---

[482] Defining Time, Franci, 2016:143
[483] Defining Time, Franci, 2016:143
[484] The Priests of Ancient Egypt, Sauneron, 2000:152

of a star will affect its visibility period. The stars used were the brightest star in the decan asterism. They were called *wnwt*-stars, hourly-stars.[485] The selected star was referred to as the doorkeeper and the other associated stars were referred to as servants. Using the decans for time-keeping was complicated by the fact that the Egyptians used a 365 day year. This resulted in a slippage of one decade every 40 years and so the star clocks needed constant revision. Analysis of the star clocks on coffins has shown that are all corrupt to some extent, probably as a result of copying errors which accumulated as copies were made from copies not the original. It is unlikely that the star clocks displayed on coffins and ceilings by the 19th dynasty were used for measuring time. They were symbolic elements retained because of their antiquity and the importance of the mythology which underlined them. The deceased did not need to know the exact time; they needed to participate in the cosmic cycle of rebirth.

TIME IN THE NETHERWORLD

The Netherworld Books depict the mysteries of rebirth and the uniting of the *ba* of Ra with Osiris. Time was very important in this critical alchemical process and there are a number of depictions of time and its passing. The temporary loss of power of the Sun God also meant that the cosmic cycles were at risk, another reason for the emphasis on the orderly passage of the stars. The preamble to the *Book of the Amduat* summarises what the book will teach including the knowledge of what is in each hour and the "*courses of the hours*".[486] It was essential that the hours of the night were determined properly because rituals were carried out to help the Sun God through the *duat*. The rituals had to tie up with the relevant hour and gate the God was passing through. The books of the Netherworld were developed at the same time as the Ramesside star clocks which might have given the astronomer priests a greater incentive to improve the accuracy of their work.

---

485 Defining Time, Franci, 2016:145
486 The Egyptian Amduat, Abt & Hornung, 2007:13

The first hour of the *Book of the Amduat* depicts the twelve Goddesses of the Hours who wear a star as a crown. They appear again in the seventh hour with different names. Their stated role is to protect and guide the Sun God. Horus addresses them as Star Hours. In the eleventh hour the passing of time is depicted, shown in red to emphasise its importance. A Goddess, Time, sits on the back of a leaping serpent called *"He who takes away the hours"*.[487] Around them are ten (sometimes eleven) stars to indicate the hours which have passed. Each hour is born and then swallowed by the time serpent.

In the *Book of Gates* the sixth hour depicts the passing of time showing the hours being generated as stars rising from a double rope pulled from the mouth of the God Aqen. A similar scene occurs in the eighth hour where a serpentine rope, named Devourer, births the hours which rise as stars. The eleventh hour shows a God named *"who belongs to the hour"* who carries a star in each hand. His role is to guide the Sun God whilst the *"hour does her duty"*.[488]

WHEN CYCLES FALTER OR PAUSE

The threat of chaos and the disruption of *maat* is ever-present. Any beautifully balanced system is an irresistible challenge to the destabilising forces of chaos. The mismatch of the lunar and civil calendar, the creation of the epagomenal days and the slippage of the decans could be explained away by the astronomer-priests not being clever enough to understand the workings of heaven. On the other hand it might be an indication of an underlying problem. The most frightening events were those that couldn't be explained by human error – eclipses being the most dramatic. The Chronicle of Prince Osorkon mentions civil unrest and adds that it occurred despite there not being an eclipse.[489] This infers that eclipses were associated with disorder whether political, social or economic. Irregular behaviour in heaven was echoed by the same on earth.

---

[487] The Egyptian Amduat, Abt & Hornung, 2007:332
[488] The Egyptian Book of Gates, Abt & Hornung, 2014:382
[489] The Ancient Egyptian Book of the Moon: Coffin Texts Spells 154-160, Priskin, 2019:16

For the Egyptians there were two main threats to *maat*. Seth, who attacks the Lunar Eye, and Apophis who attacks the Solar Barque. In the seventh hour of the *Book of the Amduat* Apophis is shown defeated and staked. There are twelve Gods and twelve Goddesses wearing stars on their heads. The Gods face an enthroned Horus whose role is to *"make the star-gods move and to set the positions of the hours in the Netherworld"*. One of the Gods is called Driver of the Stars.[490] The Goddesses are the Goddesses of the Hours. The stable orbits of the stars are a sign of the continuing cosmic order now that Apophis has been defeated.

Eclipses can only occur when the moon crosses the ecliptic, which it does twice a month at new and full moon. To get an eclipse the sun, moon and earth must align exactly, which doesn't happen very often so eclipses aren't common. Solar eclipses are fast and dramatic. Totality, the period when the moon covers the entire disc of the sun, never exceeds seven minutes. A lunar eclipse takes several hours. During its totality the moon becomes copper or red in colour but never becomes invisible. Red is the colour of anger which may be one reason why Khonsu was originally viewed as an aggressive God.

There are no records of eclipses in Pharaonic Egypt. Eclipses are dramatic and given how important the regular workings of the cosmos were and the religious significance of the sun and moon as the Eyes of Heaven, it is strange that the Egyptians left no record of their occurrence. They did have a very noticeable regard for the power of the written word. Writing something made it 'come into being' and fixed it permanently in this world. For this reason euphemisms for death were extremely common. Were they doing the same thing with eclipses, especially the dramatic and frightening total eclipse of the sun? Ignoring the temporary disruption of cosmic harmony in the written record would help to erase its power and might stop it from manifesting more strongly the next time. In that case references to eclipses had to be made oblique. In the Middle Kingdom papyrus Rhind I there is a probable reference to a lunar eclipse *"so that the sky will not swallow the moon"*.[491]

---

[490] The Egyptian Amduat, Abt & Hornung, 2007:237
[491] The Names of the Sixteenth Day of the Lunar Month, Parker, 1953:50

It is only when we get to the Greco-Roman Period that there are direct references to eclipses. There is one Ptolemaic treatise about lunar eclipses over a ten year period dating to the 1st century BCE. The style is similar to Babylonian texts of the same era. The text is only partly decipherable but it gives details of the eclipse and the position of stars and planets around it. "*The stars which were seen at the eclipse named...Saturn rise in Libra, it being on the back of the moon.*" This is purely an astronomical text, there is no reference to any deities or astrological concepts. "*The eclipse will occur on the northern face of it*" and "*the moon eclipses before Cancer*".[492] There is a reference to a solar eclipse in a Greco-Roman Period papyrus. It states that "*the sky swallowed the sun disc*" when Psamtek (26th dynasty) died.[493] It is not known if this is symbolic or factual reporting. The Greeks knew what caused eclipses and it is unlikely that the Pharaonic astronomer-priests were unaware of the physical causes. "*When the Moon is eclipsed at the full...she is entering the shadow of the earth – just as they say Osiris entered the coffin.*" The moon "*conceals the Sun and causes him to disappear, on the thirtieth, though she does not entirely destroy him, as neither did Isis Typhon...there are some however, who call the shadow of the earth into which they think the Moon falls and is eclipsed, Typhon*".[494]

There appears to be a reference to a solar eclipse in *Coffin Texts* spell 160 and its counterpart spell 108 in the *Book of the Dead*. They describe an attack on the Solar Barque by Apophis. "*After midday he turns his eyes against Re. Then a stoppage takes place in the bark and great amazement among the sailors.*"[495] The fact that the barque is halted amid "*great amazement*" infers that this attack is unexpected. Given that Apophis attacks at regular intervals it suggests that this attack refers to an eclipse where the moon takes the role of Apophis and actually halts the sun. In the *Coffin Texts* Apophis is described as being 30 cubits in length with a forepart of three cubits. These are lunar numbers aligning Apophis with the moon, 30 days in a lunar month and three days of invisibility. One lunar reference has disappeared in the *Book of the Dead*, Apophis is still 30 cubits long but his foreparts are now eight cubits. Apophis "*turns his eye*" against

---

[492] A Demotic Lunar Eclipse Text of the First Century BC, Neugebauer, 1981:312-327
[493] Astronomical chronology, Kraus, 2009:135
[494] Plutarch: Concerning the Mysteries of Isis and Osiris, Mead, 2002:224
[495] The Egyptian Book of the Dead, Allen, 2010:181 spell 108

the Solar Barque which is usually taken to mean his paralysing stare. Priskin suggests that this refers to the Eye of the Moon. Normally the moon has its Eye turned towards earth so it can be seen. During a solar eclipse the moon turns its Eye toward the sun and becomes invisible to us.[496]

Seth repels Apophis and tells him that Ra will *"set in the evening after traversing the sky…Re sets in the life-region of the horizon"*.[497] He is ensuring that the Solar Barque returns to its predetermined course so that the sun will set in the western horizon at dusk not when it is still in the sky. If Apophis tries to attack the Solar Barque during the day it might be expected that he sometimes succeeded. No one knows what goes on in the dangerous *duat* and Apophis may well have launched successful attacks on the Solar Barque. Solar eclipses are there for everyone to observe during the day. There was little reason to place the Chaos Serpent in the sky if a successful attack on the sun had never been witnessed.

In various texts there is reference to wounds on Ra's Eye. These may allude to a partial eclipse. Spell 101 in the *Book of the Dead* is to protect the Solar Barque. It refers to Ra passing by the Eye of seven cubits which has a pupil of three cubits. Priskin suggests that this refers to an eclipse with a corona or even a partial eclipse; assuming that the Egyptians had been able to view a solar eclipse without destroying their eyesight. Damage to the Eye of Horus explains the lunar cycle but could also allude to lunar eclipses. The red of the eclipsed moon is suggestive of blood.

The 30th dynasty Metternich *stele* is a healing *stele*. These are covered in healing spells and protective images. Water was poured over them and then drunk. It was believed that the water absorbed their healing magic. One spell against poison relates the story of how the young Horus child was fatally stung by a scorpion, which was actually Seth in disguise. Unable to cure him, despite her great magic, Isis *"sent her cry to the boat of millions, and the sun disk landed opposite her and did not move from his place"*.[498] Ra sends Thoth to sort

---

[496] The Ancient Egyptian Book of the Moon: Coffin Texts Spells 154-160, Priskin, 2019:160-165
[497] The Egyptian Book of the Dead, Allen, 2010:181 spell 108
[498] The Art of Medicine in Ancient Egypt, Allen, 2005:57

out the problem. He states that *"the sun disk is in its place of yesterday; darkness has happened and sunlight is repelled until Horus gets well"*.[499] Following the recitation of a long healing spell Thoth cures Horus. The reference to the abrupt halting of the sun and the darkness is very suggestive of a total solar eclipse. In an allusion to the cause of the eclipse Thoth ends his spell by telling Isis that he is *"waiting to command the Night boat and let the Day boat proceed"*.[500] Thoth is returning to the Lunar Barque, the moon will move on allowing the sun to reappear and continue on its daily course.

MAINTAINING MAAT

A major function of the temple was the maintenance of *maat* especially that of the created world, in the form of the state of Egypt. The endless cycles of nature were controlled by the deities. Accurate timekeeping honoured the divine cycles and enabled people to join in the cosmic dance which brought the harmony and *maat* of the heavens down to earth – where it was very much needed. By accurately depicting the control of the cycles, and by celebrating them at the correct time, the Egyptians echoed and hopefully amplified the work done by the deities. At the very least it showed the deities that their work was appreciated and not taken for granted. This is one reason why there wasn't a split between science and religion for the Egyptians. Understanding how the cosmos worked didn't threaten the power of any deity. This concept was so important that the king had to swear an oath at the coronation ceremony to promise that he would not alter the year as part of his duties to maintain *maat* on earth.

> *"As long as the sky will rest upon its four supports, as long as the earth will remain stable upon its foundations, as long as Re will shine during the day and the moon will shine at night, as long as Orion will be the ba of Osiris and Sothis will be the*

---

[499] The Art of Medicine in Ancient Egypt, Allen, 2005:57
[500] The Art of Medicine in Ancient Egypt, Allen, 2005:58

*ruler of the stars, as long as the inundation will come on time
and the cultivable land will produce its plants.*[501]

The astronomical ceilings depicted the work done by the deities. They regulated the processes that people had no influence over. The temple walls depicted the work done by the king, queen, priests and priestesses. They echo the actions of the deities and show that we are supporting and appreciating their efforts even if what we do can have no other effect. Cosmic renewal is critical. It is needed by the living, the deceased and the deities. Depicting events such as the progression of time made them effective and eternal. *"The cosmos is always in motion, yet always in place."*[502]

---

[501] The Astronomical Ceiling of Deir el-Haggar in the Dakhleh Oasis, Kaper, 1995:175-195

[502] Sun, Moon & Earth, Heath, 2006:26

CHAPTER 13

Depicting the Heavens

'My head has pierced the sky. I have felt the very stars, I have reached joy, so that I shine like a star, and dance like the great constellations.'[503]

MAPPING THE SKY

By the New Kingdom tomb and temple ceilings started to be illustrated with astronomical scenes. These didn't appear as a completely new form, some basic features from the ceilings can be seen in the Middle Kingdom. A fragment of a coffin lid, possibly dating to the 11th dynasty, contains details similar to that of Senenmut's ceiling from the New Kingdom. For some reason only the Greco-Roman temples have depictions of the lunar cycle. Was the moon seen as more important at this time or were the intricacies of the lunar cycle part of a more hidden knowledge during the Pharaonic Period? Or is it just a reflection of the fact that so few

---

[503] The Living Wisdom of Ancient Egypt, Jacq, 1999:53

Pharaonic astronomical ceilings and other depictions have survived?

ASTRONOMICAL CEILINGS

Some of the astronomical ceilings that have survived, and have been restored, are beautiful and awe-inspiring. All are complex and very hard to describe in detail without accompanying diagrams or photographs so I have only included descriptions of a few. There are many photographs and drawings that can be found on-line as well as in publications. The astronomical ceilings deserve, and will repay, a more detailed study. All ceilings vary but they usually conform to a basic pattern. Differences developed for a number of reasons. Firstly there was no overriding authority so temples to specific deities could emphasise different astronomical features and myths. The ceilings were not meant to be an accurate representation of the night sky. Popular themes will have changed over time and local variations in myths and deities will have been significant. Some people will have employed more skilled and accurate craftsmen and will have had more space to accommodate the design.

An elongated arching figure of Nut usually frames the border of the ceiling the same way as she forms the border of the sky. Astronomical ceilings are spilt into at least two registers. The principal positions are north and south so the northern constellations are placed in the northern register and the decans in the southern. The constellations depicted are those orientated around Ursa Major. The arrangements and the accompanying deities vary, however three are always present. These are the Meskhetyu (either as a Foreleg or as a Bull), the Hippo and the Mooring Post. They are usually accompanied by figures of men and crocodiles. On either side of the constellations are the deities of the days and months. The 36 decans are usually listed along with some of the twelve triangle decans of the epagomenal days. A few are depicted; usually the two turtles, the ovoid, the ram and the ship. The triangle decans tend to be separated by Jupiter, Saturn and Mars although Mars is sometimes omitted. This may have just been a scribal error or because of a lack of space. Was he not visible in the sky at the time when the ceiling was designed? Or, as mentioned earlier, is Mars in the aspect of Anu? Mercury and Venus follow the triangle decans. This planetary split is based on observation as Mercury and Venus are never far from the sun while the other three planets cross the ecliptic.

THE GREEKS AND THE ZODIAC

When the Greeks introduced the concept of the zodiac the decans were assimilated into them and each decan became one-third of a zodiac sign, ten degrees. They took with them their control of fate. Zodiacs only occur in the Greco-Roman Period when they are depicted in temples, tombs and on coffin lids. They are not astronomically correct and are a mixture of Greek and Egyptian components. Some show a clockwise sequence while others are anti-clockwise. They can also be rectangular and divided into strips or halves. The zodiac signs are often the Egyptian equivalent of the Greek. Shu and Tefnut appear as Gemini and Hapy (the God of the Inundation) takes the role of Aquarius. Libra has a child within a disc balanced on top of the pair of scales. Capricorn can be depicted as a sheep and Cancer as a scarab.

The Tomb of Ramesses VI (20th dynasty) in the Valley of the Kings

Two small astronomical ceilings are placed on either side of the depiction of the *Book of the Day* and *Book of the Night*. Compared to the other decorations in his tomb, as well as to the astronomical ceilings of the Greco-Roman Period, they are quite subdued. Both have the same structure; three registers showing the decans and planets, the constellations and a row of target priests and star tables. The first register is split into three columns. There are differences in the details. They are illustrated in Piankoff.[504]

The first column on the left ceiling shows Jupiter, Saturn and Mars with the Two Turtles separating them from Venus. Sothis is also present as Isis. Orion is shown in the middle column with the Womb of Nut. On the right ceiling Jupiter and Venus have been omitted. If any planet is omitted on ceilings it is usually Mars. The

---

[504] The Tomb of Rameses VI, Piankoff, 1954:428-432

middle column contains Sothis (as Isis) and Orion in barques and the Womb of Nut as the outline of a fish with stars. In both ceilings the third column shows the ship. On the right ceiling this is next to a sheep both of which are covered in stars. Only the ship is present in the left ceiling looking as if this section was left unfinished. The constellations don't dominate the ceilings and look squashed in. On the left ceiling they are based on the Sety I version although there are some differences. There is a scorpion next to the crocodile with curved tail, which may represent Serket. Anu is very small and there is no man holding the bull's rope. The position of the constellations on the right ceiling has been shifted to the right of the register. This time it is based on the Pedamenope version with an ovoid bull. Unlike the standard Pedamenope versions there is a man aiming his spear at the Crocodile. Serket is absent as is the scorpion seen on the other ceiling.

There is no obvious reason for the differences. Perhaps the two ceilings were there mainly as space fillers around the more important *Books of the Day* and *the Night*. Size and artistic requirements may have effected what was included from the constellations and the two versions might have been used as they present slightly different mythologies. Or they were just being cautious and trying to cover all eventualities. Were the ceilings completed in a hurry? Some of the scenes look as though they are unfinished or errors were made which weren't corrected.

The Temple of Hathor at Dendera

This is a Greco-Roman temple and so has a noticeable Classical influence in areas and a different composition to the astronomical ceilings of the Pharaonic Period. However, we do not have any examples of astronomical ceilings from Pharaonic temples only tombs so cannot make a direct comparison. Given that Hathor is a Sky Goddess and in view of her relationship with Nut it is totally appropriate that the best-preserved astronomical ceilings are in Hathor's temple at Dendera.

The Outer Hypostyle Hall[505]

A cleaning and restoration program of the Hypostyle Hall ceiling began in 2008 and has produced amazing results. This ceiling is decorated with a series of six astronomical scenes divided by architraves and a central panel (running north-south) consisting of alternating patterns of the vulture of Nekhbet and the winged solar disc with two *uraie*. On both outer panels Nut forms the border as she arches over the earth. The new-born sun is depicted as a winged scarab near her hips and the winged solar disc of the setting sun is next to her mouth. When the details of the panels are examined the east-west split shows the Egyptians' love of balance. The east side focuses on the day and one half of the year while the west depicts the night and the other half of the year. The eastern outer panel depicts the twelve hours of day, as Goddesses wearing a star as a crown, while the western depicts the hours of night in the same way. Each has 18 barques carrying the decans of half of the year and each has six of the Classical constellations. Those in the east are from Aquarius through to Cancer. This, together with the allusions to the New Year, may split the year into the increasing light of the sun on the eastern panel compared to its decreasing on the other panel. This is not an exact astrological match from the winter to the summer solstice. With Cancer being equated to the scarab, and hence the rising sun, it may not have been considered appropriate to place it on the night side of the ceiling.

The western outer panel depicts the five planets and the Egyptian constellations of the Hippo, Meskhetyu and the Mooring Post. Meskhetyu is shown as a foreleg with the head and torso of a bull. His chain is clearly visible. Next to the Hippo is one of the hour Goddesses who stands in front of an oryx who has been trussed up ready for slaughter. Texts at Edfu refer to an oryx being slaughtered as part of the ritual for completing the *wedjat* eye and the waxing moon.

On the eastern panel the rays of the newborn sun shine onto a Hathor Head on top of a small shrine. One of the many New Year rituals at Dendera was carried out in secret at sunrise on New Year's

---

[505] Sistra and Constellations: The House of Hathor at Dendera, Taher, 2015:24-32

day. Hathor's cult statue was carried in procession to a chapel on the roof. The rays of the first sunrise of the year shone on the statue reuniting her with her father Ra as she did in the Return of the Distant Goddess. Inscriptions on the walls of the staircase describe how she "*raises herself...at the head of her retinue and takes her place in her boat, she illuminates her temple on New Year's Day, and she unites (her) rays with (those) of her father in the horizon*".[506] The astronomical ceiling appears to depict this ritual and perhaps the sky at the New Year. Sothis and Orion are present in their barques and next to them stand Shu and Tefnut who hold hands. This represents the return of the Distant Goddess and the arrival of the inundation following the heliacal rising of Sirius.

One other theme is present on the outer eastern panel, that of conflict and its resolution. Shu and Tefnut allude to the pacification of the Distant Goddess. The sunlight streaming onto the Hathor Head confirms the reuniting of the Sun God with his Daughter and Eye Goddess. There is a God with two faces, one human the other falcon. The falcon wears the White Crown of Upper Egypt and the man the Red Crown of Lower Egypt. This symbolises the reconciliation of Horus and Seth and the unity of the Two Kingdoms. Next to this is a composite picture showing a baboon who sits back to back with a gazelle. A falcon, wearing the Double Crown, sits on the baboon's head. The gazelle represents Seth and the baboon Thoth who was the pacifier of the Two Combatants. There is a small white disc on the baboon's thigh and one on the side of his face to emphasise his lunar aspects. It may also allude to the role these Gods play in the lunar cycle. Near the sign of Pisces is a large lunar disc. Within the disc an unidentified man carries an animal by the hind legs. The animal has been identified as a pig which was associated with Seth and was abhorrent to Horus. As such it was offered as a sacrifice at certain times. Its ears and tail look similar to that of the Seth animal, a composite creature with large erect ears and a tail that is split in two at the end. The animal may be for a sacrifice but the man has no knife. Has he caught Seth at the moment that he was attacking the full moon? Seth's action

---

[506] Hathor and Thoth: Two Key Figures of the Ancient Egyptian Religion, Bleeker, 1973:89

starts the waning cycle and so is an appropriate symbol for the section depicting the waning moon.

The second panels both depict some decans, a God of wind, two Goddesses holding up the sky and the Goddesses of day and night respectively. On the eastern panel are two depictions of the Sun God in his Solar Barque. One is pulled by three jackals representing the *bas* of the east towards four worshipping baboons. In the western panel both the Solar and Lunar Barques are present indicating opposition and a full moon. There are two Lunar Barques, one contains the *wedjat* eye inside a lunar disc. It sits on a plinth and is adored by Thoth. Osiris sits enthroned in the other barque, indicating that it is the fifteenth day and he has joined with the moon.

The third western panel shows the waxing lunar cycle. Fourteen deities are shown ascending a shallow staircase. A large *wedjat* eye is depicted inside a lunar disc which rests on a crescent on a papyrus pillar. Thoth stands on the other side of the moon on a plinth of the same height. He is the fifteenth figure and the day of the full moon. He wears an *atef* crown and raises his arms in adoration.[507] Thoth personifies everything that is exact and complete, depicted here as the full moon – whole and in its correct place united with the sun. At the other end of the register is a *wedjat* eye inside a barque, the full moon is ready to sail in splendour across the night sky. Behind Thoth on his pedestal is a section with five crouching falcons receiving offerings from Thoth and an unknown Goddess. Each falcon has a flail on his shoulder. When assuming the role of the Cosmic Falcon the God Sopedu is depicted in this form. Why is he shown five times? Does he represent the planets or is it a reference to lunar invisibility, as discussed in chapter 11? Sopedu was associated with Osiris and Min which makes it more likely that it is a lunar reference.

It would be expected that both the third panels show a similar or complementary theme, but the third panel on the eastern side disrupts the symmetry. It contains three registers rather than the two of all the other panels. The central register shows the twelve

---

[507] Sistra and Constellations: The House of Hathor at Dendera, Taher, 2015:24-32

hours of day as twelve barques each with a selection of deities on board. The other two registers depict deities and other creatures in groups of three and four. These include jackals, falcons, snakes and baboons. There are *ba*-birds with human, baboon and snake heads. There are a selection of Gods including those with ibis, baboon, jackal, falcon and lion heads.

The numbers three and four were significant for the Egyptians. Three represents plurality and can stand for many rather than the actual number three. Triads, a grouping of the deities, were common. Such a grouping can show the unity of a balanced group or signify tension as two can work against the other one or one can spilt the other two. It can also show temporal change, such as the three forms of the Sun God. In many of the funerary text spells there are references to three *bas*; such as the three *bas* of Hermopolis and the three *bas* of the easterners. Four is the number of totality and completeness. It represents the cardinal points and the four quarters of the earth. Protective spells were cast to the four directions to provide all round protection. Groups of four are also common in the funerary contexts. There are four sons of Horus and four Goddesses who guard the sarcophagus.

The animal components of the scene show three distinct themes of solar, lunar and rebirth. The ibis is a lunar creature and the lion a solar one as is the falcon. Baboons can be both. Their association with Thoth gives them a lunar aspect but they are often shown as worshipping the sun. Their natural behaviour, sitting facing the rising sun to warm up after a cold night, aligned them with the Sun God. Jackals are associated with funerary rites and resurrection aligning them with the moon and Osiris. The four sons of Horus are associated with the decans and with funerary rites. They are shown as human, falcon, jackal and baboon headed Gods. The falcon can also be associated with Sopedu and the invisible moon. Snakes can symbolise most things but they have a strong association with death, rebirth and regeneration. Following the theme of the rest of the ceiling it would be expected that the eastern panel shows the waning moon and lunar invisibility. During its waning cycle the moon is increasingly diurnal and moves closer to the sun until it is lost in its light. Then it is assumed to have died and begun its process of rebirth. Is this what is being hinted at with these seemingly disparate groups of deities? They do have the look of some of the netherworld vignettes. Some of the deities are shown squatting which can be seen as a metaphor for the waning moon alluding to its fading energy and light.

The Round Zodiac[508]

There are many depictions of this online and in books. The zodiac dates to about 50 BCE. Originally it was in the chapel of Osiris but was removed to the Louvre Museum (Paris) in 1828. It is supported by four standing Goddesses at the cardinal points interspersed with four pairs of kneeling falcon-headed Gods. Deities representing the decans are shown on the outer rim in an anticlockwise procession. At the centre, signifying their lasting importance, is the Egyptian constellation group of the Hippo, the Mooring Post and Meskhetyu (as the Foreleg). The Hippo is without the crocodile, or stylized cloak on her back, the same as on the hypostyle ceiling. A hint of the ancient north-south split of the sky remains. Towards the rim is the decan group of Sothis, depicted as a recumbent cow with a star on her head, and Orion. He no longer turns his head to look at Sothis. In a loose circle around the Egyptian constellations are the zodiac figures. Scattered throughout are depictions of the sun, moon and five planets. The sun and moon are familiar; the *wedjat* eye in a disc and a falcon-headed Ra-Horakhty sitting in a barque.

A collection of animal-headed Gods show the planets. One has a bull's head so may be Saturn as Horus Bull of the Sky. Another has two heads so could be Horus-Seth as Mercury. It is believed that some of the other depictions are of the decans. Satis and Anukis are positioned behind Sothis and behind them a woman or Goddess holds a child in her hand. If this is Isis it would tie the whole group to the inundation. There is a man holding a small animal next to a decapitated animal symbolising a sacrifice. Two depictions from the Hypostyle ceiling are present. The composite baboon, gazelle and falcon as well as a disc containing a woman carrying a small animal by the leg. Lull and Belmonte suggest that the figure in the disc refers to an eclipse which took place in Pisces

---

[508] The Constellations of Ancient Egypt, Lull & Belmonte, 2009:178-184

because it is positioned directly under Pisces. This figure is placed near Pisces on the Hypostyle ceiling as well. Between the Hippo and Meskhetyu is a jackal on a hoe, similar in form to its hieroglyph sign. This is also held by a bull-headed man who hasn't been identified. Is he a duplication of Jupiter or Saturn or an amalgamation of the falcon-headed Anu and Meskhetyu as a bull? The hoe was a symbol of fertility, via grain, and was very important in mortuary rituals. It alluded to the death and rebirth of the deceased just as Osiris was present in the death and rebirth of grain. The jackal, either Anubis or Wepwawet as Opener of the Ways, was strongly associated with the afterlife journey. A relief in the temple of Dendera depicts the king using a hoe to dig the first trench in one of the foundation rituals. Given its position next to Meskhetyu the hoe with a jackal may also allude to the foundation of the temple which was aligned to this constellation. The bull-headed man with a hoe could refer to the bull of Seth as Meskhetyu.

There is a small recumbent animal on the Foreleg which is hard to decipher. One suggestion is a bear to represent Ursa Major, this seems unlikely to me as bears had no symbolism for the Egyptians. Another suggestion is that it is a ram and this figure does have a similar profile to the ram depicting Aries. Why it and the jackal are so close to the Foreleg isn't clear. Possibly they refer to specific stars in that constellation, or to a stellar alignment that appeared auspicious or was related to the temple or ceilings construction. An unknown woman holds the tail of Leo. In other zodiacs this is Virgo but here this woman stands between Virgo and Leo. She may be Serket. Leo stands on a snake barque and an unidentifiable bird sits on the stern. It is likely to be a falcon given their symbolic significance. Serpent barques are common in the Netherworld Texts which may have provided the inspiration. They give added protection and are better able to traverse the desert regions of the *duat*. Other unknown figures include what appears to be a mongoose with a human torso who wears the White Crown of Upper Egypt. She offers something to the second lion who turns his head to look at it. The mongoose was sacred to Horus and Atum as it kills snakes. The Goddess Mafdet could take the form of a mongoose. She is an ancient protective Goddess usually associated with leopards or cheetahs. Following close to Orion is a walking bird with a prominent crest and upturned tail. The nearest identification I can find is an African Hoopoe but these are usually depicted with the crest displayed. They don't appear to have any specific symbolism. These zodiacs were never intended to be an astronomical representation of the sky but a symbolic representation of the heavens as well as illustrating rituals and myths. The Egyptian artists did not like empty spaces and these would have been filled with related symbols and representations. Some of the depictions may be of asterisms which we are unaware of.

The Temple at Deir el-Hagger[509]

The astronomical ceiling of this Roman temple in the Dakhleh Oasis is dated to approximately the 2nd century CE. Most known astronomical ceilings are located where they can be seen or in rooms with mortuary significance. This one is located in the sanctuary of the temple making it unique, the only other known example was in a *mammisi* which was demolished. There is a strong lunar presence in the temple. Amun and Khonsu are given almost equal status on reliefs on the temple walls. Thoth and Amun are depicted in the *pronaos* receiving gifts from the king. Mut and Nehmataway, the consorts of Amun and Thoth, are also present on the reliefs. Mut is the Great Goddess of Thebes, a Solar Goddess. Very little is known about Nehmataway. Thoth was an important member of the pantheon in the area and there was a cult of his at a nearby temple. The pair were also venerated together at Bahriya Oasis.

The ceiling consists of four registers divided north and south by a central register while an elongated figure of Nut forms the border. The north-south split of Egyptian constellations and decans has been followed but reversed. In the southern register are the Hippo, Meskhetyu and the Mooring post while in the northern are Sothis and Orion in their barques separated by Horus as a falcon wearing the Double Crown. Above Horus, near the hands of Nut, is the sun disc. Next to Orion is a large figure in a curled acrobatic

---

[509] The Astronomical Ceiling of Deir el-Haggar in the Dakhleh Oasis, Kaper, 1995:175-195

posture thought to be Geb. It is similar in posture to one of Osiris in the *Book of Gates*. Within the space enclosed by Geb is a figure who appears to be Hapy. He stands next to a grid which may represent fields. This suggests that the vignette celebrates the fertility of the land brought by the rebirth of Osiris. The temple is located in the Dakhleh Oasis so wouldn't have been effected by the inundation. Without an annual layer of silt to fertilise the fields the emphasis on the fertilising power of Geb and Osiris is understandable. Ten figures follow. Most appear to represent decans apart from Venus as a heron on a pedestal. Due to a lack of space on the ceiling a few representative depictions have to stand for the whole.

The second register depicts the waxing lunar cycle with a procession of sixteen deities facing the *wedjat* eye in a disc. Sixteen is an unusual number, it is normally fourteen or fifteen deities shown with the waxing moon. Kaper suggests that the importance of opposition and the joint presence of both the sun and moon may have been the reason for the sixteen deities. The sun and moon are both above the horizon on the sixteenth day of the lunar month, this can only occur after the moon has become full. The extended number of deities ensures the appearance of the full moon.

One distinct feature of this ceiling is the emphasis on the opposition of the sun and moon. They unite as discs, as Amun-Re and Thoth and finally as Amun and Khonsu in person. Squashed into the central band, and impinging on the register below, are depictions of the sun and moon at conjunction and at opposition. Conjunction is shown as two figures holding hands in a barque, one wears a solar disc the other a lunar disc. To the right of this are two barques, one carries a child within a solar disc and the other a baboon inside a lunar disc. The child and baboon face each other symbolising opposition and a full moon. The Dakhleh Oasis was far from the main religious and cultural centres and so had its own strong local cult. In the Theban tradition the sun and moon act out the process of divine succession as Amun temporarily vacates his position to his son Khonsu. This may also have been the tradition followed at Deir el-Haggar given the central positioning of the depiction.

The third register depicts the night-time journey of the Sun God. At the far right of the register is a crescent moon. Next to it is a barque carrying a disc which is pulled by three jackals. Above the barque is a lunar disc. This was deliberately obscured by plaster and replaced by text. Was this the correction of a mistake, possibly the full and crescent moon shown together? Or perhaps something significant happened during the decoration of the ceiling that was taken as an omen. The lower register depicts the two winds and twelve deities who may represent the hours of the night or the months of the year. Kaper says that four of them are deities of the lunar calendar: Hathor, Khonsu, Khentykhety and Ra-Horakhty, the other eight may represent deities from the local tradition.

The Tomb at Athribis

Two zodiacs were found in a tomb at Athribis dating to the middle 2nd century CE. There are illustrations available on-line. None of the traditional Egyptian constellations are present but some of the signs of the zodiac have an Egyptian style. Differing from those previously mentioned are Libra where a falcon in a sun disc rests on the top of the scales. Sagittarius is shown with a lion's head at the back of his head and a pair of wings emerging from the back of the horse. Both zodiacs have stars scattered throughout and two lunar discs, one with a crescent attached. There are also *ba*-birds, some of which have falcon, bull or snake heads. One appears to have the head of Seth on the top of a bird's head. The composition is framed by a large number of snakes of varying forms. There are rearing snakes and cobras, human-headed cobras, falcon-headed snakes and winged snakes. The second zodiac also includes snakes with a head at each end and two wearing a solar disc and horns.

The first zodiac depicts Sothis as a recumbent cow in a barque and Orion as a man aiming a spear. Unlike the conventional depictions of the pair they are close but Orion is rotated 90° and doesn't look at Sothis. The Lunar and Solar Barques are present accompanied by worshipping deities. These are absent from the second zodiac. This depicts what appears to be Horus and Seth holding hands as they stand on the back of a walking sphinx, alluding to their reconciliation. A baboon with a bow appears to shoot at no obvious target. The Ptolemaic papyrus Leiden mentions the constellation of a baboon with a bow, which seems to represent Thoth and his role in bringing back the Distant Goddess and the inundation. *"You are the baboon with his bow."* The text then tells us that *"he hung the bow into the sky and the arrows are her stars"*.[510] This constellation does not appear on the astronomical ceilings or in the lists of decans and constellations, unless it is the unidentified Ape from the onomasticon. This is a strange given the importance of the myth of the Distant Goddess in the Pharaonic Period. There is a God with what looks like a lion or dog head at the back of his head which may have been inspired by the composite Horus-Seth figures. Another composite figure is a stork with a heavy bill who wears a wig and has a snake emerging from his tail feathers. What stories these composite non-zodiac creatures tell is largely open to speculation. Did they all have a specific meaning or were some either copied at random from Pharaonic art or inspired by them.

OTHER DEPICTIONS OF THE ZODIAC

In the Roman Period the signs of the zodiac were often painted on coffins alongside Nut. One coffin from the family tomb of Soter depicts Nut on the inside lid and she is surrounded by the twelve signs of the zodiac and the Goddesses of the Hours. On Heter's coffin the positions of the planets are given and his horoscope for October 93 CE.[511] The trio of the Hippo, the Mooring Post and Meskhetyu have disappeared either because their symbolism wasn't understood or they were considered irrelevant. Two tombs in the Dakhla Oasis contain zodiacs on their ceilings. One is the tomb of Petosiris the other of Petubastis, both dating to the Roman Period. They are a strange mix of Egyptian, Greek and Mithraic symbols. This amalgamation of different religious and cultural symbolism is quite common in the Roman Period. Like many of us in the western world, the Romans frequently appropriated or adopted what appealed to them for both religious and decorative purposes.

---

[510] A Goddess Rising 10,000 Cubits into the Air…or Only One Cubit, One Finger? Quack, 2002:288
[511] The Secret Lore of Egypt, Hornung, 2001:31

MYTHIC MAP OR ASTRONOMICAL CHART?

The astronomical ceilings were never intended to be charts of the night sky. They give a summary of the understanding of the cosmos and its cycles interspersed with important mythologies. The stories explain the science to the lay person, and make them more memorable, while the science enhances the stories. The overriding purpose of the astronomical symbols on tomb and coffin decoration was as a guide for the deceased. On temple ceilings they were a way of emphasising the importance of the night sky and its cycles, for demonstrating scientific knowledge and for the pleasure of the temple deities. The mythology and symbolism was of paramount importance as were the artistic guidelines portraying *maat*.

CHAPTER 14

Aligning with Heaven

"I hold the peg. I grasp the handle of the club and grip the
measuring cord with Seshat. I turn my eyes to the movement of
the stars. I send forth my glance to Ursa Major... I make firm
the corners of thy temple."[512]

IN TUNE WITH THE COSMOS

Aligning with heaven – whether it is done by recording and
celebrating the lunar cycle, aligning a temple with a particular star
or celebrating festivals according to the behaviour of various stars
– was, and still is, considered beneficial. It honours the deities who
reside in the heavenly bodies and who are responsible for the
celestial patterns and cycles. Working with these cycles and the
actions of the deities aligns us with the currents of heaven,
encouraging us to work with and not against cosmic *maat*. Working
with divine forces and energies is far more productive than working

---

[512] An Ancient Method of Finding and Extending Direction, Isler, 1989:191-206

against them. The Goddesses and Gods may not need their temples aligned to the star in which their *ba* resides but we do. It gives a focus for the building and the rituals as well as providing a connecting conduit between heaven and earth.

SESHAT THE LADY OF ARCHITECTS

As well as being associated with writing and notation Seshat was very much involved in the construction of temples and other monuments. *"The King himself and the goddess Seshat, the great one, established the plan."*[513] She could also be referred to as Sefkhet-Abwy which means the one of seven horns.[514] This may refer to the seven stars of the Plough or to her crown. This is very distinctive consisting of a seven pointed star or rosette on a tall stem. After the 19th dynasty it is sometimes depicted with five rays. Above this is what has been described as inverted horns, a bow or a lunar crescent but to me, and others, is more like an instrument. The form does vary considerably.

Belmonte proposes that her crown is a schematic representation of a surveying instrument which is depicted flat.[515] The seven spokes and the stem are in fact eight spokes on a horizontal wheel. Two spokes are attached to a semi-circular arc at the apex of which is a two pronged eye piece. The surveyor would align the instrument to the relevant star and the spokes would mark off the cardinal and quarter directions. This is an appropriate form for her crown as she played a vital role in the laying out the ground plan of formal buildings. She assisted the king in the *stretching of the cord* ceremony. This ritual is attested to from the 2nd dynasty and references to it continue into the Ptolemaic Period. The name of the ceremony was *pedj-sesh* providing a strong hint at the origins of her name.

The foundation ceremony was considered critical which was why Seshat was involved. She ensured that the temple was correctly aligned with whatever celestial or other object was chosen. Temple

---

[513] The Temple of Edfu, Kurth, 2004:49
[514] The Complete Gods and Goddesses of Ancient Egypt, Wilkinson, 2003:166
[515] Unveiling Seshat: new insights into the stretching of the cord ceremony, Belmonte, 2009:197

construction followed strict rules. It is reasonable to suggest that this critical process was first surveyed by the professionals and later carried out ceremonially on an auspicious date. Thutmose III *"commanded the preparation of the stretching the cord while waiting for the day of the new moon in order to stretch the cord around this building"*.[516] Texts from the temple of Horus at Edfu say that the stretching of the cord ceremony was carried out on 23rd August 253 BCE, which was on the sixth lunar day. A cord was stretched around two poles to define the axis of the temple. Texts from the temple of Hathor at Dendera explain how *"the king stretches the rope in joy. With his glance toward the Akh of Meskhetyu, he establishes the temple of the Lady of Dendera"*.[517] The *akh* may refer to the *akh* of Seth but some say that in this context it can be translated as the brilliant star of *Meskhetyu*. However the seven stars of the Plough are of similar brightness. It could refer to a specific star in the constellation or to a specific orientation of the constellation.

TEMPLE ALIGNMENT

The most common temple orientation is east-west, some temples are oriented towards points in the solar cycle others are oriented towards specific stars or constellations. Topographical alignment cannot be ignored either, such as towards a distinctive feature on the horizon. Other structures will have been aligned to important pre-existing buildings or to locations which were significant in the myths. Belmonte and his team looked at 330 temples in their study and found a high proportion were oriented to the east or to the winter solstice sunrise. For temples on the Nile it comes as no surprise that the most common orientation was on an axis perpendicular to the Nile as this was where the main gate was located.[518] The Nile symbolically flowed south-north so symbolically east-west was perpendicular to this. Orientation to the Nile might have been more important in some cases than a true east-west axis.

---

[516] Egyptian Festival Dating and the Moon, Spalinger, 2002:389

[517] Unveiling Seshat: new insights into the stretching of the cord ceremony, Belmonte, 2009:203

[518] Astronomy, Landscape and Symbolism, Belmonte et al, 2009:221

Crown of Seshat

A deity associated with a particular star was more likely to have a stellar orientation than a deity without such a connection. Alignment with a pre-existing temple might take precedence. Of the 34 temples dedicated to Goddesses most were oriented to Sirius then to Canopus whereas the 42 dedicated to the Solar Gods were mostly oriented towards key points in the solar cycle.[519]

The constellation of Meskhetyu is depicted as a bull with an ovoid body in the astronomical ceiling of Senenmut. Where its tail would be is a line which connects three stars in a row, the last one is red and encircled by a red ring. Beneath it is a very long triangular object, like a blade, whose apex is at the red star. Lull and Belmonte suggest that this is the star Alkaid (the outermost star of the Plough). It has been suggested that this star was used as a reference when aligning temples such as Dendera.[520] If this is correct then Alkaid may be the *akh* of Meskhetyu mentioned above. The fact that the triangular shape in this ceiling looks very much like the sighting stick of the *merkhet*, or merely lines of sight for triangulation purposes, suggests to me that it may well be a reference to a star used for surveying purposes but many others disagree.

Nabta Playa

Nabta Playa is located about 300km west of Abu Simbel on the shore of a former lake. It was an important religious centre about 6,000 to 6,500 years ago. The site consists of a number of features. There is a small stone circle, about 4m in diameter, made up of about 50 upright slabs. Some are arranged in a series of gates which are thought to align with the rising sun at the summer solstice. Another cluster of *stelae* appear to date to the Naqada II Period. One suggestion is that they faced the circumpolar region of the sky, the home of the imperishable stars which became so important in the *Pyramid Texts*. There are three lines of megaliths in the northern part of the site. Some investigators say that they were aligned to the rising of Ursa Major. Another double alignment is said to point to the rising stars of Orion's belt with one line and to the rise of Sirius

---

[519] Astronomy, Landscape and Symbolism, Belmonte et al, 2009:227
[520] The Constellations of Ancient Egypt, Lull & Belmonte, 2009:161

with the other at a specific time of the year.[521] The problem with the site is that the stones have collapsed and could well have been moved in antiquity. It is not possible to date exactly when they were erected so ascertaining the correct alignments is never going to be an exact science. The function of the site is highly likely to have changed over the time it was in use and stones may have been relocated, as they have been at stone circles from other cultures. What it does show is the importance of the celestial orientation of religious structures and the predecessors of temples in Ancient Egypt.

The Pyramids

The popular theory that the layout of the three pyramids at Giza mirrors Orion's belt isn't accepted by most professional Egyptologists. They argue that the similarity is just a coincidence. The human mind is good at recognising patterns but this doesn't always work in our favour, there is a risk that we see what we want to see and find a false pattern where there is no correlation just natural coincidences. Did Khufu (4th dynasty) really determine where his two successors would build their pyramids? Or did the astronomers of the third king Menkaura (4th dynasty) spot a potential pattern and follow it? Another argument is that the pyramids are aligned at their north-west corners but as they are of different sizes they appear misaligned. They were designed to be viewed from the river where they appear evenly spaced and on the horizon. As the horizon was associated with the rising sun and rebirth this was a significant feature.

The Great Pyramid is aligned to true north with an error of only $3/60^{th}$ of a degree. Spence suggests that the Great Pyramid was aligned to the cardinal points using Mizar (in Ursa Major) and Kochab (in Ursa Minor) which rotated around the pole star. These were in perfect alignment around 2467 BCE when the Great Pyramid was built. Inaccuracies in alignment of earlier and later pyramids can be correlated with the deviation of these two stars from true north.[522] The entrance and symbolic exit of most of the

---

[521] Nabta Playa Saved, Betz, 200926-30
[522] The British Museum Dictionary of Ancient Egypt, Shaw & Nicholson, 2008:45-46

pyramids were on the northern face as this is where the imperishable stars lie. Those of the Great Pyramid were angled towards Thuban, the pole star at that time.[523] The shafts of the Great Pyramid appear to have been aligned to various stars. Taylor suggests that the northern shaft was aligned to Thuban and the other to Alnitak in Orion's belt.[524]

Sirius

Belmonte suggests that the site for the temple of Hathor at Dendera was chosen because at that particular spot the Nile flowed from the direction where the helical rising of Sirius was seen.[525] However, the temple is aligned to Meskhetyu as stated in its foundation texts. There is a small temple to Isis at Dendera, located at the southwest corner of the main temple. Its axis is aligned to the heliacal rising of Sirius. References to the birth of Isis occur on the south and west walls of the main temple and in the small temple. Richter points out that the word used for the phrase 'to be born' can also mean 'helical rising' equating the birth of Isis with the heliacal rising of Sirius.[526]

An 11th dynasty temple to Horus on Thoth's Hill in Thebes was built on a 2° different orientation to the original Pre-dynastic temple. Both were orientated towards the heliacal rising of Sirius which had moved 2° further north during the intervening years. In this case the precise orientation to the star was more important than following the lines of the earlier temple. As to be expected the temple at Elephantine, the traditional source of the inundation, was oriented towards the helical rising of Sirius.[527]

The Temple of Horus at Edfu

This temple is unusual in that it is orientated north-south with the main entrance to the north. Temples on the west bank of the Nile tend to have the main entrance facing the Nile. Was this to

---

[523] Symbol & Magic in Egyptian Art, Wilkinson, 1994: 65
[524] Celestial Geometry, Taylor, 2012:172
[525] Astronomy, Landscape and symbolism, Belmonte et al, 2009:219
[526] The Theology of Hathor of Dendera, Richter, 2016:96
[527] The Complete Temples of Ancient Egypt, Wilkinson, 2000:37

differentiate it from the solar cults? Texts on the temple wall state that it was orientated by aligning two stakes on a star; Orion in the south and Ursa Major in the north.[528] The temple was inaugurated, handed over to Horus, on an auspicious date. This was *"on the day of the union of Osiris with the left eye of Ra"* on the day of the *senut* festival in the second month of *Shemu*.[529] Important as Nut was she did not have dedicated temples, as far as we are aware. The building texts from Edfu hint at an explanation for this. The open air offering court was described as the *"perfect palace of Nut"*.[530] Rather than dedicate an enclosed temple to Nut the Egyptians felt that she was best honoured through spaces which were always open to her skies.

FIXED FOR ETERNITY

The great length of Egyptian civilisation is highlighted by the fact that the stars themselves moved during that time. Aligning a temple with a star or astronomical event might have been critical at the foundation ceremony but the temple could never be physically aligned for eternity even though conceptually it was forever aligned to its guiding star. The other way of following the sacred patterns of the sky was through rituals and festivals.

STELLAR CULTS

It is unlikely that there was a general stellar cult in Egypt comparable to the lunar cult. It is more probable that various cults and mythologies were focused on a particular star or asterism. The heliacal rising of Sirius and its connection to the inundation is the prime example. The *bas* of the deities were considered to reside in the stars so the various cults will have had a stellar focus that is not always obvious to us. Hardy's work on the Cairo Calendar, discussed earlier, hints at a stellar origin or component to a number of the festivals with specific stars aligned to certain deities. In which case the stellar aspects of cults are embedded in the rituals and festivals throughout the year.

---

[528] The House of Horus at Edfu, Watterson, 1998:87
[529] The Temple of Edfu, Kurth, 2004:52
[530] The Temple of Edfu, Kurth, 2004:48

As the planets were mostly aligned to Horus and Seth, and Sirius and Orion were aligned to Isis and Osiris, the patterns and movements of the stars and planets throughout the year will have fed into their mythologies and rituals. If Apophis was aligned with Hydra the rituals against Apophis may well have originated in and been reflected by the constellation's movements throughout the year. Much of this is now buried too deep for easy identification, but religion is never intended to be dissected in such a way. All is interconnected. The stars reflect the actions of the deities and this is reflected in human lives and events on earth, both natural and manmade. Actions on earth connect to and influence divine affairs – hence the role of prayers, offerings and rituals. 11th and 12th dynasty *Coffin Texts* list offerings to stars. "*A boon which is given to the Foreleg in the northern sky; a boon which is given to Nut; a boon which is given to Orion in the southern sky.*"[531]

The Egyptians did not worship a particular star or asterism, they worshipped the Goddess or God whose *ba* manifested there. The persistence of stellar decorations and motifs in temples, tombs and coffins from the early Middle Kingdom to the Greco-Roman Period emphasises the importance of stars. An observer watching the stars along the southern horizon of the sky will see them move from the left as they rise in the east to the right where they set in the west. Locher suggests that it was this movement that became the model for religious processions.[532]

LUNAR CULTS

Triads became popular in the New Kingdom and at Thebes Khonsu formed a triad with Amun and Mut as their son. Amun was a prominent God at the time so the presence of Khonsu in a triad with him and the Goddess Mut may have raised the profile of the lunar cult. Khonsu might have been included because of the importance of the lunar cult at the time or merely because triads became popular and he acted as a counterbalance to Mut as the Solar Eye. The cult of Osiris was becoming increasingly popular

---

[531] Egypt's Dazzling Sun: Amenhotep III and his World, Kozloff & Bryan, 1992:336
[532] Gods Coming from the Left, Locher, 2016:93

and Osiris has a close connection to the lunar cycle so it may have been a way of incorporating that cult as well. Lunar cycles were popular subjects in Greco-Roman temples. Both Isis and Osiris had strong lunar attributes by that time which would have increased the moon's importance.

Amenhotep III (18th dynasty) was sometimes identified as a Lunar God while his wife Queen Tiy was identified with the Solar Eye Goddess. He built a temple at Soleb, Nubia, dedicated to Amun-Ra and Nebmaatra who was a local version of the Lunar God Khonsu. One ritual held there was *"illuminating the dais"* where Nebmaatra was invoked to ensure the regular appearance of the full moon by healing the Eye of Horus.[533] The temple held rites for the *Pacification of the Goddess.* In these the Eye of the Sun God (in the person of Queen Tiy) *"joined the deity Nebmaatra to return to Egypt and restore order to the world"*.[534] Did this lunar emphasis in the far south of the country balance the solar emphasis in the north? At these latitudes the temperatures might have been considered hot enough without the additional emphasis on the solar powers.

There is a Greco-Roman temple at Athribis dedicated to Repit and Min. Repit is a Lioness Goddess who takes the role of the Distant Goddess and the Solar Eye. Her presence gave a feminine solar balance to Min and the pair could represent the solar-lunar cycle. The eastern staircase in the temple at Athribis depicts various lunar rituals which were carried out as the priests and priestesses ascended via the staircase to the roof at the full moon. *"He who illuminates the two countries with his radiant light, after he has replaced the sun disc…after he has enlightened the ones on earth with his beaming."*[535] In one room in this temple the king is depicted worshipping a *wedjat* eye on a shrine which suggests that this was a cult object. Another shows the king offering the *wedjat* eye to Min. *"Take for you the Living Eye, equipped with its parts."*[536]

The lunar processions depicted in temples may have been acted out in rituals. In magic, counting upwards focuses on growth, as the

---

[533] The British Museum Dictionary of Ancient Egypt, Shaw & Nicholson, 2008:310
[534] Between Two Worlds, Torok, 2009:232
[535] Of Min and Moon, Altmann-Wendling, 2017:10
[536] Of Min and Moon, Altmann-Wendling, 2017:9

numbers increase so does the object under the spell. This sympathetic magic may have been an important part of waxing moon rituals. According to Clement of Alexandria (150-215 CE), some of the priests would carry books describing the movements of the sun and moon in processions during the Osiris festivals. The Egyptians were always happiest when both Eyes of Heaven were present, balanced and equal. In the astronomical ceiling of the Ramesseum the king is included in the procession of lunar deities which may indicate that he was part of a lunar cult. One lunar cult object comes from the Fayum, it is formed of a half cylinder split into five compartments. Each end is decorated with a disc containing a pig surrounded by fifteen dots. Both the pig and the number fifteen have strong lunar connections.[537] The cylinder would have been used in waxing cycle rituals and each compartment filled as the days passed and the moon waxed to full. A variety of monthly rituals will have been performed to ensure that the Lunar Eye was filled and then to celebrate the full moon. One *Coffin Texts* spell refers to a "*vessel containing the factional components of the eye*".[538] This vessel was probably filled with grain, or something similar, in parts equal to the Horus fractions as the waxing progressed.

In one spell from the *Book of Two Ways* the deceased say that they celebrated the monthly and midmonth festivals and "*examines the eight*".[539] Faulkner translates this as the eighth-garment. It may be a reference to ritual clothing used during the lunar rituals. Was it added to and taken away from a statue to reflect the waxing and waning of the moon? Was it an offering based on the lunar cycle? We can only speculate.

Sennefer's statue refers to himself as "*one pure of hands and pure of fingers when offering to Iah-Thoth*".[540] Ritual purity was essential for those taking part in any ceremony, but the reference to fingers as well as hands seems unnecessary unless it was relating to specific

---

[537] The Ancient Egyptian Book of the Moon: Coffin Texts Spells 154-160, Priskin, 2019:14
[538] The Ancient Egyptian Book of the Moon: Coffin Texts Spells 154-160, Priskin, 2019:46
[539] The Ancient Egyptian Book of Two Ways, Lesko, 1977:47 spell 1151
[540] The Moon god Iah in ancient Egyptian Religion, Garcia-Fernandez, 2017:224

rituals associated with completing the Lunar Eye using his fingers as Thoth will have done.

In funerary spells the deceased often claim knowledge of names, *bas* and places. Such as knowing the *bas* of Hermopolis and of the New Moon for example. In one of the lunar *Coffin Texts* spells the deceased claim to know more than the High Priest in Heliopolis, hinting at secrets of an exclusive lunar cult. This is followed by statements regarding initiation, keeping their secrets and participating in festivals. Funerary spells were also relevant to the living, according to their claims. "*It is good for the dead to have this knowledge, but also for a person on earth, a remedy – a million times proved.*"[541] Knowledge is gained in two ways; by study and by practical application and experience. The spells merely give basic details or a summary of the key parts. As with any profession, entrants into the cult would learn the basic details of the subject and basic practical skills, becoming more skilled and gaining a deeper understanding as they progressed along their path. Rituals may have been followed without understanding at first. Parts of the liturgy might have been unspoken and known only by the cult leaders. Initiation would be the first step to acquiring mystical knowledge and ritual experience.

The secret knowledge of the moon obviously has to be more than astronomical facts that any layperson could work out if they were diligent in their moon watching. The secret knowledge is mythical and mystical knowledge and would have involved using the lunar cycle as the key to entering into the presence of the deities or communicating with them. As the initiates, priests and priestesses carried out the physical rituals their *ba* did the same in the divine realm. Opening the doors to the shrine was paralleled by the opening of the doors of earth and heaven so that the *ba* could travel through. Vast amounts of incense were used in the temples and music and song accompanied rituals. One consequence of this was that it could induce the participants to enter into a trance-like state or altered consciousness. The myth explains about the divine realm while the ritual creates a way to access it.

---

[541] Knowledge for the Afterlife, Abt & Hornung, 2003:9

Rituals acted out at key points in the lunar cycle, or even every night, opened the portal to the deities behind the cycles. Observing the moon rising in the *mentjat-bowl* or participating in the processions enacting the filling of the Lunar Eye would have been more than just physical actions for the initiates. Sacred experience is frequently impossible to put into words. It must be both experienced and then interpreted. *"Praise to Thoth...who knows the secrets and interprets their words."*[542]

Secret knowledge, allowing a person to connect to the divine world, needed to be protected and restricted. Sometimes this is for the good; it is too dangerous for the uninitiated to attempt and could result in harm to the individual, to society or to creation. At other times it is for elitist reasons. Knowledge is power and is restricted for the sole benefit of a chosen few. Secret could also mean something sacred and difficult. Something that can only be accessed through ritual and understood within a sacred environment. Knowledge that would evaporate like a dream if used or accessed in the physical world. One version of *Coffin Texts* spell 156 ends *"it is something difficult to understand at night, it is known only in the temple at night"*.[543]

LUNAR FESTIVALS

There were two basic types of festivals. Seasonal ones were based on the civil calendar or the actual event and held annually, such as harvest and inundation. Religious ones were based on the lunar calendar and could be held monthly, such as every fifteenth day, or annually such as the first full moon of a particular season. Feast lists were inscribed on walls in temples and tombs from the Old Kingdom. The phase of the moon sometimes affected the nature of festivals which were based on the civil calendar. A list from the temple of Edfu states that the eighteenth day of the first month of *Akhet* (Inundation) was a feast for Shu and Tefnut but if it coincided with a full moon it became a full festival day.

---

[542] Secrets, Knowledge and Experience in Ancient Egyptian Religion, Joergensen, 2006:69

[543] Secrets, Knowledge and Experience in Ancient Egyptian Religion, Joergensen, 2006:34

The Blacked-out Moon festival was held on the day when the moon was not visible. The Monthly Festival, also called the Head of the Month or New Crescent, was the day of the first crescent. At full moon came the Half Moon festival which was called the Fifteenth Day festival in the New Kingdom. There was no definitive list at any period and the popularity of lunar festivals varies considerably. The Middle Kingdom coffin of Ma from Beni Hassan lists the first to sixth days, the fifteenth, seventeenth, twenty-ninth and thirtieth days as festivals. Other lists give the Coming Forth of the *Sem* Priest (the fourth day) and the Coming Forth of Min (the thirtieth day).[544]

The sixth day isn't a significant point in the lunar cycle so its origin is unclear. Was this a solar festival which was inserted into the lunar cycle? One suggestion is that it was originally called the sixth part festival and was held at the summer solstice. As there are six months between the solstices and six parts to the *wedjat* eye, the Solar Eye could be viewed as having six parts as well. These decreased as the sun moved south in winter and increased as it moved north. The Cairo Calendar's entry for the summer solstice reads *"celebrate your god and satisfy your akh since this eye of Horus has arrived, filled and healed while nothing remains to be counted"*. [545] Alternatively it might have been a local full moon festival at Heliopolis, perhaps one nearest a solstice. When Heliopolis became dominant it was added to the monthly lunar calendar.

Te Velde suggests that the sixth day was important because of the Eye fractions. On the first day 1/64 was added to the dark moon. On the second day 1/32 was added, continuing in this manner until the sixth day when 1/2 was added.[546] This sums to 63/64 which fills or completes the Eye with the exception of the $1/64^{th}$ which has to be provided by Thoth. Given the importance of the Eye fractions and the emphasis on filling the Eye this seems a reasonable explanation to me.

---

[544] Monthly Lunar Festivals in the Mortuary Realm: Historical Patterns and Symbolic Motifs, Eaton, 2011:229-245

[545] Secrets, Knowledge and Experience in Ancient Egyptian Religion, Joergensen, 2006:17

[546] Seth, God of Confusion, te Velde, 1967:49

In the funerary texts the deceased confirm that they have celebrated the various lunar festivals. One spell in the *Book of the Dead* was to be recited on the last day of the second month of winter *"when the Sacred Eye has been reckoned up…and it stands complete and contented"*.[547] The text says that the spell has to be recited over a *wedjat* eye made of lapis lazuli or carnelian and decorated with gold. It mentions that a festival of all the deities is celebrated that day and offerings made to the Sacred Eye. By including this in the funerary text the deceased could participate in, and benefit from, the offerings made on that day and the rebirth associations of completing the Eye.

Some spells in the *Pyramid Texts* associate lunar festivals with purification rites as well as with offerings for the deities and the deceased. The moon may have been considered purified as it apparently passes through the sun during its days of invisibility. *"May you be pure at the monthly festival, may you be manifest at the New Moon, may the three-day festival be celebrated for you."*[548] Lunar festivals were strongly tied to the cult of Osiris. One text from a Greco-Roman papyrus states that it is to be recited *"at the sixth day festival, the half-month and monthly festivals and at every festival of Osiris by the chief lector priest of this temple"*.[549] One calendar from Edfu gives details of festivals for Hathor. The fifteenth day feast was a *"day of full moon; a great feast in all the land…a pig is cut up and placed on an altar at the river bank"*.[550] Another festival for Horus and Hathor in the third month of *Shemu* was the *"day of the New Moon; performing Opening of the Mouth before this noble god Horus"*.[551]

In the *Book of the Dead* spell 125 refers to the filling, or completing, of the Sacred Eye in Heliopolis on the last day of the second month of *Peret*. A full moon on this day would have been symbolically significant as it split the year in half. Given Thoth's love of balance it may have been considered sacred to him.

---

[547] The Ancient Egyptian Book of the Dead, Faulkner, 1989:132 spell 140

[548] The Ancient Egyptian Pyramid Texts, Faulkner, 2007:170 utt 483

[549] Monthly Lunar Festivals in the Mortuary Realm: Historical Patterns and Symbolic Motifs, Eaton, 2011:229-245

[550] Temple Festival Calendars of Ancient Egypt, el-Sabban, 2000:173

[551] Temple Festival Calendars of Ancient Egypt, el-Sabban, 2000:179

At the festival of the Beautiful Union the cult statue of Hathor was taken in her barque to the temple of Horus of Edfu. It was held in the month of *Epiphi* and was carefully timed to arrive at Edfu for the new moon. The entire festival lasted fourteen days. It was in part a fertility rite as well as a celebration of the first harvest. It also had lunar associations, hence the timing to coincide with the new moon and the fourteen day duration of the festival. These are just a few of the references to lunar festivals. The religious calendar was the lunar calendar so a festival might not relate directly to the phase of the moon; it was just that it was a convenient marker.

WRITTEN IN THE STARS?

The need and desire to predict the future is common practise in all cultures as is using the stars to do so. The development of astrology came from simple observations. The cycles of the sun and moon correlate with the seasons and the tides. The helical rising of Sirius coincided with the inundation. It was logical to look to the heavens to try and find other patterns of cause and effect.

The concept of the planets and constellations influencing an individual's destiny wasn't present in Pharaonic Egypt. It was introduced from Mesopotamia in the Ptolemaic Period. For the Egyptians there were a number of deities who determined a person's destiny. The Goddess Meskhenet presided over the birth and determined the child's fate at the moment of birth while the Cobra Goddess Renenutet, responsible for the harvest, allocated an individual's lifespan. Seshat, Thoth and Khonsu had their parts to play. In the later periods Isis was the Mistress of the Sky who had power over fate as well as embodying cosmic order. She acquired a lot of her fate aspect through the assimilation of Renenutet. The decan stars were associated with fate and retribution but acted more as emissaries sent by the deities to act out destiny rather than to foretell or determine it.

Calendars listing lucky and unlucky days were popular and the festivals of various deities appear to have been aligned with the positions of certain stars. Many of the days were given a comment as to whether they were auspicious or not. This suggests that the concept of astral influence on people's fate was present from the

New Kingdom. Much of a magician's work was an attempt to change the destiny of an individual. In the stories of *Setne I* there is a magician who could *"enchant the heaven"* to achieve the desired outcome.[552]

Part of the Ptolemaic papyrus Berlin is a text used for compiling horoscopes. *"He who was born when Mercury was in the descendant...he will enchant the human heart...he will happen unto a hidden thing."* While for someone born when Venus was in the ascendant *"he will be foremost in the house of his fathers and will do his upmost"*. In classical astronomy the houses equate to the signs of the zodiac. Some of the houses listed in this text include; Brother, Lake of the Underworld, Nobility, Evil Genius, Death, God and Fate. These have not been identified. *"He who was born when Mercury was in the house 'Nobility': He will be one happy as to fate, giving commands to many men."* But if Mercury was in the house of Evil Genius life did not look particularly kind. *"He is malformed. A hidden malady occurs within him while he is small."*[553]

Greco-Egyptian magical papyrus include lists of the types of magic which work best under specific star signs. They developed elaborate theories which linked the energies of individual stars and planets with material objects such as precious stones and parts of the body. A talisman to cure gout was to be made when the moon was in Leo. The Greeks and Romans often viewed the moon with suspicion and this is reflected in a number of anti-social spells invoking Selene, the *"only ruler, Swift Fortune of daimons and gods"*. The practitioner is warned in a number of these to be careful how and why they use these spells. *"Do not use it frequently to Selene unless the procedure which you are performing is worthy of its power...do not approach the procedure carelessly or else the goddess is angry."*[554] One spell aligns her with Hekate calling her *"triple-headed, triple-voiced Selene"* in a charm using a stone carved with *"a three-faced Hekate"*.[555]

Divination was very popular in the Greco-Roman Period and there are a number of texts relating to this. One addresses Khonsu

---

[552] The Ancient Egyptian Book of Thoth, Jasnow & Zauzich, 2005:427
[553] An Astrologer's Handbook in Demotic Egyptian, Hughes, 1986:55-58
[554] The Greek Magical Papyri in Translation, Betz, 1996:85-86
[555] The Greek Magical Papyri in Translation, Betz, 1996:91-92

as "*O silver, lord of silver…the great god who is in the disc…the great god who is in the sound eye*".[556] Another divination spell, from the Leiden papyrus, invokes the seven stars of the constellation of Meskhetyu. "*Set up your planisphere and you stamp on the ground seven times and recite these charms to the Foreleg, turning to the North seven times.*"[557]

THE ENDURING SKY

Although it is not always obvious the stellar aspects of Egyptian religion permeate the cults, with the exception of the solar ones. The night sky is illuminated by the presence of the deities. "*The sky contains your ba. The earth contains your effigies.*"[558] The assignment of stars and asterisms to the Gods and Goddesses is illustrated in this funerary spell for "*knowing the names of the Gods of the Southern sky, the Gods of the Northern sky*".[559] Nut was prominent in mythology and vital to the deceased but didn't have a cult, as far as the evidence shows. In virtually all societies lunar cults preceded solar ones. Solarisation of a religion tends to be associated with the rise of agriculture and then with increasing patriarchy and royalty. One king to rule on earth, one Sun God to rule in heaven. Ancient Egypt never abandoned polytheism (excluding that imposed by the heretic Akhenaten). The lunar influence remained strong largely through its association with Osiris and rebirth and with the equilibrium of the Eyes of Heaven.

---

[556] The Greek Magical Papyri in Translation, Betz, 1996:209
[557] The Leyden Papyrus, Griffith & Thompson, 1974:45
[558] Traversing Eternity, Smith, 2009:132
[559] The Egyptian Book of the Dead, Allen, 2010:225, spell 141A

CHAPTER 15

Beyond the Sun

*"Can you rise? Can you reach up to Heaven
like a great star rising in the East?"*[560]

For the Egyptians knowing and worshipping Thoth meant understanding the cycles of the moon. Lunar science glorified him and helped bring his devotees closer to him. This is the complete antithesis to the modern relationship between science and religion. Throughout history the powerful leaders of the various religions, and their supporters, viewed scientific explanations of the natural world as a direct threat to their jealous god. Fundamentalists continue to reject science and logic for the same reason. The Egyptians took the opposite view. In order to develop a deep relationship with someone you have to get to know them. Astronomy allows you to get closer to the Celestial deities, especially Nut and Thoth. Science does not remove the awe. Astronomers describe their subject in terms of chemistry,

---

[560] The Living Wisdom of Ancient Egypt, Jacq, 1999:53

mathematics and physics yet they still have boundless enthusiasm for the night sky and its wonders.

From the point of view of a Sky Goddess the sky is where the sun is born and where it dies. Nut is the all-encompassing female regenerative power. She is fixed and enduring and contains within herself all her transient children – the sun, the moon, the stars and all life including ourselves. This concept wasn't always reflected in the theology. The solar cults transformed her into an impassive waterway on which the Solar Barque sails. The sky became the place where the Sun God rules and Nut is not even his daughter but his granddaughter. The wiser and friendlier Gods, such as Thoth and Osiris, are not involved in this battle for power. They understand the cyclical nature of everything that is created. All are born, they live for a time and then they fade away and die, to be replaced by something else or to be reborn. This is just as true for suns and Gods as it is for people and grain.

"*I am Nut, the Sky, the haven at the zenith.*"[561] Sky wisdom is knowing that there are many ways and forms not just the one. Beyond the concept of the one dominant God in heaven who outshines all others lies a deeper way of many stars and a dancing moon. The diurnal sky can obscure their dance but it is always present as a total solar eclipse, by the lesser moon, reminds us. It shows Nut behind the daytime Sun God as she always was and always will be, lasting long after our sun has finally succumbed to the eternal cycle of life and death.

The night sky is an awe-inspiring place to observe but what you can see only hints at what is concealed. "*Men received all manner of things from the day sky; from the night sky they had all manner of things to learn.*"[562] Standing under a starry sky can be a numinous and uplifting experience and the skies in Ancient Egypt provided excellent viewing conditions which few can appreciate or experience today. Schweizer describes such an experience as creating a mysterious longing. "*A consciousness that is still weak needs the protection of night to be thus moved by its light.*"[563] It is at night, or in

---

[561] Hymns, Prayers and Songs, Foster, 1995:20
[562] Daily Life of Egyptian Gods, Meeks & Meeks, 1999:113
[563] The Sun God's Journey Through the Netherworld, Schweizer, 2010:7

the equivalent *duat*, that new or renewed life occurs and with it a soft longing for the gentle light before it can reach for the dawn and the full light of being.

Space is not our natural environment. It is chaotic and hostile with its radiation, near-vacuum and temperatures hovering above absolute zero. To date none of the planets or exoplanets found so far are suitable for human habitation without some serious technology. It is not our body which long for the stars it is our *ba*. It was with great understanding that the Egyptians depicted the *ba* as a free-flying bird. We need to have a longing for the light in order to grow and be reborn. But the longing for the stars, and to escape the pull of earth, is more than a longing for the light. We have more than enough light each day from our own star. Schweizer talks of a component of the *ba* which *"longs for the celestial, the spiritual, and the distant and that desires to wander and travel; it is the ba that makes psychic flights into the distance and the heights"*.[564] When we long for the stars it is the cosmic and freedom-loving *ba* expressing herself in our earthbound lives.

> *Let us join the cosmic dance of the Great Goddess Nut.*
> *She who holds within her galaxies beyond our seeing and marvels beyond our understanding.*
> *Whose star-jewelled sky uplifts our souls with its splendour and beauty.*
> *Whose night-soft wings enfold us in comfort and protection.*
> *Who holds out her hands to lift us back to the stars.*
> *There is no ending of the Great Goddess Nut.*
> *No ending of her wonders and of her embrace.*
> *She will never be far from us, ever.*

---

[564] The Sun God's Journey Through the Netherworld, Schweizer, 2010:42

Bibliography

Abdala, A. (1991) *A Greco-Roman Group Statue of Unusual Character from Dendera*. In *Journal of Egyptian Archaeology*, Vol 77:189-193

Abt, T. & Hornung, E. (2003) *Knowledge for the Afterlife*. Zurich, Living Human Heritage Publications

Abt, T. & Hornung, E. (2007) *The Egyptian Amduat*. Zurich, Living Human Heritage Publications

Abt, T. & Hornung, E. (2014) *The Egyptian Book of Gates*. Zurich, Living Human Heritage Publications

Aderin-Pocock, M. (2018) *Book of the Moon*. London, BBC Books

Aelian & Scholfield, A.F. (trans) (1957) *On the Characteristics of Animals Vol I*. London, William Heinemann Ltd

Allen, J (1989) The Cosmology of the Pyramid Texts. In Simpson, W. (Ed) (1989) *Religion and Philosophy in Ancient Egypt* New Haven, Yale Egyptological Studies 3

Allen, J. P. (1988) *Genesis in Egypt: The Philosophy of Ancient Egyptian Creation Accounts*. Connecticut, Yale Egyptological Studies 2

Allen, J. P. (2005) *The Art of Medicine in Ancient Egypt*. New York, Metropolitan Museum of Art

Allen, T. A. (2011) *The Egyptian Book of the Dead*. Chicago, University of Chicago Press

Almanso-Villatoro, M. V. (2019) *The Cultural Indexicality of the N41 sign for b3j: the metal of the sky and the sign for metal*. In *Journal of Egyptian Archaeology*, Vol 105:73-81

Altmann-Wendling, V. (2017) *Of Min and Moon – Cosmological Concepts in the temple of Athribis (Upper Egypt)*. In Rosati, G. & Guidotti, M. C. (2017) *Proceedings of the XI International Congress of Egyptologists. 2015. Museo Egizio Firenze*. Oxford, Archaeopress.

Andrews, C. (1994) *Amulets of Ancient Egypt*. London, British Museum Press

Apuleius & Walsh, P. G. (trans.) (1994) *The Golden Ass*. Oxford, Oxford University Press

Assman, J. (2005) *Death and Salvation in Ancient Egypt*. Ithaca, Cornell University Press

Azzazy, M. & Ezzat, A. (2016) *The Sycamore in Ancient Egypt – Textual, Iconographic & Archaeopalynological Thoughts*. In Guilhou, N. (Ed.) (2016) *Nut Astrophoros: Papers Presented to Alicia Maravellia*. Oxford, Archaeopress Publishing Ltd

Barring A & Cashford J, (1993) *The Myth of the Goddess: Evolution of an Image*. London, Penguin Books

Bastijns, B. (2017) *The Sky at Night: Astronomical Knowledge in the New Kingdom*. In *Ancient Egypt*, Vol 18:24-30

Belmonte, J. A. (2009) *The Egyptian Calendar: keeping Ma'at on Earth*. In Belmonte, J. A. & Shaltout, M. (Ed.) (2009) *In Search of Cosmic Order*. Cairo, Supreme Council of Antiquities Press

Belmonte, J. A. et al. (2009) *Unveiling Seshat: new insights into the stretching of the cord ceremony*. In Belmonte, J. A. & Shaltout, M. (Ed.) (2009) *In Search of Cosmic Order*. Cairo, Supreme Council of Antiquities Press

Belmonte, J. A., Molinero, M. A. & Miranda, N (2009) *Astronomy, Landscape and symbolism: a study into the orientation of ancient Egyptian temples*. In Belmonte, J. A. & Shaltout, M. (Ed.) (2009) *In Search of Cosmic Order*. Cairo, Supreme Council of Antiquities Press

Betz, H. D. (Ed.) (1996) *The Greek Magical Papyri in Translation. Volume I: Texts*. Chicago, University of Chicago Press

Betz, R. (2009) *Nabta Playa Saved*. In *Ancient Egypt* Vol 10:26-30

Billing, N. (2002) Nut: The Goddess of Life in Text and Iconography. Uppsala, Uppsala University

Billing, N. (2006) *The Secret One. An Analysis of a Core Motif in the Books of the Netherworld*. In *Studien zur Altägyptischen Kultur* 34:51-71

Billing, N. (2016) *The Dialogue of Geb and Nut in Relation to the Royal Sarcophagus in the Pyramid of King Pepy I*. In Guilhou, N. (Ed.) (2016) *Nut Astrophoros: Papers Presented to Alicia Maravellia*. Oxford, Archaeopress Publishing Ltd

Bleeker, C.J. (1973) *Hathor and Thoth: Two Key Figures of the Ancient Egyptian Religion*. Leiden, E.J. Brill

Bomhard, A (2016) *The Genesis of the Stars in Ancient Egypt, According to the Naos of the Decades*. In Guilhou, N. (Ed.) (2016) *Nut Astrophoros: Papers Presented to Alicia Maravellia*. Oxford, Archaeopress Publishing Ltd

Bomhard, A. S. (1999) *The Egyptian Calendar: A Work For Eternity*. London, Periplus Publishing

Borghouts, J. F. (1978) *Ancient Egyptian Magical Texts*. Leiden, E J Brill

Boylan, P. (1922) *Thoth Or The Hermes Of Egypt*. New York, Kessinger Publishing (Reprints) 1922.

Buhl, M. (1947) *The Goddesses of the Egyptian Tree Cult*. In *Journal of Near Eastern Studies*, Vol 6:80-97

Cashford, J (2003) *The Moon: Myth and Image*. London, Cassell Illustrated.

Cerny, J. (1957) Ancient Egyptian Religion. London, Hutchinson's University Library

Clagett, M. (1995) *Ancient Egyptian Science Volume II: Calendars, Clocks and Astronomy*. Philadelphia, American Philosophical Society

Darnell, J. C. & Darnell, C. M. (2018) *The Ancient Egyptian Netherworld Books*. Atlanta, SBL Press

David, R. (2016) *Temple Ritual at Abydos*. London. Egypt Exploration Society

Eaton, K. (2011) *Monthly Lunar Festivals in the Mortuary Realm: Historical Patterns and Symbolic Motifs*. In *Journal of Near Eastern Studies*, Vol 70:229-245

El-Leithy, H., Leitz, C. & von Recklinghaussen, D. (2019) *The Ancient Colours of Esna Return*. In *Egyptian Archaeology*, Vol 55:20-23

el-Sabban (2000) *Temple Festival Calendars of Ancient Egypt*. Liverpool, Liverpool University Press

Erman, A. (1995) Ancient Egyptian Poetry and Prose. New York, Dover Publications

Etz, D. V. (1997) *A New Look at the Constellation Figures in the Celestial Diagram*. In *Journal of the American Research Centre in Egypt*. Vol 34:143-161

Ezzat, A. (2016) *Staircases in Ancient Egyptian Pools*. In Guilhou, N. (Ed.) (2016) *Nut Astrophoros: Papers Presented to Alicia Maravellia*. Oxford, Archaeopress Publishing Ltd

Faulkner, R. O. & Goelet, O. (2008) *The Egyptian Book of the Dead*, San Francisco, Chronicle Books

Faulkner, R. O. (1937) *The Bremner-Rhind Papyrus III: The Book of Overthrowing Apep*. In *Journal of Egyptian Archaeology*, Vol 23:166-185

Faulkner, R. O. (1989) *The Ancient Egyptian Book of the Dead*. London, British Museum Publications

Faulkner, R. O. (2007) *The Ancient Egyptian Coffin Texts*. Oxford, Aris & Phillips

Faulkner, R. O. (2007) *The Ancient Egyptian Pyramid Texts*. Kansas, Digireads.com Publishing

Foreman, W. & Quirke S. (1996) *Hieroglyphs & the Afterlife in Ancient Egypt*. London, Opus Publishing Ltd

Foster, J. L. (1995) *Hymns, Prayers and Songs*. Atlanta, Scholars Press

Foster, J. L. (2001) *Ancient Egyptian Literature*. Austin, University of Texas Press

Franci, M. (2016) *Defining Time*. In Guilhou, N. (Ed.) (2016) *Nut Astrophoros: Papers Presented to Alicia Maravellia*. Oxford, Archaeopress Publishing Ltd

Frankfort, H. (1948) *Ancient Egyptian Religion*. New York, Harper & Row

Freed, R. E. et al (2009) *The Secrets of Tomb 10A*. Boston, MFA Publications

Galan, J. M. (2013) *The Book of the Dead in Djehuty's burial chamber*. In *Egyptian Archaeology*, 42:21-24

Galfard, C (2015) *The Universe in Your Hand*. London, Pan Books

Garcia-Fernandez, G. (2017) *The Moon god Iah in ancient Egyptian Religion*. In Rosati, G. & Guidotti, M. C. (2017) *Proceedings of the XI International Congress of Egyptologists. 2015. Museo Egizio Firenze*. Oxford, Archaeopress.

Goodison, L. & Morris C. (Ed) (1998) *Ancient Goddesses*. London, British Museum Press

Graves-Brown, C. (2006) *Emergent Flints*. In Szpakowska, K. (Ed.) (2006) *Through a Glass Darkly*. Swansea, The Classical Press of Wales

Griffith, F. L. & Thompson H. (1974) *The Leyden Papyrus*. New York, Dover Publications

Griffiths, J. G. (1964) *An Appeal to Nut in a Papyrus of the Roman Era*. In *Journal of Egyptian Archaeology*, Vol 50:182-183

Griffiths, J. G. (1976) *Osiris and the Moon in Iconography*. In *Journal of Egyptian Archaeology*, Vol 62:153-159

Habachi, L. (1952) *The Naos with the Decades (Louvre D 37 and the Discovery of Another Fragment*. In *Journal of Near Eastern Studies*, Vol 11:251-263

Hardy, P. A. (2003) *The Cairo Calendar as a Stellar Almanac*. In *Archaeoastronomy*, Vol XVII:48-63

Hart, G. (2005) *The Routledge Dictionary of Egyptian Gods and Goddesses*. Abingdon, Routledge

Heath, R. (2006) *Sun, Moon & Earth*. Glastonbury, Wooden Books Ltd.

Herodotus & Selincourt, A. (Trans.) (2003) *The Histories*. London, Penguin Books

Horning, E. (2001) *The Secret Lore of Egypt*. Ithaca, Cornell University Press

Hornung, E. (1999) *The Ancient Egyptian Books of the Afterlife*. Ithaca, Cornell University Press

Hughes, G. R. (1986) *An Astrologer's Handbook in Demotic Egyptian*. In Lesko, L. H. (Ed) (1986) *Egyptological Studies in Honour of Richard A Parker*. London, Brown University Press

Isler, M. (1989) *An Ancient Method of Finding and Extending Direction*. In Journal of the American Research Centre in Egypt. Vol 26:191-206

Jackson, L. (2018) *Sekhmet & Bastet: The Feline Powers of Egypt*. London, Avalonia Books

Jackson, L. (2020) *The Cobra Goddess and the Chaos Serpent*. London, Avalonia Books

Jacq, C. (1999) *The Living Wisdom of Ancient Egypt*. London, Simon & Schuster

Jasnow, R. & Zauzich, K (2005) *The Ancient Egyptian Book of Thoth*. Harrassowitz Verlag 2005.

Joergensen, J. (2006) *Secrets, Knowledge and Experience in Ancient Egyptian Religion – the spells of knowing the powers of the sacred sites*. MA Thesis, University of Copenhagen. Academia.edu accessed 04/07/2020

Kakosy, L. (1981) *The Astral Snakes of the Nile*. In Mitteilungen Des Deutschen Archäologischen Instituts, Abteilung Kairo 37. 62:255-260

Kaper, O. E. (1995) *The Astronomical Ceiling of Deir el-Haggar in the Dakhleh Oasis*. In *Journal of Egyptian Archaeology*, Vol 81:175-195

Kemp, B. (2005) *100 Hieroglyphs: Think Like an Egyptian*. London, Granta Books

Kemp, B. (2007) *How to Read the Egyptian Book of the Dead*. London, Granta Books

Kozloff, A. P. & Bryan, B. M. (1992) *Egypt's Dazzling Sun: Amenhotep III and his World*. Cleveland, Cleveland Museum of Art

Kraus, R. K. (2009) *Astronomical chronology*. In Belmonte, J. A. & Shaltout, M. (Ed.) (2009) *In Search of Cosmic Order*. Cairo, Supreme Council of Antiquities Press

Kurth, D. (2004) *The Temple of Edfu*. Cairo, The American University in Cairo Press

Lamy, L. (1986) *Egyptian Mysteries: New Light on Ancient Knowledge*. London, Thames & Hudson

Lesko, B. S. (1999) *The Great Goddesses of Ancient Egypt*. Norman, University of Oklahoma Press

Lesko, L. H. (1977) *The Ancient Egyptian Book of Two Ways*. California, University of California Publications.

Lesko, L. H. (1991) *Ancient Egyptian Cosmogenesis and Cosmology*. In Shafer, B. E. (ed.) *Religion in Ancient Egypt*. Ithaca, Cornell University Press.

Lichtheim, M. (2006) *Ancient Egyptian Literature Volume II*. California, University of California Press

Lichtheim, M. (2006) *Ancient Egyptian Literature Volume III*. California, University of California Press

Lindsay, J. (1968) *Men and Gods on the Roman Nile*. London, Frederick Muller Ltd

Locher, K. (2016) *Gods Coming from the Left – Possible Astronomical Origins of Religious Processions*. In Guilhou, N. (Ed.) (2016) *Nut Astrophoros: Papers Presented to Alicia Maravellia*. Oxford, Archaeopress Publishing Ltd

Lull, J. & Belmonte, J. A. (2009), *The constellations of ancient Egypt*. In Belmonte, J. A. & Shaltout, M. (Ed.) (2009) *In Search of Cosmic Order*. Cairo, Supreme Council of Antiquities Press

Martin, G. T. (2012) *The Tomb of Maya and Meryt I*. London, Egypt Exploration Society

McDermott, B. (1998) *Death in Ancient Egypt*. London, Cheltenham, The History Press

Mead, G. R. S. (2002) *Plutarch: Concerning the Mysteries of Isis and Osiris*. Montana, Kessinger Publishing (Reprints)

Meeks, D. & Favard-Meeks, C. (1999) *Daily Life of Egyptian Gods*. London, Pimlico

Nemes, G. W. (2020) *The mythological importance of the constellation Mshtjw in mortuary representations until the end of the New Kingdom*. In *Egypte Nilotic et Mediterraneenne*, Vol 13:1-61.

Neugebauer, O. & Parker, R. A. (1960) *Egyptian Astronomical Texts I: The Early Decans*. London, Brown University Press

Neugebauer, O. & Parker, R. A. (1969) *Egyptian Astronomical Texts III: Constellations and Zodiacs*. London, Brown University Press

Neugebauer, O. (1981) *A Demotic Lunar Eclipse Text of the First Century BC*. In *Proceedings of the American Philosophical Society*, Vol 125:312-327

Nyord, R. (2014) *Permeable Containers: Body and Cosmos in Middle Kingdom Coffins*. In Sousa, R. (Ed) (2014) *Body, Cosmos and Eternity*. Oxford, Archaeopress

O'Rourke, P. F. (2016) *An Ancient Egyptian Book of the Dead*. London, Thames & Hudson Ltd

Oakes, L. & Gahlin, L. (2004) *Ancient Egypt*. London, Hermes House

Ouda, A. M. M. (2017) *The Canopic Box of NS-'3-RWD (BM EA 8539)*. In *Journal of Egyptian Archaeology*, Vol 98:127-138

Parker, R. A. (1953) *The Names of the Sixteenth Day of the Lunar Month*. In *Journal of Near Eastern Studies*, Vol 12:50

Parker, R. A. (1974) *Ancient Egyptian Astronomy*. In *Philosophical Transactions of the Royal Society of London. Series A, Mathematical and Physical Sciences*, Vol 276:51-65

Parkinson, R. (2008) *The Painted Tomb-Chapel of Nebamun*. London, British Museum Press

Parkinson, R. B. (1991) *Voices from Ancient Egypt*. London, British Museum Press

Piankoff, A. (1934) *The Sky-Goddess Nut and the Night Journey of the Sun*. In *Journal of Egyptian Archaeology*, Vol 20:57-61

Piankoff, A. (1954) *The Tomb of Rameses VI*. New York, Pantheon Books.

Piankoff, A. (1964) *The Litany of Re*. New York, Pantheon Books.

Pinch, G. (2002) *Egyptian Mythology*. Oxford, Oxford University Press

Pinch, G. (2004) *Egyptian Myth: A Very Short Introduction*. Oxford, Oxford University Press

Pinch, G. (2006) *Magic in Ancient Egypt*. London, British Museum Press

Poo, M. (1995) *Wine and Wine Offering in the Religion of Ancient Egypt*. London, Kegan Paul International

Priskin, G. (2016) *The Depictions of the Entire Lunar Cycle in Graeco-Roman Temples.* In *Journal of Egyptian Archaeology*, Vol 102:111-144

Priskin, G. (2019) *The Ancient Egyptian Book of the Moon: Coffin Texts Spells 154-160.* Oxford, Archaeopress Publishing

Priskin, G. (2019) *The Constellations of Egyptian Astronomical Diagrams.* In *Egypte Nilotic et Mediterraneenne*, Vol 12:137-180

Quack, J. F. (2002) *A Goddess Rising 10,000 Cubits into the Air…or Only One Cubit, One Finger?* In Steele, J. M. & Imhausen, A. (2002) (Ed) *Under One Sky.* Munster, Ugarit-Verlog

Richter, B. A. (2016) *The Theology of Hathor of Dendera.* Atlanta, Lockwood Press

Ritner, R. K. (1985) *Anubis and the Lunar Disc.* In *Journal of Egyptian Archaeology*, Vol 71:149-155

Roberts, A. (1995) *Hathor Rising.* Rottingdean, Northgate Publishers

Roberts, A. (2000) *My Heart My Mother.* Rottingdean, Northgate Publishers

Roberts, A. (2019) *Hathor's Alchemy.* Rottingdean, Northgate Publishers

Sauneron, S. (200) *The Priests of Ancient Egypt.* Ithaca, Cornell University Press

Schweizer, A. (2010) *The Sungod's Journey Through the Netherworld.* Ithaca, Cornell University Press

Shaw, G. J. (2014) *The Egyptian Myths.* London, Thames & Hudson

Shaw, I. & Nicholson, P. (2008) *The British Museum Dictionary of Ancient Egypt.* London, British Museum Press

Simpson, W. K. et al (2003) *The Literature of Ancient Egypt.* New Haven, Yale University Press

Smith, M. (1993) *The Liturgy of Opening the Mouth for Breathing.* Oxford, Griffith Institute

Smith, M. (2009) *Traversing Eternity.* Oxford, Oxford University Press

Sousa, R. (2014) *Spread Your Wings Over Me.* In Sousa, R. (Ed) (2014) *Body, Cosmos and Eternity.* Oxford, Archaeopress

Spalinger, A. (1991) *Remarks on an Egyptian Feast Calendar of Foreign Origin.* In *Studien zur n zur Altägyptischen Kultur*, Vol 18:349-373

Spalinger, A. (1995) *Some Remarks on the Epagomenal Days in Ancient Egypt.* In *Journal of Near Eastern Studies*, Vol 54:33-47

Spalinger, A. (2002) *Egyptian Festival Dating and the Moon.* In Steele, J. M. & Imhausen, A. (2002) (Ed) *Under One Sky.* Munster, Ugarit-Verlog

Stemmler-Harding, S. (2016) *Devil in Disguise – On the Stellar Mythology of Apophis.* In Guilhou, N. (Ed.) *Nut Astrophoros: Papers Presented to Alicia Maravellia.* Oxford, Archaeopress Publishing Ltd

Strabo & Jones, H.L. (trans) (1932) *Geography Vol VIII.* New York, Cornell University Press

Symons, S. (2007) *Astronomical Ceilings.* In *Egyptian Archaeology*, Vol 30:11-13

Taher, A. W. (2015) *Sistra and Constellations: The House of Hathor at Dendera.* In Ancient Egypt, Vol 16:24-32

Taylor, J. H. (2001) *Death & the Afterlife in Ancient Egypt.* London, The British Museum Press

Taylor, J. H. (2017) *Sir John Soane's Greatest Treasure.* London, British Museum Press.

Taylor, K. (2012) *Celestial Geometry.* London, Watkins Publishing

Te Velde, H (1967) *Seth, God of Confusion.* Leiden, Brill

Toomer, G. J. (1988) *Mathematics and Astronomy.* In Harris, J. R. (Ed) (1988) *The Legacy of Egypt.* Oxford, Clarendon Press

Torok, L. (2009) *Between Two Worlds.* Leiden, Brill

Wainwright, G. A. (1936) *Orion and the Great Star.* In *Journal of Egyptian Archaeology*, Vol 22:45-46

Wainwright, G. A. (1939) *Seshat and the Pharaoh.* In *Journal of Egyptian Archaeology*, Vol 25:104

Watterson, B. (1998) *The House of Horus at Edfu.* Stroud, Tempus Publishing Ltd

Wells, R.A. (1992) *The Mythology of Nut and the Birth of Ra.* In *Studien zur Altägyptischen Kultur* 19:305-321

Wendrich, W. (2006) *Entangled, Connected or Protected? The Power of Knots in Ancient Egypt.* In Szpakowska, K. (Ed.) (2006) *Through a Glass Darkly.* Swansea, The Classical Press of Wales

Wernick, N. (2009) *Timekeeping in Ancient Egypt*. In *Ancient Egypt* Vol 9:29-32

Wilkinson, R. H. (1994) *Symbol & Magic in Egyptian Art*. London, Thames & Hudson

Wilkinson, R. H. (2000) *The Complete Temples of Ancient Egypt*. London, Thames & Hudson

Wilkinson, R. H. (2003) *The Complete Gods and Goddesses of Ancient Egypt*. London, Thames & Hudson

Wilkinson, R. H. (2011) *Reading Egyptian Art*. London, Thames & Hudson

Wilkinson, T. (2003) *Genesis of the Pharaohs*. London, Thames & Hudson

Wilkinson, T. (2016) *Writings from Ancient Egypt*. London, Penguin Books

Zabkar, L. V. (1988) *Hymns to Isis in Her Temple at Philae*. Hanover, University Press of New England

Index

Q

R

S

T

U

V

W

Y

OTHER BOOKS BY LESLEY JACKSON

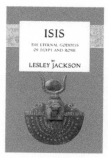

Isis: The Eternal Goddess of Egypt and Rome

A thought-provoking study of one of the most enduring and enigmatic ancient goddesses. Isis was known as a great magician, healer and associated with events of cosmic significance.

This extensive work draws on the texts of the Ancient Egyptians and Classical writers.

ISBN: 978-1-910191-21-7

Hathor: A Reintroduction to an Ancient Egyptian Goddess

A comprehensive and thought-provoking study of Hathor's different roles and titles, associations with other deities, alter-egos and assimilations, temples, worship, and festivals.

Hathor is reintroduced to us as a sovereign, powerful, beautiful and lovely goddess, she 'whose ba is powerful'.

ISBN: 978-1-910191-22-4

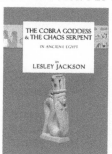

The Cobra Goddess and The Chaos Serpent

An in-depth investigation of snakes in ancient Egyptian religion, encompassing their roles in the divine, earthly and afterlife realms, including both the arch-fiend and sun-stealing Chaos Serpent Apophis, or Apep, the ultimate destructive force in the universe and representative of total disorder, and the *uraeus*, or Egyptian cobra, the ultimate protector of deities and royals

ISBN: 978-1-910191-24-8

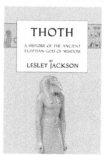

Thoth: The History of the Ancient Egyptian God of Wisdom

Drawing on research from magical papyri and stelae to statues and wall carvings, this book explores Thoth's diverse functions including as god of writing, magic and wisdom, creator god, judge, healer, psychopomp, reckoner of time and lunar god.

Long overdue, this is an unmissable work on this most enduring of gods.

ISBN 978-1-910191-23-1

www.avaloniabooks.com

Lightning Source UK Ltd.
Milton Keynes UK
UKHW011319040422
401065UK00006B/1488